Human Rights and Sustainability

T0330901

The history of human rights suggests that individuals should be empowered in their natural, political, social and economic vulnerabilities. States within the international arena hold each other responsible for doing just that and support or interfere where necessary. States are there to protect these essential human vulnerabilities, even when this is not a matter of self-interest. This function of human rights is recognized in contexts of intervention, genocide, humanitarian aid and development.

Human Rights and Sustainability develops the idea of environmental obligations as long-term responsibilities in the context of human rights. It proposes that human rights require recognition that, in the face of unsustainable conduct, future human persons are exposed and vulnerable. It explores the obstacles for long-term responsibilities that human rights law provides at the level of international and national law and challenges the question of whether lifestyle restrictions are enforceable in view of liberties and levels of wellbeing typically seen as protected by human rights.

The book will be of interest to students, researchers and policymakers in the areas of human rights, sustainability, and law and philosophy.

Gerhard Bos is a postdoctoral researcher at Utrecht University.

Marcus Düwell is the Director of the Ethics Institute at Utrecht University.

Routledge studies in sustainability

Human Rights and Sustainability

Moral responsibilities for the future

Edited by Gerhard Bos
and Marcus Düwell

Routledge
Taylor & Francis Group

LONDON AND NEW YORK

First published 2016 by Routledge

2 Park Square, Milton Park, Abingdon, Oxfordshire OX14 4RN
711 Third Avenue, New York, NY 10017

Routledge is an imprint of the Taylor & Francis Group, an informa business

First issued in paperback 2017

British Library Cataloguing-in-Publication Data
A catalogue record for this book is available from the British Library

Library of Congress Cataloging-in-Publication Data
Names: Bos, Gerhard, editor. | Dèuwell, Marcus, 1962– editor.
Title: Human rights and sustainability : moral responsibilities for the future / edited by Gerhard Bos and Marcus Dèuwell.
Description: Abingdon, Oxon ; New York : Routledge is an imprint of the Taylor & Francis Group, an Informa Business, [2016] | Series: Routledge studies in sustainability
Identifiers: LCCN 2015035185 | ISBN 9781138957107 (hb) | ISBN 9781315665320 (ebook)
Subjects: LCSH: Human rights–International cooperation. | Human rights–Moral and ethical aspects. | Sustainability. | Environmental justice.
Classification: LCC JC571 .H768854 2016 | DDC 179/.1–dc23
LC record available at http://lccn.loc.gov/2015035185

ISBN: 978-1-138-95710-7 (hbk)
ISBN: 978-0-8153-5566-3 (pbk)

Typeset in Goudy
by Wearset Ltd, Boldon, Tyne and Wear

Contents

Contributors

Deryck Beyleveld is Professor of Law and Bioethics at the Durham Law School, Durham University and Professor of Moral Philosophy and Applied Ethics at the Department of Philosophy and Religious Studies, Utrecht University. He has written many books and articles defending and interpreting the moral theory of Alan Gewirth and applying it, in particular to various areas of law and bioethics.

Gerhard Bos is a postdoctoral researcher at the Ethics Institute, Utrecht University. Currently, his research involves looking at the conceptual underpinnings of human rights and the implications for long-term responsibilities. He coordinated the ESF-funded networking programme 'Rights to a Green Future' (2011–2015). He is currently co-editing a number of books, including *Human Dignity in Philosophy and Applied Ethics – China and the West.*

Rutger Claassen is Associate Professor of Ethics and Political Philosophy at the Department of Philosophy, Utrecht University. His research interests include: socio-economic justice (especially the capability approach); economic and ethical theories about regulating and limiting markets; conceptions of freedom and autonomy; and the limits of state interventions in private life.

Marcus Düwell is Professor of Philosophical Ethics and Director of the Ethics Institute at Utrecht University. His research is focused on questions of moral justification, human dignity, human practical self-understanding, bioethics and the ethics of climate change. He is co-editor of the *Cambridge Handbook on Human Dignity.*

Sandor Fulop, PhD, is the Chair of the Environmental Management and Law Association (EMLA) in Hungary. He participated in the drafting of the Aarhus Convention and was a member of its Compliance Committee. He was also the first Parliamentary Commissioner for Future Generations of Hungary, a position he held from 2008 until 2012.

Emilie Gaillard's PhD is entitled 'Future Generations and Private Law' (LGDJ 2011, 673 pp., and was awarded the Charles Dupin Prize in 2010 by the

French Academy of Political and Moral Sciences). Her works highlight the emergence of a new temporal paradigm which not only tends to reconfigure legal imagination but also initiates new legal logics. She writes articles on legal theory, human rights, the preservation of the environment and rights for future generations.

Lukas Köhler holds three positions at the Munich School of Philosophy. He is a lecturer in environmental ethics, a member of the Institute for Social and Development Studies and Manager of the Centre for Environmental Ethics and Environmental Education. His main interests are environmental ethics, (intergenerational) justice, democracy and participation.

Peter Lawrence is a senior lecturer at the University of Tasmania (UTAS) Law School and the author of *Justice for Future Generations, Climate Change and International Law* (2014). He previously worked for the Australian Department of Foreign Affairs and Trade, including as First Secretary to the Australian Mission to the UN in Geneva.

Franck L.B. Meijboom is an assistant professor affiliated to both the Ethics Institute and the Department of Animals in Science and Society at the Faculty of Veterinary Medicine, Utrecht University. He focuses on agricultural and food ethics, animal ethics and the role of public trust and debate in these domains. In addition, he is chair and a member of a number of ethics committees and Secretary of the European Society for Agricultural and Food Ethics (EurSafe).

Tim Meijers is a doctoral researcher at the Hoover Chair of Economic and Social Ethics at the Université Catholique de Louvain, Belgium and a lecturer in political philosophy at Leiden University. In his PhD project (funded by the *Fonds pour la Recherche en Sciences Humaines*) he is working out the implications of egalitarian theories of justice for questions of population size and family policies. He writes about intergenerational justice, family ethics, reproductive rights and the ethics of migration. In addition, he is interested in transitional justice, particularly in international criminal justice.

Elina Pirjatanniemi is the Director of the Institute for Human Rights at Åbo Akademi University in Turku, Finland. She is also the Chair in Constitutional and International Law at the same university. Her research interests include fundamental and human rights, asylum and migration, and environmental issues.

Jos Philips is an assistant professor in political philosophy and ethics at the Ethics Institute, Utrecht University. His research interests are in the areas of global justice, human rights and sustainability. He has published various articles on individual responsibilities in relation to poverty, on nongovernmental organization (NGO) responsibilities and on conceptual questions of human rights.

Adina Preda is a lecturer in political theory at the University of Limerick. She works on questions related to rights, on which she has published several articles, as well as to distributive and global justice, and justice and health.

Michael Reder is the Chair of Practical Philosophy with a Focus on Intercultural Understanding at the Munich School of Philosophy, a member of the Institute for Social and Development Studies and Director of the Centre of Environmental Ethics and Environmental Education. His main interests are ethics of globalization, political philosophy and democracy, and environmental ethics.

Stephen Riley received his PhD in law from Lancaster University and is currently a postdoctoral researcher on an NWO-funded (Netherlands Organization for Scientific Research) project concerning human dignity as the foundation of human rights. He main interest is the philosophy of law, and his research focuses on human dignity as a component of legal systems. This is addressed in publications on human rights foundations, the rule of law and the sources of international law.

1 Human rights and future people

An introduction

Gerhard Bos and Marcus Düwell

Introduction

From a normative perspective, although one of the main problems related to climate change is that CO_2 emissions are too high, perhaps the primary issue is that global and local institutions are failing to address this urgent issue.

On 24 June 2015, the environmental organization Urgenda 'and nine hundred co-plaintiffs were victorious in the climate case ..., forcing the Dutch government to adopt more stringent climate policies'. A court based in The Hague demanded

> that the Dutch government do what the government itself has already deemed necessary in order to avert dangerous climate change. The court is ordering the Netherlands to reduce CO_2 emission by a minimum of 25% (compared to 1990) by 2020, while current ambitions are hovering at 16%
>
> (Urgenda 2015)

This verdict is unique for several reasons, most of which are to do with the fact that a legal institution has taken a position in a new and perhaps unexpected way by giving a future-oriented interpretation of the state's responsibility to protect its citizens facing climate change. The verdict is surprising, at least for anyone who understands environmental concern as a private, if not insignificant, affair and as something that should not be on the agenda of politicians, whose main task is to protect personal liberty. The idea that climate change is a threat to many of our future interests and liberties will require a quite radical reframing of the approach to climate policy.

Furthermore, the verdict implies a stance on the distribution of authority and responsibilities within a state facing climate change. In addition, the verdict respects the idea that law and politics should be independent, emphasizing that lawyers do not make policy and that politics does not apply the law. However, it does imply that the government should respect law and that law should have the authority and the responsibility to make sure the government does so, especially when it comes to the government's legal responsibility to protect its citizens. If the government does not do what on the basis of our best scientific knowledge would be required to protect its citizens against a threatening future, law can be used to require governments to generate and choose between policy options that meet this requirement. According to what can be implied from the verdict, science has a distinctive role to play with regard to law and politics. The question of whether the state fulfils its legal responsibility is decided by a judge on the basis of the effects of the actual policy interpreted in the light of scientifically predicted scenarios.

The idea of the state having responsibility to protect its citizens is not a peculiarity of the Dutch legal system. That is why this case is perceived as a test case for lawsuits against governments of different nations. So there is more to come. The general questions raised by this case are what responsibility a state has for people living in the future and, primarily, to what extent this is a responsibility grounded in rights.

Climate change is a global challenge that has a global cause and a global impact and that requires a global solution. Of course, any solution to it should be implemented via different national policies and diverse local practices of realization that take local side-constraints and the cultural and social peculiarities of different countries into account in order to enable an effective and broadly accepted realization. However, an adequate and effective response to climate change requires the distribution of the responsibility for implementing climate policy between relevant nations and probably the concerted action of global institutions. Hence, addressing climate change also requires international recognition of a common responsibility for climate policy as well as the distribution of climate policy between nations. Climate negotiations aimed at creating binding agreements for such distribution have thus far not been particularly successful – because of scepticism about climate change, because of a failure to agree on the distribution of responsibilities, because of tensions between rich and poor countries and because of different judgements with regard to the weight historical emissions should have when distributing responsibilities in the future.

However, if one thing is suggested in the Dutch context, it is that protecting the basic rights of people living in the future is not up for negotiation – neither at the local nor the global level. The air of optionality has disappeared, and a normative orientation towards the protection of basic rights has been provided as a basis from which to negotiate climate policy and distribute responsibility for implementing it.

From a philosophical perspective, the central question is whether national and international institutions that are building on basic rights require protection of these rights for the future. In this book, we explore whether and to what extent international human rights practice requires protection of the basic interests of vulnerable human beings that will exist in the future. The practice, and in particular what is legally binding in it, may have been developed in a context in which nobody would have thought that it would one day be used to address climate change. However, its normative commitment, understood as the responsibility to progressively secure the basic interests of vulnerable human beings, seems to invite application to climate change. It is crucial to see how anthropogenic climate change exposes human vulnerability within the lifetime of future generations, if not already within our current generation's future. Hence, a coherent commitment to human rights practice requires that the question of what can be done about climate change be asked in terms of it.

The leading research question in this book is whether long-term environmental responsibility is implied by an account of human rights. To address this question, our focus will be on spelling out to what extent human rights – conceived as a legal institution built on a moral idea – require respect for people living in the near or distant future. In doing so we will refer to the interpretation of long-term responsibilities in the contemporary, legally valid human rights regime. But primarily, the book will deal with philosophical conceptualizations and attempts to justify the normative authority of human rights in this regard. This strong focus on the philosophical perspective is motivated by the insight that a reinterpretation of human rights as a response to ecological challenges is of such fundamental importance that we have to refer to the basic understanding of what human rights are about, which has primarily and extensively been the topic of philosophical debate for quite a while.

The first part of the book will be legal in focus, explaining to what extent long-term environmental concern is consistent with, and can be framed in terms of, existing human rights practices and documents. In Chapter 2, *Elina Pirjatanniemi* addresses the issue of the obstacles to and promises for long-term environmental protection, with a focus on the European Convention of Human Rights. Via the idea of sustainable development, she distinguishes four forms of sustainability, ranging from very weak to very strong, and explores the extent to which these can be covered by the convention. Pirjatanniemi shows that the weaker forms of sustainability are more easily recognized under the convention, whereas stronger forms could be recognized but only if the scope of those with legal standing is widened and precautionary reasoning is more emphasized.

In Chapter 3, *Peter Lawrence* develops the idea of an 'atmospheric trust' as a reform option in international human rights law. Starting with an interpretation of international human rights, which advocates that its underlying ethical principles apply to future generations, Lawrence spells out a utopian human rights law that would protect the environment for future generations in terms of its scope, structure and effectiveness. The upshot of this is a utopian right to a healthy environment that can be claimed on behalf of future generations by an atmospheric trust, but that will continue to face challenges associated with balancing it against other interests, including the distribution of mitigation burdens between generations. The chapter ends by explaining the reform options of international human rights law in view of this utopian understanding.

In Chapter 4, *Emilie Gaillard* identifies the development of legal recognition of future generations and pleads that we need to change our mode of thinking in relation to contemporary human rights law so that it protects future generations. Here, the central ideas seem to be that various notions, justifications, divisions and symmetrical relations currently important in the theory and practice of human rights have to be rethought if we are to anticipate and prevent a human rights tragedy for future people.

In Chapter 5, *Stephen Riley* explores the possibility of having human rights-based sustainability duties via the idea of human rights law as an international constitution. Human rights have legal and moral dimensions that, although distinct in a relevant sense, are interdependent. Conceived as constitutional, international human rights law is the self-projection of an international community of human rights in the future. From this follows the recognition of duties that concern the rights of future human individuals. The chapter ends with an evaluation of this approach in terms of the specification of sustainability duties, the duty holder, the whole range of addressees of human rights and the claimants of such rights. The conclusion is that international human rights law has its own potential to transcend the generational limits it encounters today.

This chapter ends the part of the book that is about recognizing long-term environmental responsibility within existing human rights frameworks. The take-home message is twofold: there are obstacles to doing this, but – with creative will and effort – various reform options are possible, if not required, that would safeguard a healthy environment in terms of rights for future generations that could be justified in terms of core ideas of human rights law. The second part of the book will identify at a conceptual level the argumentative possibilities and obstacles that there are for framing long-term implications of human rights, primarily highlighting the extent to which central concepts in the analysis of human rights could imply long-term responsibilities.

In Chapter 6, *Marcus Düwell* argues that it should be recognized that human rights imply duties in terms of the protection of vulnerable human agents. The guiding idea behind this is that dignity, as the normative principle underlying human rights, requires acceptance of a responsibility to protect vulnerable human agents of the future. Düwell explores the conceptual possibilities and implications of a human rights regime from an intergenerational perspective.

Jos Philips, in Chapter 7, argues that a human rights approach to climate change fits the central requirements that basic rights are there to offer rightholders protection against standard threats up to a threshold level. The chapter starts with an explanation of the basic idea, followed by a positioning in relation to alternatives in order to clarify it further and understand its distinctive strengths and weaknesses. The chapter closes by rejecting the application to it of some of the general objections of sufficientarianism.

In Chapter 8, *Adina Preda* considers environmentally sustainable policies as elements of intergenerational justice, environmental justice and global justice. More specifically, she addresses the question of whether, in the contexts of these three forms, a sustainable policy would be required as a matter of rights or whether it should be framed differently. To answer that question, Preda operationalizes the distinction between an Interest theory and a Choice theory of rights. From this, she infers that the idea of future people's rights against us is best understood in terms of an Interest theory, and then notes how this may imply that future people will have rights, but not in the form of rights against us. Preda rejects the idea of a rights-based approach to environmental justice, and argues that a rights-based approach in the context of global justice, when taken to imply (long-term) environmental responsibilities, is problematic in view of the nature, content and addressees of the obligations.

In Chapter 9, *Gerhard Bos* argues that our individual status as a subject of human rights is connected with the possibility of future human persons having this status too. He identifies the challenges of thinking about long-term responsibility generationally, and claims that the first question we should ask about such a responsibility should concern individual and collective respons-ibility in relation to future people's future rights. Bos introduces the idea of a 'chain of status' as a compatible alternative line of argument to (i) the direct approach, which asserts that future people have rights against us and (ii) the chain style approach, which holds that we have duties regarding future people in terms of duties to specific interests or rights of contemporaries. Bos argues that the chain of status argument justifies enforceable and overriding long-term responsibilities without having to address the objections to the two approaches just mentioned.

This ends the part of the book in which the possibilities of a rights-based approach to long-term responsibility are explored on conceptual grounds. Com-bining this with the take-home message of the first part of the book, we find that – despite the challenges related to the existence and identity of future people – there appears to be a sufficient moral and philosophical reason to attribute human rights to future people. There may be disagreement about how environmental responsibilities in relation to future people have to be justified, but there are different ways of arguing that we should be concerned with future human persons and their interests.

The third part of the book considers various ways in which a rights-based approach to long-term responsibility makes a distinctive contribution. In this part, the pros and cons of a rights-based approach to long-term responsibility are assessed with regard to various forms that thinking about sustainability in terms of human rights could have in practice.

Michael Reder and *Lukas Köhler* argue in Chapter 10 that rights have a use apart from their function in legal review or courts in that they produce norms in a public sphere that accepts rights. The authors explore this function of human rights in a global sphere, in particular with regard to norms in the context of climate change. They emphasize that, interpreted in terms of the need for a decent life, freedom, equality, solidarity and participation give orientation to a global politics that is facing global challenges. As such, they should also give direction when responding to climate change at the global level.

In Chapter 11, *Deryck Beyleveld* advances an argument illustrating why and how a theory of rights, because of its internal logic, would demand recognition of the rights of future generations that would also entail duties towards them. Beyleveld introduces Alan Gewirth's Principle of Generic Consistency and two justifications of it, and shows how these address a variety of normative concerns and lack of clarity when it comes to recognizing and identifying duties to future generations.

Rutger Claassen, in Chapter 12, addresses the question of what the content of the rights of future generations is, focusing primarily on the function of rights to protect capabilities of future agents. Arguing for capability protection across generations, Claassen points out that this leaves open the issue of what resources should be left to future generations. He then goes on to criticize the total capital conception of such resources, and advances the idea that the preservation of specific forms of natural capital fits best with the capability approach to the rights of future generations.

Chapter 12 ends the part of the book that illustrates what the distinctive qualities would be of a human rights approach to long-term responsibility. Human rights have a use apart from their legal function, giving normative orientation in terms of their presuppositions. Furthermore, they can be used to decide substantial normative issues in the context of long-term responsibilities, primarily by accounting rationally for human rights and their content.

The fourth part of the book discusses what requirements long-term responsibilities based on human rights would entail for human rights practice itself. Could perceived liberties, protected as human rights, be limited for the sake of human rights of future people? How would it be possible to make human rights institutions incorporate the rights of future generations?

In Chapter 13, *Franck Meijboom* interprets the consumption of food as a matter of human rights and discusses various options for making it sustainable with respect to future people. Conceived as a human right, the right to food is quite basic, but is not only a matter of nutrition but of identity and private choice too. This complicates the question of what should be secured as a matter of right – including the right to food – for future generations. Meijboom discusses several reservations concerning restricting food consumption, emphasizing how difficult it can be to reconcile current consumption patterns with the rights of future generations, but also explaining that reducing food waste can diminish the unsustainable dimension of the food sector significantly.

Tim Meijers argues in Chapter 14 that long-term environmental responsibilities should be addressed in full awareness of all dimensions of unsustainability, drawing attention to its demographic dimension. Recognizing the distinctive value of rearing children, Meijers emphasizes that population size is a decisive factor in terms of the impact we have on the earth's potential to sustain human persons in the future. Meijers objects to an unlimited interpretation of the right to procreate because he believes that it would be problematic, while recognizing the importance of a right to protection of the freedom to procreate.

We end the volume with the perspective of a practitioner. *Sandor Fulop* was the Ombudsman for Future Generations in Hungary and serves on various international committees that deal with questions of long-term responsibilities. Fulop argues in Chapter 15 that important UN legal documents concerning sustainability and future generations spell out the functions that an international institution representing future generations should have as well as the conditions for its effective operation.

Chapter 16 concludes the book, pointing out the urgency and challenges of a human rights approach to long-term responsibility.

We would like to thank NWO for supporting the project 'Human Dignity as the Foundation of Human Rights'. This book has been realized in the context of both this project and the ESF-funded networking programme 'Rights to a Green Future' (2011–2015). The scholars who participate in this network are from various disciplines and come from all over Europe; they aim to identify long-term environmental responsibilities in the context of human rights and to discuss related governance issues with regard to their legal, political, ethical and philosophical dimensions.

Reference

Urgenda (2015) *Urgenda wins the case for better Dutch climate policies* [press release], Available at www.gwec.net/urgenda-wins-the-case-for-better-dutch-climate-policies/, Accessed 17 July 2015.

Part I

Obstacles and promises in contemporary human rights law

2 Greening human rights law

A focus on the European Convention on Human Rights

Elina Pirjatanniemi

1 Introduction

The 1948 *Universal Declaration of Human Rights* (UDHR) continues to inspire peoples of the world, but it nevertheless has one substantial lacuna: it is silent about our relationship to the environment. The Covenants that were designed to give legally binding status to the rights listed in the UDHR, the 1966 *International Covenant on Civil and Political Rights* (ICCPR) and the 1966 *International Covenant on Economic, Social and Cultural Rights* (ICESCR), share this silence, as does the 1950 *European Convention on Human Rights* (ECHR).

With some exceptions, human rights instruments have not linked human rights and the environment at a textual level. However, human rights treaty bodies, and especially regional human rights courts, have been innovative in interpreting human rights provisions as protecting environmental interests. The European Court of Human Rights (ECtHR) has been particularly active and has developed an extensive case law on environmental issues by way of its dynamic interpretation of the ECHR.

The inherent tension between the protection of human rights on the one hand and environmental values on the other is still a source of controversy. Documented by others too (Boyle 2012; Francioni 2010), the contemporary human rights regime has limits in this respect. It is primarily focused on violations of individuals' human rights, and even when it recognizes the collective dimension of rights, it nonetheless concentrates on the interests of particular identifiable human beings. Many environmental problems would instead necessitate actions to protect the environment for the benefit of those not yet born.

Nevertheless, significant progress has been made in illuminating the relationship between human rights and the environment, but many intriguing questions still remain. One of them is whether the concept of sustainable development could integrate human rights and the environment. The aim of this chapter is to delve into this question. The more specific focus will be on the possibilities of operationalizing long-term responsibility within the ECHR regime.

Sustainable development is a powerful concept, and it is often used without analytical reflection. At the same time, it has gained support thanks to its ability to simultaneously take into account several important interests (Barr 2008, 21).

Accordingly, sustainable development can be given different meanings. As Bosselmann (2008, 52) vividly puts it, the concept "is caught between political vagueness and legal ambition." However, if sustainable development is to be made enforceable and operational, it must be given a solid normative core (Bosselmann 2008, 52).

Sustainable development is usually defined as "development that meets the needs of the present without compromising the ability of future generations to meet their own needs" (World Commission on Environment and Development 1987, 41). An essential element of it is a linkage between economic, social, and environmental aspects of development. The need to integrate these has been acknowledged recently in the political outcome of the 2012 UN Conference on Sustainable Development (United Nations 2012).

As a consequence of this, sustainable development is hampered by a dilemma. If these three elements of development are seen as equally relevant, the concept loses its ability to guide us. This is also the limit of the concept. It does not provide definitive solutions; it only gives us instruments with which to understand the consequences of our deeds.

Researchers have created different methods of analyzing the assumptions embedded in different understandings of sustainability. On the basis of these, Barr has developed a sustainability continuum ranging from weak to strong forms of sustainability. A strong version desires to maintain critical levels of different forms of natural resources. A weak form argues that natural capital can be traded off and replaced with human capital, so long as the total capital that passes on from the present generation to the next is constant or growing (Barr 2008, 44). These opposites can be further divided into two groups which results in a spectrum ranging from very weak to weak, and from strong to very strong sustainability. Every category has its distinctive features as regards type of economy, management strategies and, most importantly in this context, ethics (Barr 2008, 46).

This typology is used here as a heuristic tool in order to provide a better understanding of the possibilities and limits human rights can have in our quest for the achievement of sustainable development. The main argument is that when promoting sustainable development the role of human rights should not be overstated. As will be shown, human rights in general and the ECHR in particular are currently capable of enhancing merely the weaker forms of sustainability. The ECHR seems to have specific problems in providing tools for long-term responsibility.

2 Weak forms of sustainable development

2.1 The delicate art of balancing

According to the sustainability spectrum presented by Barr, sustainability is very weak if the relationship between human beings and the environment is based on what Barr (2008, 46) calls "traditional ethical reasoning." It is mainly concentrated on the rights and interests of contemporary individual humans. Nature is valuable as long as it is of recognized value to humans. Very weak sustainability exploits natural resources and focuses on maximizing economic growth without limitations.

As stated earlier, the ECtHR has developed an impressive case law concerning environmentally relevant questions. For a detailed analysis of this body of law we will refer to work done by others (Boyle 2012, 626–33; Desgagné 1995; Francioni 2010, 48–51; Pedersen 2010). On a general note, the case law illustrates that the ECtHR is not a proponent of a very weak sustainability. But the case law also shows how demanding it is to adequately address the three competing elements of sustainable development. On the other hand, as Blanco and Razzaque (2009, 720) have emphasized, a rights-based approach can also be useful in this respect, because it is created in assigning responsibilities to, as well as allocating benefits among different actors.

We can take the case of *Dubetska and Others v Ukraine* as an example of how the ECtHR reasons. The applicants were two Ukrainian families who lived near to a coal mine and a coal-processing factory. They claimed that their right to respect for private and family life (Art. 8) was violated because of continued pollution originating from the industrial unit. The Court referred to its well-established case law according to which no provisions of the ECHR guarantee the right to preservation of the natural environment as such. Moreover, it stated that no issue will arise if the disadvantage complained of is insignificant in comparison to the environmental hazards inherent in modern life. An arguable claim may nonetheless arise "where an environmental hazard attains a level of severity resulting in significant impairment of the applicant's ability to enjoy his home, private or family life" (*Dubetska and Others v Ukraine* (2011), para. 105).

After establishing a causal link between the pollutant emissions and the state's actions, the Court continued to analyze whether the actions at hand had been justified pursuant to the limitation clause in Art. 8(2).[1] The Court emphasized that in environmental cases the state must be allowed a wide margin of appreciation and, accordingly, be given a choice between different ways of meeting its obligations. The key issue is whether a state

> has succeeded in striking a fair balance between the competing interests of the individuals affected and the community as a whole.... In making such an assessment all the factors, including domestic legality, must be analysed in the context of a particular case (para. 141)

The Court also underlined the fact that "the complexity of the issues involved with regard to environmental policymaking renders the Court's role primarily a subsidiary one" (para. 142).

When the Court examined whether the state's actions were justified, it analyzed whether the authorities had conducted adequate studies to evaluate the risks of a potentially hazardous activity. Moreover, it examined whether the state had developed a sufficient policy vis-à-vis polluters, and whether all essential measures had been taken to enforce this policy. Likewise, it examined to what extent the individuals affected by the policy were able to contribute efficiently to the decision making (para. 143). All things considered, the ECtHR found that there had been a breach of Art. 8 (para. 155).

Needless to say, there can be diverse opinions on what constitutes a fair balance between economic interests and individual rights. Such a judgment is inevitably subjective (Boyle 2010, 22). The fact that human rights law allows this type of weighing can be seen as both a strength and a weakness. On the one hand, human rights law is flexible and allows room for different aspects of sustainability, the environmental dimension included. On the other hand, human rights law is unable to definitively solve the tension between the three elements of sustainability.

As far as long-term responsibility is concerned, the essential question is what kind of balancing in a given society is seen as fair. This analysis is not made in a vacuum. Changes in the way we understand fairness are reflected in court judgments, within the limits of what is legally possible. The battle between the status quo and legal certainty on the one hand and dynamic interpretation on the other is nonetheless constantly present in the courts. New openings may first occur in dissenting opinions or in landmark cases that are tightly linked to the circumstances of a specific case. Societal development via courtrooms is often a step-by-step exercise.

2.2 On the rights of future generations

2.2.1 Sustainability as responsibility

As described above, very weak sustainability relies on traditional ethical reasoning and gives nature only instrumental value. When we move along the sustainability spectrum, the next stage entails the extension of ethical reasoning to include inter- and intragenerational dimensions too (Barr 2008, 46).

According to many scholars, the debate on sustainable development is primarily a discourse on our responsibility to future generations (Gündling 1990, 208). This linkage has also been identified by all the major UN conferences on sustainable development organized since 1972. The rights and interests of future generations are still seen as an important element in sustainable development which was also emphasized in Rio + 20 (United Nations 2012).

The concept of the rights of future generations has been the subject of lively debate among scholars. Its core essence is nonetheless simple. As Brown Weiss does in her work, we can start from an assumption that humans have the natural environment in common with all members of our species: past, present, and future generations. The present generation holds the earth in trust for future generations (Brown Weiss 1990, 198–9).

Three basic principles guide our relationship to future generations. First, each generation is required to conserve the diversity of the natural and cultural base so that it does not excessively restrict the options available for future generations.

Second, each generation should also be required to maintain the quality of the planet and pass it on in no worse condition than it was received. Finally, each generation should provide its members with a right of access to the legacy of past generations and should conserve this access for future generations (Brown Weiss 1990, 201–2).

A more elaborate analysis is outside the scope of this study. The three principles nevertheless necessitate some remarks. Unfortunately, they are more and more difficult to live up to. In fact, they are beyond reach. It is, for example, evident that we have already lost species and, consequently, it is impossible to provide anyone with access to that legacy. These observations of facts do not, however, make the concept useless in legal deliberations. Implementing law is a pragmatic exercise, and it is often utilized to provide more decisive content for vague political and moral standards. Law can thus be used to give more specific meaning to the idea of intergenerational equity (Nickel and Magraw 2010, 462).

Legally speaking, the logical starting point is to deliberate over whether rights are necessarily temporal. The answer is in the negative. All claims of right are to some extent future oriented, because their primary aim is to question or change existing norms, practices, and institutions. Equivalently, all declarations of rights presume that individuals in the future will benefit from them as well. Laws and regulations concerning environmental protection obviously invoke the future as justification for conservation (Hiskes 2005, 1355–6).

The idea of the rights of future generations is not foreign to human rights documents either. The UDHR recognizes in its preamble the inherent dignity and equal and inalienable rights of all members of the human family. Many other human rights documents disclose a fundamental belief in the dignity of all, and in an equality of rights that goes beyond time and space (Brown Weiss 1990, 201; Hiskes 2006, 92). However, the most difficult legal problems involve situations in which one right meets another right. This is the case with long-term responsibility toward future generations. If it is accepted, it can only modify, not cancel out, the duties toward existing generations.

2.2.2 Intertemporal balancing

The balancing between different elements of sustainability is hard for the present generation, and the task is even more difficult when rights are looked at in terms of temporal considerations (see also Maggio 1997, 171). Legal traditions constitute the first obstacle. Legal conventions, such as the perception of who can be a rights holder, change slowly (Stone 1972, 450–7). The legal audience is thus easier to convince using arguments that are based on traditional interpretations. The rights of future generations need to be argued for in this kind of scenario. In a case in which, say, property rights of living individuals are in conflict with the rights of future generations, the proponent of the latter group starts with an uphill battle.

Another element that makes the task demanding is that many of the risks we face are not known. Consequently, it is difficult to create efficient mechanisms to prevent them. The legal toolbox nevertheless includes an instrument through which the future with its unknown challenges can be taken into account. The precautionary principle states that where there are threats of serious or irreversible damage, a lack of full scientific certainty should not be used as a reason for suspending cost-effective measures to prevent environmental deprivation (United Nations 1992). One could say that the principle encourages a discussion on what kind of human-induced harm can be seen as acceptable (Cameron and Abouchar 1991, 3).

The significance of precaution is obvious for future generations. One of the challenges relating to their rights is that the more remote the future generation is, the more difficult it is to consider its needs. Simultaneously, we cannot assume that future generations will develop the knowledge or technology necessary to cope with all the problems they inherit. Both these aspects support precaution (Gündling 1990, 211).

Importantly, precautionary action involves a shift in the burden of proof toward those who wish to act, since they need to demonstrate that the potential harm is not serious or irreversible (Cameron and Abouchar 1991, 12). The principle is nonetheless feasible for the present generation, because it requires that measures to prevent damage are cost-effective. The precautionary approach appears to be beneficial in construing long-term responsibility.

But how does precautionary logic fit into the ECHR system? This question is linked to the concept of victim. The ECtHR used to exclude the possibility that a risk of future violation confers on an individual the status of a victim. It required instead that the applicant was able to produce reasonable and convincing evidence of the likelihood that a violation affecting him/her would occur (*Asselbourg and 78 and Greenpeace v Luxemburg* (1999), para. 1). It is noteworthy that future harm as such has not been the hurdle, but the likelihood of the negative consequences of it has. The judgment in the famous death row case of *Soering* demonstrates that the ECtHR has been able to take into consideration future harm if the risk of the violation has attained a particular level of certainty (*Soering v the United Kingdom* (1989), para. 111).

The environmental case law also shows that states have positive obligations to act, for example by engaging in risk and/or impact assessments, if there is a risk that a certain activity poses a danger to human health. As soon as the risk ought to have been foreseen, there is a duty to act (Boyle 2010, 16; de Wet and du Plessis 2010, 357). Recent case law even seems to take this a step further. In *Tatar v Romania*, the ECtHR ruled that the government must adopt adequate measures even when scientific certainty is lacking (*Tatar v Romania* (2009), paras 107–24). The Court also stated that the precautionary principle is, on the European level, a legally binding norm (para. 69).

It is thus probable that the principle of precaution will get a more significant role in the future, at least in cases where serious or irreversible harm is at stake. It is too early to say how far the measures of precaution should be taken, but it is safe to conclude that they need to be determined in accordance with the extent and the social acceptability of the risk involved (Boyle 2010, 16; Shelton 2010,

106). It is also doubtful whether human rights litigation is suitable to promote precautionary measures based on risk assessments, except in cases where risks involve an imminent threat to the rights of particular individuals (Boyle 2010, 37).

3 Strong forms of sustainability

3.1 *Preferring the rights of future generations*

Strong forms of sustainability presuppose a further extension of ethical reasoning in the sense that collective interests take precedence over those of the individual. They thus move beyond the instrumentalist view on nature that is typical in relation to the weaker forms of sustainability. This triggers two questions that have been difficult for human rights regimes. First, we need to explore the possibility of the ECtHR taking into account collective interests and rights. In addition, we must analyze whether the ECtHR can offer protection for the environment. The latter question, if answered in the affirmative, would suggest that human rights can also support very strong forms of sustainability. This argument will be developed in section 3.2.

Environmental degradation may violate the enjoyment of several individual rights. The individualistic approach is nevertheless ill-suited to address the subtle effects of environmental degradation of society as a whole (Desgagné 1995, 294; Francioni 2010, 44). This is relevant with regard to long-term responsibility, as rights of future generations are by nature collective rights.

The common argument against collective rights is that they devalue the notion of human rights and distract attention from individual rights (Boyle 2010, 2; Hiskes 2006, 82). It is nonetheless interesting that the only existing human rights convention that includes a specific right to a satisfactory environment has formulated it as a collective right. According to the *African Charter on Human and Peoples' Rights*, "[a]ll peoples shall have the right to a general satisfactory environment favorable to their development" (Art. 24). This demonstrates that, at the very least, the individualistic approach is not the only available option.

The Inter-American system has also shown an understanding of collective rights. The context has been somewhat specific, being that of indigenous peoples. Doelle (2004, 208) has suggested that the development could have implications beyond indigenous rights. Indigenous communities undoubtedly have a special connection to nature and depend on its conditions more than the general population. At the same time, argues Doelle, similar claims can be made by others who live in a way that makes them vulnerable to changes in the condition of the environment. This could open possibilities for similar claims from nonindigenous claimants, as long as they are able to show comparable dependence on nature and its resources.

The essential element in group rights seems to be the identity of the rights holder. If that is in dispute, talking about rights can be difficult. But as Waldron

(1987, 320) has emphasized: "[i]n cases where the identity of a group is not seriously disputed, talk of group rights is perfectly intelligible, and may be a useful vehicle for the expression of so called third generation claims." Emerging environmental rights of indigenous peoples verify the validity of his statement. They also offer an interesting analogy that supports the rights of future generations.

The tension between individualism and collectivism also has consequences for litigation processes. The approach of the ECtHR entails that only those directly affected by a violation can be victims. Even if the notion of victim has been expanded so as to also cover potential or eventual victims, the applicants must still show that an act or omission has an impact on their individual rights. The ECtHR has explicitly rejected the possibility of public interest litigation, or *actio popularis* (*Kyrtatos v Greece* (2003), para. 53; *L'Erablière A.S.B.L. v Belgien* (2009), paras 28–9).

This is inconsistent in an environmental context, considering that broader participation is a central element in sustainable development. In order for long-term responsibility to become enforceable, there must be a way to broaden the scope of those who can act on behalf of future generations. The recent land-mark decision in the *Centre for Legal Resources on behalf of Valentin Câmpeanu v Romania* case is interesting in this respect. The case concerned a Roma boy who had been abandoned at birth. He had grown up in orphanages, and had also been infected with HIV. After he turned 18 he was moved to an institution that denied him proper medication. When his health worsened, he was transferred to a psychiatric hospital, where the staff of the Centre for Legal Resources met him in horrifying circumstances. He died some time later. No investigation was conducted and nobody was held accountable for his death. As he had no relatives, the Centre applied to the ECtHR on his behalf.

The Court concluded that the Centre had legal standing. It noted that at the time of his death Mr Câmpeanu had no known next of kin. Nobody had been appointed by the state to take care of his interests. The Court concluded that in these exceptional circumstances the Centre should be allowed to represent Mr Câmpeanu. According to the ECtHR,

> [t]o find otherwise would amount to preventing such serious allegations of a violation of the Convention from being examined at an international level, with the risk that the respondent State might escape accountability under the Convention as a result of its own failure to appoint a legal representative to act on his behalf as it was required to do under national law (*Centre for Legal Resources on behalf of Valentin Câmpeanu v Romania* (2011), paras 110–12)

It is dangerous to jump to conclusions on the basis of one case. Nevertheless, the ECtHR was willing to speak out on behalf of Mr Câmpeanu because he had no voice. It broadened the concept of legal standing in order to guarantee the interests of justice. By analogy, the same logic could be used to support the rights of future generations. In the face of an environmental catastrophe, they can be seen as just as vulnerable as those who are maltreated in locked institutions. Without a guardian with legal standing, access to justice remains only a fiction for future generations.

3.2 Toward very strong sustainability?

The original intention of those who drafted the ECHR was not to guarantee a right to a sound, quiet, and healthy environment. The awareness of environmental problems came later. Regardless of the progress marked by the case law, the ECtHR still fails to recognize an independent right to a decent environment. Its approach is illustrated by the *Kyrtatos v Greece* case, in which the applicants brought a complaint under Art. 8 alleging that urban development had led to the destruction of a swamp close to their property and that as a consequence the area around their home had lost its picturesque beauty. The Court found no violation and emphasized that none of the articles of the ECHR "are specifically designed to provide general protection of the environment as such; to that effect, other international instruments and domestic legislation are more pertinent in dealing with this particular aspect" (*Kyrtatos v Greece* (2003), para. 52; see also *Fadeyeva v Russia* (2005), para. 68).

A very strong approach to sustainability would entail that environmental values are valuable in their own right. In the opinion of the ECtHR, environmental harm is not itself a cause for complaint, but must be linked to some sort of impact on humans. On another note, the ECtHR's strong focus on strengthening the rule of law has led to indirect protection of environmental values proper. As Shelton (2010, 106) has described, if the protection of nature is guaranteed under national law, there may be a separate claim in the ECtHR for failure to enforce that law. This is remarkable, as there is a growing tendency to, first, adopt laws that protect the environment and, second, formulate constitutional guarantees for environmental values (Pedersen 2010, 577–81).

The question of the intrinsic value of the environment still remains unanswered in the context of human rights. Without disparaging the relevance of the issue, one can argue that our fundamental dependence on the environment makes the difference between instrumental and intrinsic merely a question of degree, not a difference in essence. At the same time, lawyers understand that dynamic interpretation has its limits. To cross the line and conclude that the ECHR should be used in order to protect the environment per se should be left to those democratically responsible to decide.

4 Concluding remarks

Each legal vocabulary, whether it relates to human rights, trade law, or environmental law, is likely to emphasize some solutions, actors, and interests. Accordingly, the human rights regime is imprisoned within its own way of perceiving the world (see also Koskenniemi 2009, 10–11). Also, lawyers differ in their approaches to the role of law. An interpretation criticized by one is praised by another. When the possibilities and limits of human rights law are evaluated, these disagreements are always present.

Keeping these disclaimers in mind, we can present the potential of human rights in protecting environmental values. It is apparent that the relationship between human rights and environmental protection has not evolved by accident. They have many common objectives, such as keeping the planet as a place in which we can all live and guaranteeing that everyone participates in environmental decision making. Human rights have gradually developed into a common language of ethical discourse, which means that a human rights approach to environmental problems can rely on a fairly coherent and well-developed set of norms (Knox 2014, 23). The existence of legal and institutional mechanisms of implementation and enforcement is an additional asset alongside the pragmatic approach that is common in relation to legal rights (Hiskes 2005, 1362; Knox 2014, 23–5).

As repeatedly stated, the adaptability of the human rights system has been remarkable. Human rights bodies, such as the ECtHR, obviously accept the primacy of the texts of human rights treaties, and their main aim is the protection of the rights of the individual. They nevertheless interpret the rights in a dynamic manner. In addition, international conventions must always be considered along with other treaties, customary international law, and general principles of law relevant to the issue.[2] This legal cross-fertilization, together with the flexibility of the ECtHR, can be beneficial for the environment.

On the other hand, human rights law has its limitations as well. It covers only certain parts of the whole story. As human rights translate conflicts into rights entitlements and legal duties, they not only solve societal dilemmas, but also actively select the legally relevant aspects of the reality. Conflicts are framed as rights conflicts, which are displaced from their everyday locations and transferred to formal institutions specialized in rights problems. Conflicts are certainly cooled down, but the political–social dimension of them may get lost in translation (Frankenberg 2014, 51–2). This is also reflected in the way in which the ECtHR emphasizes the importance of a wide margin of appreciation in environmental issues. The Court has been cautious regarding redirecting environmental conflicts to become rights conflicts.

The aim of this article was to analyze whether the concept of sustainable development could provide tools that could be used to better integrate human rights and the environment. As the concept of sustainable development can be understood in many different ways, we found it important to define its essence to the extent that this is possible. We decided to systematize the development that has taken place in the European human rights regime with the help of the sustainability spectrum presented by Barr. The spectrum consists of a continuum ranging from weak to strong forms of sustainability. The strong versions of sustainability aim to maintain the critical levels of different forms of natural capital. The weaker forms, for their part, assume that natural capital can always be traded off and replaced with human capital, as long as the total capital that passes on from the present generation to the next is constant or growing. These two opposites were further divided into two subgroups, and the result was a spectrum ranging from very weak to weak and from strong to very strong sustainability. As described above, all these categories have their distinctive features as regards the type of economy, management strategies, and ethics involved. This categorization is of course one of many, but it nevertheless helps to manage the inherent tensions that are characteristic of the concept of sustainable development.

On the basis of the study, it is evident that in promoting sustainable development the role of human rights should not be overstated. Human rights in general and the ECHR in particular are currently capable of enhancing merely the weaker forms of sustainability. The environmental jurisprudence mainly bears a resemblance to traditional ethical reasoning. The focus is on individual rights of contemporary individuals, and the environment is taken into account via these rights. This is especially tangible in the balancing that takes place between the rights and interests at stake. At the same time, it is fair to argue that the European human rights system is greening, and it certainly puts emphasis on environmental values. In other words, environment matters, but it comes in second.

As we move along the sustainability spectrum from very weak to weak, the question of operationalizing intergenerational equity becomes pressing. Long-term responsibility as a legally enforceable responsibility requires first of all that we can overcome the question of causality. In addition, the scope of those having standing should be widened. Regarding the former question, we have identified some interesting signals, such as the emerging importance of the precautionary principle. A stronger emphasis on the role of precaution would shift the burden of proof to those who want to engage in actions that have long-term consequences. This would strengthen the role of *ex ante* impact assessments which, together with a broader understanding of legal standing, could support the situation of those not yet born. On a negative note, the shifting of the burden of proof might be perceived as unfair and unreasonably limiting, for example in relation to industrial activities. Development toward *actio popularis* could entail the risk of burdening the ECtHR's already pressing workload.

When approaching the stronger forms of sustainability, one can only find possible openings toward them. Human rights systems have been reluctant to accept collective rights, and this can also be seen in the case law at hand. Outside Europe, the emerging right to a satisfactory environment for indigenous peoples is still a development worth following. Their vulnerabilities have much in common with those of future generations.

Human rights, with their inevitable anthropocentric bias, have sometimes been regarded as a significant cause of environmental problems. Certainly, it is challenging to link individual human rights with the idea of intrinsic value in nature. It is up to us to decide whether we let this tension paralyze us or whether we choose to become more pragmatic. As part of nature, we can accept our fundamental dependence on the environment and decide to work for environmental protection. In many national constitutions, this dilemma is solved one-sidedly. For example, the Finnish Constitution declares that nature and its biodiversity are the responsibility of everyone. Not a word is said about the rights of nature. This solution is perhaps unsatisfactory for philosophers, but it is legally enforceable. Seen from a legal perspective, it shows that it is possible to create obligations without having identifiable rights holders.

Present environmental problems are everyone's concern, and we also have the responsibility – common but differentiated – to mitigate the negative effects of our actions and omissions. Above all, we need courageous political decisions. Courtrooms should not be a substitute for politicians. But there is also a lot of work for progressive lawyers to do. The potential of human rights to protect the environment has not yet been fully discovered.

Notes

1 Art. 8(2):

> There shall be no interference by a public authority with the exercise of this right except such as is in accordance with the law and is necessary in a democratic society in the interests of national security, public safety or the economic well-being of the country, for the prevention of disorder or crime, for the protection of health or morals, or for the protection of the rights and freedoms of others.

2 I refer to the rules concerning treaty interpretation, codified in the 1969 *Vienna Convention on the Law of Treaties*. See, in particular, Art. 31(3), according to which there shall be taken into account in interpretation, together with the context, a) any subsequent agreement between the parties regarding the interpretation of the treaty or the application of its provisions, b) any subsequent practice in the application of the treaty that establishes the agreement of the parties regarding its interpretation, and c) any relevant rules of international law applicable in the relations between the parties. This approach has also been emphasized by the ECtHR in the case of *Demir and Baykara v Turkey* (2008), para. 85.

References

Monographs, articles, and official publications

Barr S. (2008) *Environment and society: sustainability, politics and the citizen* Aldershot, Ashgate.

Blanco E. and Razzaque J. (2009) "Ecosystem services and human well-being in a globalized world: assessing the role of law" *Human Rights Quarterly*, 31 692–720.

Bosselmann K. (2008) *The principle of sustainability. Transforming law and governance* Aldershot, Ashgate.

Boyle A. (2010) *Human rights and the environment: a reassessment* UNEP paper (18), Available at www.unep.org/environmentalgovernance, accessed 4 April 2015.

Boyle A. (2012) "Human rights and the environment: where next?" *The European Journal of International Law*, 23(3) 613–42.

Brown Weiss E. (1990) "Our rights and obligations to future generations" *The American Journal of International Law*, 84(1) 197–207.

Cameron J. and Abouchar J. (1991) "The precautionary principle: a fundamental principle of law and policy for the protection of the global environment" *Boston College International and Comparative Law Review*, 14(1) 1–27.

de Wet E. and du Plessis A. (2010) "The meaning of certain substantive obligations distilled from international human rights instruments for constitutional environmental rights in South Africa" *African Human Rights Journal*, 10(2) 345–76.

Desgagné R. (1995) "Integrating environmental values into the European Convention on Human Rights" *The American Journal of Human Rights*, 89(2) 263–94.

Doelle M. (2004) "Climate change and human rights" *The Macquarie Journal of International and Comparative Environmental Law*, 1 179–216.

Francioni F. (2010) "International human rights in an environmental horizon" *The European Journal of International Law*, 21(1) 41–55.

Frankenberg G. (2014) "Human rights and the belief in a just world" *International Journal of Constitutional Law*, 12(1) 35–60.

Gündling L. (1990) "Our responsibility to future generations" *The American Journal of International Law*, 84(1) 207–12.

Hiskes R. (2005) "The right to a green future: human rights, environmentalism, and intergenerational justice" *Human Rights Quarterly*, 27 1346–64.

Hiskes R. (2006) "Environmental human rights and intergenerational justice" *Human Rights Review*, 81–95.

Knox J.H. (2014) "Climate ethics and human rights" *Journal of Human Rights and the Environment*, 5 22–34.

Koskenniemi M. (2009) "The politics of international law – 20 years later" *The European Journal of International Law*, 20(1) 7–19.

Maggio G.F. (1997) "Inter/intra-generational equity: current applications under international law for promoting the sustainable development of natural resources" *Buffalo Environmental Law Journal*, 4 161–223.

Nickel J. and Magraw D. (2010) "Philosophical issues in international environmental law" in Besson S. and Tassioulas J. eds, *The philosophy of international law* Oxford, Oxford University Press 453–71.

Pedersen O.W. (2010) "The ties that bind: the environment, the European Convention on Human Rights and the rule of law" *European Public Law*, 16(4) 571–95.

Shelton D. (2010) "Developing substantive environmental rights" *Journal of Human Rights and the Environment*, 1(1) 89–120.

Stone C.D. (1972) "Should trees have standing? – Toward legal rights for natural objects" *Southern California Law Review*, 45 450–501.

United Nations (1992) *Report of the United Nations Conference on Environment and Development* A/CONF.151/26, Vol. I, Annex I, held at Rio de Janeiro, Brazil, 3–14 June 1992, Available at www.un-documents.net, accessed 2 April 2015.

United Nations (2012) *The future we want* Resolution adopted by the General Assembly, A/RES/66/288, Annex, Available at http://daccess-dds-ny.un.org/doc/UNDOC/GEN/N11/476/10/PDF/N1147610.pdf?OpenElement, accessed 20 October 2015.

Waldron J. (1987) "Can communal goods be human rights?" *European Journal of Sociology*, 28 296–322.

World Commission on Environment and Development (1987) *Report of the World Commission on Environment and Development: our common future*, Available at www.un-documents.net, Accessed 2 April 2015.

Cases

Free online access to the cases of the ECtHR is provided by the European Court of Human Rights Case Database (HUDOC) [Online]. All cases are available from http://hudoc.echr.coe.int/sites/eng/Pages/search.aspx# [Accessed 2 July 2015].
Asselbourg and 78 and Greenpeace v Luxemburg, Application no. 29121/95, Decision of 29 June 1999.
Centre for Legal Resources on behalf of Valentin Câmpeanu v Romania, Judgment of 17 July 2011 [Grand Chamber, GC].
Demir and Baykara v Turkey, Judgment of 12 November 2008 [GC].
Dubetska and Others v Ukraine, Judgment of 10 May 2011.
L'Erablière A.S.B.L. v Belgium, Judgment of 24 May 2009.
Fadeyeva v Russia, Judgment of 9 June 2005.
Kyrtatos v Greece, Judgment of 22 May 2003.
Soering v the United Kingdom, Judgment of 7 July 1989.
Tatar v Romania, Judgment of 6 July 2009 (available in French only).

Conventions and declarations

African Charter on Human and Peoples' Rights 1981, 1520 UNTS 217.
Convention for the Protection of Human Rights and Fundamental Freedoms 1950, *European Convention on Human Rights*, as amended, CETS No. 005.
International Covenant on Civil and Political Rights 1966, 999 UNTS 171.
International Covenant on Economic, Social and Cultural Rights 1966, 993 UNTS 3.
Universal Declaration of Human Rights 1948, UNGA Res 217 A(III), adopted 10 December 1948.
Vienna Convention on the Law of Treaties 1969, 1155 UNTS 679.

3 An atmospheric trust to protect the environment for future generations?

Reform options for human rights law

Peter Lawrence

1 Introduction

Law rests on fictions. Christopher Stone (1972) pointed this out forcefully in his seminal article, written 40 years ago: 'Should trees have standing? Toward legal rights for natural objects'. Examples of such fictions are easy to find. 'Corporations' are given 'personality' as though they possess characteristics common to natural persons. Even the notion of natural legal persons under the law involves fictions in that an assumption is made that a person has the capacity to exercise rights regardless of whether that person is infirm or profoundly disabled. International law is also replete with fictions. For example, customary international law requires states to express consent to a particular rule – the so-called requirement of *opinio juris* – implying that a state somehow embodies a natural person (Shaw 2008, 75).

Stone points out that these legal fictions, while initially strongly resisted, eventually find acceptance because they conform to particular shared ends or values which are being pursued by society. This chapter is inspired by Stone in imagining possibilities for a reformed international human rights (IHR) law which would flow from a set of assumptions entailing ethical obligations towards future generations in relation to the environment. This is used as a springboard for critiquing current IHR law in terms of its treatment of the preservation of the environment for the benefit of future generations. A particular legal fiction – that of the 'trust' found in common law but also in fragmentary form in current international law – is argued to be a particularly useful mechanism for giving weight to future generations' interests in the IHR legal system. In recent US litigation, attempts have been made to extend the notion of a 'public trust' to the atmosphere with non-governmental organisations (NGOs) purporting to represent particular young people and future generations seeking declarations that the government in question (state and national) be required to urgently curtail greenhouse emissions. This is argued to be pursuant to the government's obligation as a trustee to respect the atmosphere as a public resource for the benefit of the public, including future generations. These cases provide interesting possibilities for cross-fertilisation with IHR law.

The context of this discussion includes a number of global environmental challenges which can only be addressed through international cooperation, including climate change, ozone depletion, disposal of nuclear waste, transboundary atmospheric pollution and marine pollution. These issues have an intergenerational justice dimension, in that a failure by current generations to adequately address them creates greater harm and costs for future generations.

The other important context of this chapter is the increasingly complex relationship between IHR law and institutions and global environmental issues. One example of this has been the taking up of the issue of climate change within the UN human rights system, while human rights discourse has largely been absent from the *United Nations Framework Convention on Climate Change* (UNFCCC) negotiation process itself.

My argument has three parts. In section 2, I address the content of human rights, sketching an argument for a moral right to a healthy environment which generates obligations on governments to preserve the global ecological system – including the climatic system.

In section 3, I outline what a *utopian* IHR law would look like if it reflected the ethical obligations towards future generations set out in section 2. This is done by a focus on its scope, structure and effectiveness. By *scope* I am referring to the *content* of human rights: do human rights law obligations extend to the environment as such in addition to more traditional human rights? By *structure* I am referring to both the legal subjects of human rights, i.e. the bearers of human rights obligations, and the addressees of human rights, i.e. those entities subject to obligations, to ensure that human rights are respected. Indeed, if human rights rest on the bedrock of a person's humanity rather than her or his citizenship, how would a utopian IHR law reflect this? Do IHR law obligations extend to harm occurring to the citizens of other states – so-called extraterritorial harm? By *effectiveness* I am referring to what impact the reformed IHR law would have in addressing the particular environmental problem at hand. I illustrate this with reference to climate change.

In section 4, I contrast the utopian vision of international human rights law set out in section 3 with IHR law as it currently stands. In conclusion, I argue that there is no inherent obstacle in IHR law as such which limits the possibility of it moving towards the utopian vision set out in section 3. Law reflects the values of society. This applies equally to international as well as to national law. I strike, however, a note of caution in terms of the limits of IHR law in addressing global environmental issues such as climate change, which depend upon effective treaties and minimal agreement on the distributive justice questions at stake. The latter involve, for example, how climate change mitigation burdens should be distributed between current and future generations. The less mitigation that occurs now, the greater the burden of mitigation and the greater the impact for future generations. Human rights law, by its nature, cannot resolve these distributional justice issues.

2 Ethical responsibility for a healthy environment for future generations

This part addresses the content of human rights, developing an argument for an ethical obligation on current generations to preserve a minimum level of ecological integrity essential for the welfare of future generations (Lawrence 2014). My approach is pragmatic in seeking to ground such an obligation in widely shared values. My starting point is that one can distinguish human rights as a system of morality from IHR law. Besson (2012, 231) points out that human rights are inherently both moral and legal. She defines human rights as a 'subset of universal moral rights (a) that protect fundamental and general human interests against (b) the intervention, or in some cases non-intervention, of (c) national, regional, or international public institutions' (see also Sen 2004, 327). She adds to this interest-based notion of rights the idea that human rights have an independent moral basis and depend on the notion of each individual being a member of the community and possessing equal status; thus, human rights are a means of consolidating an abstract notion of equality (Besson 2012, 233).[1]

Human rights as moral rights protect particularly important human interests and generate corresponding ethical obligations on states not to harm these interests (Raz 1984, 183). Traditionally, IHR law has not included the environment as a discrete right, but has included other rights – particularly economic and social rights – which may be violated by environmental harms. These include human rights to life (physical security), subsistence, property and health, which are clearly threatened by climate change (Caney 2009, 167). There has also been recognition of the human right to water in the UN human rights system.[2] Human beings are dependent on a healthy environment in terms of water, food and shelter, which are essential for human flourishing (Hiskes 2009, 39). This dependence also extends to a stable climate, which is currently threatened by climate change (Vanderheiden 2008, 252). Bearing this in mind, it is logical to posit a 'right to a healthy environment' as a moral human right that protects human interests of equal importance to human flourishing as the more traditional human rights (Hayward 2005, 54). An alternate approach is to argue that the environment can be protected incidentally to the protection of other rights. For example, implementation of the right to subsistence can arguably only be achieved through governments ensuring protection of the environment. However, this, in my view, is insufficient in capturing the crucial importance of environmental protection as an independent value. Given the current global environmental crisis and threat to the interests of future generations, an explicit right to a decent environment could help ensure that governments explicitly focus on meeting the preconditions for sustainable development (Boyle 2012, 641).

As mentioned, climate change threatens traditional human rights, such as the rights to life, health and subsistence. Unmitigated climate change threatens the rights of persons alive today with increasingly harmful impacts into the future. If one imagines a person born today, that person in 2050 will be 35 years old. A 50-year-old politician now will be 85 years old in 2050. Thus, climate change will seriously impact current generations within their lifetime, with increased mortality from extreme weather events and tropical diseases (Intergovernmental Panel on Climate Change 2014). But the most severe impacts will be felt by unborn generations, and these future generations will face risks of irreversible harm to the global ecological system and climate. The recently released IPCC Fifth Assessment Report highlights some of these risks, including the likelihood of the Greenland ice sheet melting (Intergovernmental Panel on Climate Change 2013). A right to a healthy environment would capture more fully the range of threats posed by these developments.

An obligation on contemporaries towards future generations in relation to the environment rests on three central principles. These principles are not fully elaborated here and stand as assumptions.

They are as follows:

P1 _Equality principle_: Flowing from human dignity as the basis of all human rights, all persons born now and in the future are entitled to certain core human rights to life, health and subsistence (Caney 2009, 168) and a healthy environment.
(Hayward 2005)

P2 _Harm avoidance principle_: Contemporaries have an ethical obligation to avoid harm, including to the interests and core human rights of future generations, including their right to a healthy environment.
(see Lawrence 2014, 29–66; Vanderheiden 2008, 137)

P3 _Precautionary principle_: The third principle is an extension of the harm avoidance principle and requires contemporaries to refrain from action which causes irreversible harm to the global ecological system upon which both contemporaries and future generations depend.

I would emphasise that these three ethical principles rest on widely shared values. The notion of all persons being equally entitled to core human rights is found in the near universal support for the _Universal Declaration of Human Rights_ (UDHR) and the major human rights treaties (Donnelly 2007). The UDHR links this equality principle with the notion of human dignity expressed as 'recognition of the inherent dignity and of the equal and inalienable rights of all members of the human family'.[3] These treaties and the UDHR enjoy near-consensus support from the international community. All states now accept the universality of human rights, while some states, such as China, place emphasis on 'survival rights of subsistence' – socio-economic rights – over civil and political rights (Sceats and Breslin 2012, 8).[4] The right to a healthy environment expressed in P2 has not found universal agreement (see section 3 below), but is nevertheless embodied in some non-binding instruments enjoying widespread support, such as the Stockholm Declaration of 1972[5] and, as mentioned above, could be argued to be implicitly entailed in a number of other rights.

It should be noted that the three principles set out above are anthropocentric in nature. The global ecological system does not have a value in itself but is valued in terms of its value for human beings. This approach rests on an assumption that one is more likely to be able to develop the required consensus for international action on global environmental problems by taking it, rather than deep ecology approaches.[6] Moreover, as Norton (as cited in Hay 2002, 60) points out, given that human beings share with other species a requirement for clean air, water and sustainable ecosystems, 'weak anthropocentrism' can ground a 'strong sustainability' approach: long-term human values require protection of the ecological system.

If we now turn to the potential claimants of a reformed human rights, does the human rights analysis sketched above fail, however, in relation to future generations, on the grounds that such persons cannot possess rights prior to being born? This issue is dealt with elsewhere in this book (see Chapter 6 by Düwell, Chapter 8 by Preda, Chapter 9 by Bos and Chapter 11 by Beyleveld). I put this issue aside, on the basis that it is sufficient to ground an ethical obligation towards future generations in the context of global environmental threats such as climate change on the assumption that current generations should refrain from action which will harm future persons' humans rights upon being born (Vanderheiden 2008).

Turning now to the addressees of a reformed human rights, does the notion of 'sustainable development' supply the necessary content in terms of obligations on contemporary governments extending into the future? The Brundtland notion of sustainable development as 'development that meets the needs of the present generations without compromising the ability of future generations to meet their own needs' (World Commission on Environment and Development 1987, 43) is widely supported in international instruments, at least at a political level (Sands and Peel 2012, 206–9). This concept of sustainable development implies a notion of intergenerational justice. The Brundtland definition, however, leaves key questions unanswered, including what precisely is to be sustained and whether the obligation is to maintain overall human well-being or merely to ensure that one's successors lead reasonable lives above a basic subsistence level (Page 2006, 11). The Brundtland concept combined with the notion of equality points in the direction of strong sustainability being applied, at least in relation to elements of the ecosystem upon which human beings depend that are not substitutable (Carmody 2012, 73). Anything less than this would impinge upon the equality principle P1, set out above, by implicitly according less value to the interests of future generations.

The three ethical principles sketched above seem vague in answering the difficult question of how much environmental quality must be preserved for future generations. Put differently, how do policymakers strike a balance between current and future generations' interests in relation to, for example, biological diversity where these conflict? In the context of mitigation of climate change, for example, this involves the question of how quickly mitigation should occur given the conflict in interests between current generations' dependence on fossil-fuel-related energy sources and future generations' interests in having a stable climate system. Distributional-justice-related principles are required to address this issue, and human rights cannot by themselves answer this question.[7]

In summary, the three ethical principles which I have outlined require for their implementation, as a minimum, that current generations avoid action which is likely to cause irreversible harm to irreplaceable elements of the global ecosystem, including the climate system, upon which future generations depend for their human rights. This is a version of a strong sustainability approach. Such an approach flows from the equality principle, as a failure to observe a strong sustainability approach would entail according less weight to the interests of persons born in the future because, according to our current state of knowledge, future generations will be as dependent upon a functioning global ecological system as current generations.

3 A utopian international human rights law for the protection of the environment for future generations

How would the ethical principles sketched above be reflected in a utopian IHR law? This question is addressed in terms of the *scope*, *structure* and *effectiveness* of this 'ideal' law. By *scope* I am referring to the content of this utopian IHR law. By *structure* I am referring to its subjects, addressees and potential claimants.

In terms of scope, an ideal IHR law would contain a 'right to a healthy environment' in order to give effect to the 'harm avoidance' and 'equality principles' sketched in the previous section. As argued above, this would help pressure governments to specifically focus on the environment in policy-making, essential given the current global environmental crisis. Such a right would be embedded in an IHR instrument with a corresponding obligation on governments to progressively implement this right in accordance with their capabilities. Boyle makes a good case for inclusion of such a right in the *International Covenant on Economic, Social and Cultural Rights* (ICESCR) rather than in the *International Covenant on Civil and Political Rights* (ICCPR) (Boyle 2012, 613). He points out that inclusion of such a right would entail an obligation on governments, when making policy decisions, to give sufficient weight to environmental concerns, while allowing them to retain policy discretion in terms of how the balance is struck between competing environmental and economic factors.

Incorporating a right to a healthy environment would help ensure that increased weight is given to the environmental interests of current generations in terms of the *scope* of IHR law. It would also benefit future generations if interpreted consistently with the sustainability requirements outlined above.

Furthermore, a utopian IHR law would entail the notion of a 'right to a healthy environment' being used as a benchmark, generating obligations of prevention on governments (Caney 2006; Rajamani 2010, 424). While inherently vague, the right to a healthy environment could be further elaborated and refined over time to ensure that the thresholds were sufficiently clear in order to have the desired impact on policymakers.

The *structure* of contemporary IHR litigation is limited in terms of potential claimants (see section 4 below) in that obligations are generally only able to be invoked if a person can show actual or imminent damage to their rights. This would seem to preclude claims being brought on behalf of future unborn generations. But an IHR environmental trust mechanism could more directly ensure that future generations' interests are given equal weight, reflecting the equality principles set out in section 2 above.

Recent atmospheric trust cases in the US are instructive in this regard. In these cases, minors and their guardians brought legal actions coordinated by the not-for-profit organisation Our Children's Trust in 50 states of the US and under federal jurisdiction. The claimants invoked the common law public trust doctrine, according to which governments have a duty to preserve the quality of rivers and some other natural resources for the benefit of current and future generations (Wood 2013, 128).[8]

In these cases, the petitioners claimed that the public trust extended to the atmosphere and that the courts should make declarations requiring government action to reduce greenhouse gas emissions in accordance with the prescriptions of climate scientists. An example of such a case is *Robin Blades v State California*. In this case, the complainants comprised Californian children and young adults. They did not purport to represent future unborn generations but based their claims on the impact which greenhouse gas emissions would have on their own lives. Thus, for example, Robin Blades (14 at the time of the petition) described the impacts that climate change was projected to have on California, including in relation to water scarcity, noting that he would be 50 years old in 2050.[9]

A similar attempt to invoke the public trust doctrine and extend it to the atmosphere has been attempted under US federal law, to date without success.[10] The US Supreme Court rejected a claim of this nature in *PPL Montana, LLC v Montana* on the grounds that the public trust doctrine was a matter of state law and even if it formed part of federal law, it had been displaced by US federal legislation in the form of the Clean Air Act.[11] Further litigation raising these issues has continued in the US District Court of Columbia. Various youth groups have sought an order compelling the Obama administration to immediately implement sharp reductions in greenhouse gas emissions.[12] These groups have argued that the failure of the US administration to take the necessary mitigation action breaches the US Constitution's requirement to guarantee 'equal protection before the law' (Fourteenth Amendment to the US Constitution) as young people and 'posterity' were disproportionately impacted by climate change compared to current generations.[13] This argument mirrors the equal entitlement notion discussed in section 2 above.

To date, these US atmospheric trust cases have had no direct impact on climate policy, and are likely to continue to have limited success owing to the view taken by the US courts that climate change mitigation is a policy issue for the executive and not the judiciary.[14] Nevertheless, these cases may increase political pressure on governments to take mitigation action. For our purposes, these cases are interesting in that they suggest a possible trust-based model for potential incorporation in IHR law. Indeed, other areas of international law already contain examples of trust-based mechanisms. These include, for example, the UN Law of the Sea Convention's designation of certain high seas areas as 'common heritage of mankind', with the resources of these areas of the seabed to be administered so as to be 'vested in mankind as a whole, on whose behalf an International Seabed Authority ... shall act' (Birnie, Boyle and Redgwell 2009, 197).

A utopian IHR law could incorporate a trust mechanism whereby the ICESCR is amended to provide that NGOs representing young people and future generations have a right to invoke the obligation on states to ensure implementation of the right to a healthy environment. Such a provision could include a right for individuals or groups to invoke this right against the government in question and could also include the option of individual petitions to the UN Human Rights Committee (Alston and Goodman 2013, 808). To protect the rights of future generations, these provisions could make clear that NGOs which met certain criteria could bring claims on behalf of future generations, thus expanding the range of potential claimants.

Indeed, the notion of giving NGOs a pivotal role in compliance with international treaties already has a strong precedent in the (regional) 1998 Aarhus Convention.[15] This Convention provides for a right to participate in environmental decision-making and extends to NGOs playing a key part in cases of non-compliance. A mechanism similar to the Aarhus mechanism could be incorporated in IHR law to give substance to the equality principle outlined in section 2 by allowing NGOs that represent future generations a right to participate in environmental decision-making. This would ensure increased weight being given to environmental interests in policy-making for the benefit of future generations while not intruding on governments' discretion in balancing competing interests. In this respect, such a mechanism would be largely procedure but with the potential to improve policy in substance.

A possible objection to the proposal to include a right to a healthy environment in the ICESCR is that it would be too vague to be justiciable. Moreover, it would arguably involve the courts in social policy issues which should be more appropriately dealt with by the executive branch of government. Jurisprudence in South Africa is interesting in this respect. South Africa has incorporated in its constitution a provision based on the ICESCR which provides that '[e]veryone has a right to have access to adequate housing', with the state required to take 'reasonable legislative and other measures, within its available resources, to achieve the progressive realisation of this right' (Anton and Shelton 2011, 256). The South African Constitutional Court has interpreted this provision as requiring that reasonable provision be made for persons in desperate need following evictions, while emphasising that 'the national government bears overall responsibility for ensuring that the state complies with the obligations imposed upon it by section 26'.[16] This jurisprudence suggests that it would be feasible to implement a right to a healthy environment which would appear to be no less vague than a right to adequate housing. A total disregard for the environment would breach such a provision, but governments would be left to balance the interests at stake within this constraint.

A further important structural element to be included in a utopian IHR law would be provisions establishing that the ICESCR and ICCPR generate duties of prevention for governments which apply to extraterritorial harms that occur in places under the control or jurisdiction of the parties to these treaties. Under current IHR law it is unclear whether governments have such duties (see below). Thus, where environmental harm occurs outside the territory of a state, victims could invoke the breach of human rights norms in the courts of the state which caused the harm. Indeed, utopian IHR law could include provisions which established the rights of NGOs to invoke these provisions on behalf of young people and future generations. These extraterritorial provisions, again, would reflect strongly notions of equal entitlement and non-discrimination. Those outside the state causing the harm should have the same rights of access to remedies as victims inside the state (Boyle 2012, 639).

In summary then, a utopian IHR law could reflect the ethical principles of avoiding harm to the environment and equal entitlement to a human right to the environment for future generations. This would be attained by, first, expanding IHR law in *scope* or content to include a right to a healthy environment. Second, in terms of *structure*, IHR law would recognise duties of prevention in relation to future generations and across national boundaries. It would also expand the category of potential claimants by incorporating a trust mechanism whereby NGOs representing young people and future generations could invoke this right to a healthy environment against governments, including on behalf of future generations.

Such a utopian human rights law would, however, have important limitations. While it would aim to ensure that greater weight is given to the environmental interests, including those of future generations, in government decision-making, it would not, however, displace governments' retention of primary responsibility for balancing competing environmental and other interests. In this sense, it would have a largely procedural dimension. This inherent limitation also includes the obstacle that human rights cannot by themselves address the distributional justice issues involved in, for example, the distribution of mitigation burdens across generations needed to address climate change. These limitations mean that in terms of *effectiveness*, even a utopian IHR law could only partially solve the particular global environmental issue in question.

4 Existing international human rights law for the protection of the environment for future generations

In this part, I examine the broad contours of existing IHR law in terms of the protection of the environmental interests of future generations. The analysis again proceeds in terms of scope, structure and effectiveness. Existing IHR law is contrasted with the utopian IHR law outlined in the previous section.

In terms of scope or content, current IHR law does not generally include a 'right to a healthy environment'. The key UN human rights treaties do not include such a right; however it is found in regional human rights treaties for Africa[17] and South America.[18]

A 'right to sustainable development' is not embedded in a legally binding treaty at the global level as a freestanding obligation. The 1992 *Rio Declaration on Environment and Development* contains a controversial 'right to development' providing that 'the right to development must be fulfilled so as to equitably meet developmental needs of present and future generations'.[19] The 1993 Vienna human rights declaration (*Vienna Declaration and Programme of Action*) similarly states that 'the right to development should be fulfilled so as to meet equitably the developmental needs of present and future generations' (para. 11),[20] but it is a non-binding political instrument. The UNFCCC incorporates 'a right to sustainable development' and a corresponding obligation on state parties 'to promote sustainable development'.[21]

So in terms of *scope*, current IHR law is limited in that it does not include a right to a healthy environment for the benefit of future generations. However, as mentioned above, global environmental threats such as climate change infringe a range of well-established human rights, including rights to life, health, subsistence and property.[22] In the European human rights system, these rights have been invoked for environmental purposes (see Pirjatanniemi, Chapter 2 section 2.1 in this volume).

In terms of the *structure* of contemporary human rights litigation,[23] typically this entails a citizen of a state bringing a claim against its government for a breach of a particular human rights obligation. There are both *temporal* and *spatial* limits to this typical schema. A temporal limit is the requirement that victims of human rights violations establish actual or imminent harm to their interests as a precondition for bringing a claim against their government. This is what lawyers describe as 'standing'. This poses an obvious obstacle in relation to future unborn generations, restricting the class of potential claimants.

It is instructive in this context to examine these issues in the jurisprudence of the *European Convention on Human Rights* (ECHR). In the case of *Noel Narvii v France* (1995), some residents of French Polynesia claimed that the right to life of their descendants under the ECHR was threatened by France's resumption of nuclear testing in the Pacific.[24] The claimants pointed to the risk of potential birth defects which they and their descendants would likely suffer. The European Commission of Human Rights held, however, that only in 'highly exceptional circumstances' could an applicant claim to be a victim of a breach of the Convention owing to a 'risk of future violation'[25] and that 'evidence needed to be produced demonstrating the likelihood that the violation would impact on her or him personally'.[26]

In *Kolyadenko v Russia*,[27] the European Court of Human Rights held that the measures taken by the authorities in Russia were inadequate to discharge that country's obligations to take positive steps to safeguard the right to life required under article 2 of the Convention. The case concerned the release of water from a reservoir which had put at risk the lives of the complainants. The Court held that the authorities knew that it may be necessary to release the water and the potential consequences should have been foreseen (paras 163–5). The authorities had failed to put in place adequate measures to address this risk (paras 169–73). The Court affirmed the doctrine of 'margin of appreciation' (para. 160), according to which member states are given some discretion as to exactly how they implement particular rights in the Convention. But the Court made clear that this doctrine will not apply where the preventive measures taken by a government are totally inadequate to address a foreseeable risk. While the issue has not come directly before the Court, the rationale of this decision would seem applicable to climate change measures where a government took measures that were totally inadequate to protect against a foreseeable risk, e.g. storm surges.

Thus, a *structural* difficulty under current IHR litigation is that to establish standing, claimants must demonstrate actual or imminent harm to their interests. This is clearly not possible for future unborn generations. However, the *Kolyadenko* case, by emphasising the obligation on states to take preventive measures to secure rights in the face of anticipated and predictable threats,[28] may have opened up new possibilities in this field (Cox 2014). Further claims could provide a basis for putting political pressure on policymakers to take preventive mitigation action in relation to climate change and other critical environmental threats.

A further *structural* limitation in current IHR law is that it is unclear under jurisprudence relating to these instruments whether the relevant obligations on governments extend to cover harm outside the control or jurisdiction of the particular state party. This makes it uncertain whether, for example, a citizen of Tuvalu could bring a claim against the US or have its government bring such a claim in relation to damage sourced from US greenhouse gas emissions. Such a claim would face other obstacles such as those relating to causation (see below). Jurisprudence on this issue is conflicting, and to date there has not been a case which considers this issue in terms of transboundary environmental issues (Knox 2009).

A final structural difficulty relates to causation. In relation to global environmental issues such as climate change, it is difficult to attribute causation to any particular state. One could argue that liability should be apportioned according to current greenhouse gas emissions. But this would still leave unresolved how much weight should be given to historic emissions (Knox 2009, 191).

The causation challenge reflects the more general problem that human rights litigation cannot be a substitute for international law-making in the form of effective environmental treaties. Such treaties need to incorporate rules which operate on a preventive rather than a reactive basis and have, for example, binding emissions targets and timetables in relation to greenhouse gas emissions and restrictions on ozone-depleting substances. We have seen that IHR law as a benchmark may, however, supplement environmental treaties and may assist by increasing political pressure on governments. In terms of *effectiveness*, IHR litigation to date has had a limited impact in terms of adequately addressing global environmental problems. States remain reluctant to bring claims against each other involving IHR law (Office of the High Commissioner for Human Rights n.d.). This is probably due to concerns about the adverse consequences which a state bringing such a claim could suffer in terms of relations with its powerful trading partners. While standing on behalf of future generations remains problematic, under the ECHR there have been signs of a preventive approach that may open up fruitful possibilities.

5 Conclusion

In this chapter, I have explored the promise of contemporary human rights law to achieve sustainability by describing a utopian IHR law which reflects some key principles, including a moral right to a healthy environment and the notion that all persons possess such a right regardless of when and where they are born. Law reflects societal values. I have sought to show that if we ascribe a particular value to the global ecological system, then there is nothing inherent in the nature of IHR law which would prevent this law from being reconfigured to reflect this value. Just as the notion of a 'corporation' services particular ends in domestic law (facilitating investment through limited liability of shareholders), IHR law could incorporate the notion of an atmospheric or environmental trust that reflects the value of a stable climate system for human existence. This utopian IHR law would incorporate standing rights for NGOs to enforce an atmospheric trust against governments, thereby ensuring that environmental values were accorded greater weight by them in policy-making. It could do this without impinging unduly on the role of governments in balancing environmental and economic interests. Such a utopian IHR law could include obligations of prevention extending into the future and also extending across national boundaries to cover extraterritorial harms, reflecting the notion of equality of access to justice.

In contrasting this utopian IHR law with current IHR law, we have seen that there are, however, inherent limitations to IHR law which would be difficult to overcome even if the utopian vision sketched above became a reality. A reformed IHR law would remain limited in addressing global environmental issues such as climate change, as even an IHR law with broader content cannot by itself resolve the distributional justice issues involved in addressing issues such as mitigation of climate change. Despite these limitations, there is value in pursuing reform of IHR law. The urgency of the global ecological crisis requires nothing less.

Acknowledgements

I wish to thank Gerhard Bos and Marcus Düwell for their helpful comments in finalising this chapter. All errors and omissions remain my responsibility.

Notes

1 Both the foundation of human rights and whether it makes sense to talk about *moral* human rights at all remain highly contested (see, for example, Campbell (2014)).
2 *Resolution on Human Rights and Access to Safe Drinking Water and Sanitation*, UN GAOR Res. 16309, UNHRC, 15th sess., agenda item 3, UN Doc A/HRC/15/L.14 (28 July 2010).
3 *Universal Declaration of Human Rights*, GA Res. 217A (III), UN GAOR, 3rd sess., 183rd plen. mtg, UN Doc A/810 (10 December 1948) Preamble paragraph 1.
4 I do not intend to deny that a longer list of human rights may be justifiable, but it is unnecessary for the argument presented here, which is limited to those human rights essential for addressing environmental threats such as climate change. See Caney (2009, 166).
5 *Declaration of the United Nations Conference on the Human Environment*, UN Doc. A/CONF/48/14/REV.1 (16 June 1972) ('*Stockholm Declaration*') Principle 1.
6 See Hayward (2005, 35), who points out that there is no single ecocentric approach.
7 For an analysis of the distributive justice options of 'equality', 'prioritism' (priority to the poor) and 'sufficientism' (minimum level of welfare) in this context, see Page (2006).
8 Wood (2013) traces the history of the public trust doctrine in the US context, drawing out its links to sovereignty and democracy.
9 *Robin Blades v State of California*, Complaint of 4 May 2011, Available at www.eenews.net/assets/2011/05/05/document_gw_04.pdf, paragraph 8, accessed 13 August 2012.
10 In May 2015, a Lane County Circuit Court held that the public trust doctrine in Oregon did not extend to the atmosphere. See *Chernaik & Ors v State of Oregon*, Case No. 16–11–09273, Available at http://ourchildrenstrust.org/sites/default/files/15.05.11.OregonCircuitCtOpinion.pdf, accessed 6 July 2015.
11 *PPL Montana*, U.S., 132S. Ct. 1215, 1235, 182 L. Ed. 2d 77 (2012).
12 See memo to reconsider, filed 28 June 12, *Alec L., et al. v Lisa P. Jackson, et al.*, US District Court for the District of Columbia, Case No. 1: 11-cv-2235 (RLW) at 21.
13 *Ibid.*, 21.
14 *Massachusetts v EPA*, 549 U.S. 497, 127 S. Ct. 1438, 1457 (2007).
15 *Convention on Access to Information, Public Participation in Decision-making and Access to Justice in Environmental Matters*, opened for signature 25 June 1998 (entered into force 30 October 2001), Available at http://ec.europa.eu/environment/aarhus/, Accessed 6 July 2015.
16 *Republic of South Africa v Grootboom*, Constitutional Court of South Africa, (1) SA 46 (CC) (2001) judgment of Yacob J. cited in Anton and Shelton 2011, 258.
17 *African Charter on Human and Peoples' Rights*, opened for signature 27 June 1981, 21 ILM 58 (entered into force 21 October 1986) Article 24.
18 *Additional Protocol to the American Convention on Human Rights in the Area of Economic, Social and Cultural Rights*, opened for signature 17 November 1988, OASTS No. 69 [Protocol of San Salvador] Article II.
19 *Declaration of the United Nations Conference on Environment and Development*, UN Doc. A/CONF.151/26/Rev.1 (3–14 June 1992) ('*Rio Declaration*') Principle 3.
20 *Vienna Declaration and Programme of Action*, adopted by the World Conference on Human Rights in Vienna on 25 June 1993, UN Doc. A/CONF.157/23.
21 *United Nations Framework Convention on Climate Change*, opened for signature 9 May 1992, 1771 UNTS 107 (entered into force 21 March 1994) Article 3(4).
22 United Nations High Commissioner for Human Rights, *Report of the Office of the United Nations High Commissioner for Human Rights on the relationship between climate change and human rights*, UN GAOR, Human Rights Council, 10th sess., agenda item 2, UN Doc. A/HRC/1061 (15 January 2009).

23 IHR also involves the practice of international diplomacy, which is important but not considered here.
24 *Noel Narvii Tauira and Eighteen Others v France* (1995) 83 – B Eur Comm HR 112 315.
25 *Ibid.*, 130.
26 *Ibid.*, 131.
27 (2013) 56 E.H.R.R. 2.
28 See survey of relevant ECHR cases in Cox 2014.

References

Alston P. and Goodman R. (2013) *International human rights* Oxford, Oxford University Press.

Anton D.K. and Shelton D.L. (2011) *Environmental protection and human rights* Cambridge, Cambridge University Press.

Besson S. (2012) 'Human rights: ethical, political … or legal? First steps in a legal theory of human rights' in Childress D.E. ed., *The role of ethics in international law* New York, Cambridge University Press, 211–45.

Birnie P., Boyle A. and Redgwell C. (2009) *International law and the environment*, 3rd edn Oxford; New York, Oxford University Press.

Boyle A. (2012) 'Human rights and the environment: where next?' *The European Journal of International Law*, 23(3) 613–42.

Campbell T. (2014) 'Human rights: moral or legal?' in Kinley D., Sadurski W. and Walton K. eds, *Human rights: old problems, new possibilities* Cheltenham, UK; Northampton, MA, US, Edward Elgar, 1–26.

Caney S. (2006) 'Cosmopolitan justice, rights and global climate change' *Canadian Journal of Law & Jurisprudence*, 19 255–78.

Caney S. (2009) 'Climate change, human rights and moral thresholds' in Humphreys S. ed., *Human rights and climate change* Cambridge; New York, Cambridge University Press. Reprinted in Gardiner S., Carney S. and Jamieson D. eds (2010) *Climate ethics essential readings* Oxford; New York, Oxford University Press, 163.

Carmody C. (2012) 'Considering future generations – sustainability in theory and practice' *Economic Roundup*, Issue 3 65–91, Available at www.treasury.gov.au/PublicationsAndMedia/Publications/2012/Economic-Roundup-Issue-3/Report/Considering-future-generations-8212-sustainability-in-theory-and-practice, Accessed 26 September 2012.

Cox R. (2014) 'Case note: the liability of European states for climate change' *Utrecht Journal of International and European Law*, 30(78) 125–35.

Donnelly J. (2007) 'The relative universality of human rights' *Human Rights Quarterly*, 29 281–306.

Hay P. (2002) *Main current in Western environmental thought* Sydney, Australia, University of New South Wales Press.

Hayward T. (2005) *Constitutional environmental rights* New York, Oxford University Press.

Hiskes R.P. (2009) *The human right to a green future: environmental rights and intergenerational justice* Cambridge; New York, Cambridge University Press.

Intergovernmental Panel on Climate Change (2013) "Summary for policymakers" in *Climate change 2013: the physical science basis. Contribution of Working Group I to the Fifth Assessment Report of the Intergovernmental Panel on Climate Change* Cambridge;

New York, Cambridge University Press, Available at www.climatechange2013.org/images/report/WG1AR5_SPM_FINAL.pdf, accessed 7 May 2014.

Intergovernmental Panel on Climate Change (2014) 'Summary for policymakers' in *Climate change 2014: impacts, adaptation, and vulnerability. Part A: global and sectoral aspects. Contribution of Working Group II to the Fifth Assessment Report of the Intergovernmental Panel on Climate Change* Cambridge; New York, Cambridge University Press, 1–32, Available at http://ipcc-wg2.gov/AR5/images/uploads/IPCC_WG2AR5_SPM_Approved.pdf, accessed 7 May 2014.

Knox J. (2009) 'Climate change in human rights law' *Virginia Journal of International Law,* 50 163–218.

Lawrence P. (2014) *Justice for future generations: climate change and international law* Cheltenham, UK, Edward Elgar.

Office of the High Commissioner for Human Rights [n.d.] *Human rights bodies – complaints procedure,* Available at www.ohchr.org/EN/HRBodies/TBPetitions/Pages/HRTBPetitions.aspx#interstate, accessed 6 July 2015.

Page E.A. (2006) *Climate change, justice and future generations* Northampton, MA, US, Edward Elgar.

Pirjatanniemi E. chapter 2 in this volume.

Rajamani L. (2010) 'The increasing currency and relevance of rights-based perspectives in the international negotiations on climate change' *Journal of Environmental Law,* 22(3) 391–429.

Raz J. (1984) 'Right-based moralities' in Waldron J. ed., *Theories of rights* Oxford, Oxford University Press, 182–200.

Sands P. and Peel J. (2012) *Principles of international environmental law* New York, Cambridge University Press.

Sceats S. and Breslin S. (2012) *China and the international human rights system* London, Chatham House, Available at www.chathamhouse.org/sites/default/files/public/Research/International%20Law/r1012_sceatsbreslin.pdf, accessed 23 August 2013.

Sen A. (2004) 'Elements of a theory of human rights' *Philosophy and Public Affairs,* 32(4) 315–56.

Shaw M. (2008) *International law,* 6th edn Cambridge; New York, Cambridge University Press.

Stone C.D. (1972) 'Should trees have standing? Toward legal rights for natural objects' *Southern California Law Review,* 45 450–501.

Vanderheiden S. (2008) *Atmospheric justice: a political theory of climate change* New York, Oxford University Press.

Wood M.C. (2013) *Nature's trust, environmental law for a new ecological age* New York, Cambridge University Press.

World Commission on Environment and Development (1987) *Our common future* Oxford, Oxford University Press.

4 Avoiding the tragedy of human rights

How complex thought may open the way to recognising human rights for future generations

Emilie Gaillard

1 Introduction

The expression "tragedy of human rights" enables us to insist on the urgent necessity of giving respect for the future a foundation in law. A failure of the system of human rights was put on the agenda by Amnesty International when it denounced half a century of petroleum pollution in the Niger Delta (Amnesty International 2009).[1] This is a relevant case in this context because elementary rights to access to food, water, non-polluted air or even health cannot be claimed any more in that area.[2] These facts are enough to embitter people kept in abject poverty while oil multinationals have speedily acquired great wealth during several generations and, at the same time, have polluted the environment and the health of the population for half a century. Such disgraceful irresponsibility can intuitively be thought of as a crime, in both economic and ecological terms, against people of the past, present and future in that country. But what can be said about this in legal terms? For those who doubt the need to formulate in law some kind of responsibility towards the future, it is important to point out that even now the Fukushima catastrophe is continuing to cause an irreversible chain of transgenerational pollutions. In both these cases, the environment and living beings are being polluted over particularly extended timescales. By keeping these instances in mind we can legitimately affirm that from now on it is clearly becoming irresponsible to blindly maintain past attitudes regarding the place that future generations have in law. Wherever a return to the previous status quo is impossible, and where even conditions for life are adversely affected, the very concept of human rights becomes downgraded into obsolescence. However, if these examples make it possible to highlight the interest in daring to imagine and formulate human rights for future generations, it remains true that the number of obstacles, both conceptual and practical, is legion.

What could the tragedy of human rights be? The notion may seem astonishing, but it indicates the idea that one day even the concept of human rights may become an anachronism. The pollution of food chains by heavy metals and carbon nanotubes, genetic mutations caused by radioactive contamination and the process of bio-accumulations of chemical substances in living organisms are very real threats of long-term harm to environmental rights, to health and life and finally to all human rights of future generations. The intuition that it is legitimate to take future beings into account by way of legal measures seems to be rallying support from an increasing number of UN member states (and, more widely, members of the "human family", to repeat the term used in the *Universal Declaration of Human Rights*), and therefore it is all the more necessary to press ahead boldly to open a way to protect the future by law. What can be done so that future generations can see human rights as meaningful for them if they are not even able to enjoy those goods that human rights ought to protect or give access to? How is it possible to attribute human rights to future generations? How could we ascribe human rights to an entity such as future generations that is so vague, indefinable and non-existent and, moreover, is without an elected representative? These are some of the challenges which have to be met. Are the epistemological obstacles we may face sufficient to prevent us from ascribing those rights to future generations, even when our historical context is constantly reminding us of the need to do so? Does not the growing international support for the need for legal protection of the environment open up a way to widen the field of possibilities for future generations? Faced with future threats to humans and all living things which are already deeply rooted today, I am convinced that including a higher level of complexity in our legal thinking will do much to help the progress that is needed[3] (Morin 1994). In order to imagine and conceive human rights for future generations, it is necessary to reform our thought process. Under the influence of simplifications, human rights thought appears disconnected from multiple transformation processes at work in the contemporary legal field. Such a reform would then change the course of thinking, taking it from a path leading towards the tragedy of human rights (section 2) to a promise of recognition of human rights for future generations (section 3).

2 From a tragedy of human rights for future generations

Thinking about human rights for future generations involves an intellectual exercise of the most delicate and sensitive kind in relation to legal positivism. In fact there are numerous theoretical and practical obstacles preventing one even getting to the point of imagining such a thing. This can be demonstrated by a generational and contextualised account of contemporary human rights law (section 2.1). A clearly defined overview of human rights, formulated for those now living and excluding any compulsory protection in the future does inevitably herald a tragedy for human rights (section 2.2).

2.1 A generational and contextual overview of contemporary human rights

I.   In French law, it is possible to present contemporary human rights in chronological, even genealogical order. The Declaration of the Rights of Man and of the Citizen of 1789, the cornerstone of so-called first generation rights, proclaims rights and freedoms such as the freedom to move, freedom of conscience and expression, the presumption of innocence and even the right to own property. It was adopted after the French Revolution and signalled France's entry into the modern era. Moreover, it was influenced by the individualistic ideas of Enlightenment philosophy[4] (Chevallier 2008, 12) and ideas about a teleological concept of historical progress, quite common in that period (Chevallier 2008, 12).[5] At that time there was no room for developing ideas about extending the rights that are proposed in the declaration towards future generations (Delmas-Marty 1988, 317).[6] Those rights were thought to exist only because they were recognised and respected by living people. There is then a temporal gap between the concept of human rights and future generations. At the end of the Second World War, a new wave of human rights began to take shape in France. These concerned economic and social rights, carefully enumerated in the preamble to the Constitution in 1946 which instituted the Fourth Republic. Notably, they covered the right to social security, the right to strike and the right to education. These second generation rights are binding the state. At the same time, major progress in terms of the legal implementation and recognition of human rights was taking place. From 1946, it became possible to invoke human rights in the courts.[7] More than ever, the concept of human rights needs to be understood as rights that are applied, validated and enforceable. Therefore, if the state's will and justiciability are sufficient to uphold claims of liberty and creditability, a temporal matrix is inevitably in place here, which at the same time creates a problem for a transgenerational perspective on human rights. Since future generations do not exist, they are not seen as protected by human rights. In French law, the main theoretical and practical obstacles to opening up human rights law to future generations consist of the importance of the paradigm of autonomy and freewill, the necessity of justiciability and the short-term vision of these rights, which are nonetheless often described as non-temporal, inalienable or even sacred. Here, the problem is obvious.

II.   At the international level, the genealogy of human rights is somewhat different. In 1948, the United Nations adopted the *Universal Declaration of Human Rights*. The intention behind this text was to put the concept of human rights on to the international stage, but it was not directly legally enforceable; this was a real juridical revolution in itself. It was only in 1966 that the first binding international texts were adopted: the ICCPR and the ICESCR.[8] The two international agreements are part of a genealogical and binary approach to human rights: on the one hand, they include civil and political rights, and on the other, economic and social rights. Though recognised internationally, these rights are firmly linked to and dependent on the expression of human willingness to fulfil the obligations corresponding to those rights. It is, however, clear that they are rights of already existing people. These are rights which are proclaimed and recognised at an international level where only inter-state relationships are applicable.

III.   At the end of the Second World War, Europe put in place the foundation of two juridical systems which have today become the European Union and the Council of Europe. The first system, founded on the solidarity of economic interests, has had a binding Charter of Fundamental Rights since 2007.[9] The classic list of rights and freedoms is enumerated in it and brought up to date by including rights that are relevant in the age of the internet and biotechnology, including items such as the sequencing of the human genome. It is important to highlight article 37, which deals specifically with the protection of the environment.[10] The Council of Europe has a juridical system that is considerably larger than that of the European Union. At its core there is a common conception of human rights. Besides traditional human rights, the Council of Europe played a major role in the 1980s in setting up human rights as a juridical rampart against certain biomedical advances (De Vel 2003, 347). Some raised their voices to ensure that the rights of the fourth generation be taken into consideration. This concerned *"those who must protect human dignity from some abuses by science"* (Marcus-Helmons 2000, 552). These two systems are, moreover, endowed with jurisdictions responsible for applying, in accordance with different norms, human rights law recognised at the European level.

Contemporary human rights law does not work with any idea of human rights for future generations; implicitly, human rights laws seem to make the conceptual presuppositions that human rights have to be respected without enforcement and on the basis of reciprocity. A silent and dominant juridical paradigm is present: juridical reciprocity. By virtue of this paradigm, every right entails a corresponding obligation. This paradigm tends to enclose the law in a temporal frame which excludes the distant future and human beings who do not yet exist. Since the twenty-first century is characterised by new actions of humankind that are harmful for future generations (directly by posing a threat on their human condition or indirectly by mortgaging their natural resources in particular), isn't it necessary to take the future into account? Not envisaging the possible integration of a defence of future generations through human rights law might well become part of a potentially terminal threat.

2.2 An account of the obsolescence of human rights law?

How is it possible that the failure to respect the interests of future generations in law could lead to a tragedy for human rights? Since law is now compartmentalised in the way described above, it lacks a long-term perspective. This situation could result in doubts being raised about the inner sense of human rights. If human rights law proves incapable of providing answers to current environmental challenges, the question of whether it is still the appropriate legal framework to use will arise.

There was a breakthrough in the early 1990s. Professor Karel Vasak identified a third generation of human rights in international law. These are human rights relating to solidarity between peoples, across and beyond state boundaries and time limits. This opened the way for a possible conceptual link between the concept of human rights and that of future generations. Without being exhaustive, these rights cover the right to a healthy environment, the right to the common heritage of humanity and the right to peace and development. Many juridical arguments have been raised in order to deny them any legal validity. For many, these rights only amount to "pseudo-human rights" which risk "contaminating" real human rights. Some highlight a major philosophical incompatibility with the classical conceptual construction of these rights (Amor 1986, 76);[11] others consider that rights of solidarity have an imprecise objective and that the specific holder of those rights and those who have the corresponding duties are hard or even impossible to identify. The presupposition of the legal construction by virtue of which every right entails a corresponding obligation that has to be respected cannot be applied (Loschak 1984, 54–5).[12] It follows that since rights to solidarity are impossible to implement legally, they cannot be considered a part of the human rights regime. This paradigm of legal reciprocity deserves to be updated here. The result is that third generation human rights are somewhat scorned, since there are no binding legal texts that give them any valid support. It is mainly because of the ascendancy of a binary logic that the rights of the third generation have long been relegated to a place outside the field of human rights. It is true that the rights of humankind for the third generation have been thought through and formulated "outside traditional frameworks". These are laws that fall outside the scope of the legal framework only designed for regulating relationships between individuals or nation states. They are also open to the idea of recognising legal duties. Since they apply to humanity's future through trans-temporal and trans-spatial law, binding duties become necessary (Dupuy 1984, 199, 201).

One problem seems to be a binary distinction between subject and object according to which an entity is either a legal subject (endowed with human dignity) or a legal object (subjected to *usus*, *fructus* and *abusus*). By virtue of this, there is a human right only if there is intervention of positive law and when a legal implementation is organised and enforceable before the courts (Sudre 2012, 53).[13] Since future generations do not exist, they cannot have the status of a subject in law. The consequence is that no limits to the exercise of present rights and freedoms can be enacted. The legal concept of "the subject" in law seems to form an impassable theoretical barrier preventing human rights from achieving the goal of the preservation of the environment for the future and future generations.

In such a binary approach, only enforceable rights can be considered to be human rights. If this division between "subject" and "object" in law prevents any defence of the rights of future generations due to their "non-existence", the result is that existing generations are free to ignore the interests of future generations. If freedom consists of not doing anything to harm others, the fact of understanding this within the limits of the present time leads to the real possibility of having unlimited power over the future. The fact that no boundaries regarding the consequences for future generations exist that would limit the exercise of rights and liberties for those now living means that humanity, living beings and ecological systems may be subjected to irreversible pollution; this, however, leads more or less inevitably to a tragedy for human rights. We are witnessing a tipping point in the abuse of human rights as peoples, states and enterprises act today against the interests of those who will live tomorrow. This abuse of law and of power has no other justification than the priority of temporal existence. Moreover, the logic of simple thought can only cope with a causality which affirms that a given cause leads to an invariable effect and cannot take into consideration transgenerational or evolutive harms. How, then, can space be given for human rights, when living beings and whole areas undergo continual exposure to many types of pollution including that coming from chemicals and crude oil derivatives and also genetic pollution? This can be carried out with complete impunity in the name of freedom to undertake research projects in a way which does not take the future of the planet into account. In other words, it seems that to a considerable extent, linear causality fosters a measure of blindness towards the future. The tragedy of human rights, therefore, consists of the impossibility of enjoying elementary rights, which up to now have been considered immutable and obvious, just because the challenges arising from environmental precariousness or the human condition cannot be formulated using either classical theory in law or the traditional philosophical concept of human rights. Binary logic leads to support of the Physiocrats' principle of "*laisser-faire, laisser-passer*". If this is transposed into the realm of technology, it leads to judging that anything which can be done should be done. From then on, a science without a conscience is possible, and the direction taken invokes the adage "*après nous le deluge*" (Ost 2003).

That said, the opening of the "era of catastrophes" heralds all the more strongly the prospect of a slippery slope towards shrinking horizons for human rights. Denying the need for environmental health and ignoring the fact that humans are part of an ecosystem will close future horizons for human rights. From now on, the challenge confronting us is to undergo a reversal of our perspectives in order to promise future generations that they will be able to enjoy human rights. Stepping into the logical framework of complex thought may shift the tragedy into a promise of human rights for future generations.

3 Towards a promise of human rights for future generations

Avoiding the tragedy of human rights law implies the adoption of a new intellectual mindset so that future generations will one day benefit from the protection of their rights. The Declaration of the Rights of Man and of the Citizen of 1789 makes specific reference to "natural, inalienable and irrevocable rights" of man. To avoid the alienation of tomorrow's rights because of the demands of today's economic logics, we must consider a systemic and complex study of human rights law for future generations on the bases outlined in 3.1. Looking at the issue from a certain distance, it becomes possible to contextualise our view and bring to light a real convergence of the dynamics of transgenerational protections (3.2).

3.1 Bases of a systemic and complex analysis of human rights for future generations

Undoubtedly, we need to realise a complex process of transformation in the way we think about human rights. This is possible when we accept the complexity of the transgenerational questions and create awareness of the implications of transgenerational harms or disasters from philosophical and anthropological points of view.

Edgar Morin vigorously denounces what he calls "the compartmentalisation of knowledge in the planetary era" (Morin 1999, 21). In a time when total interdependence is obvious, a multidisciplinary approach is needed in order to face the challenges of the twenty-first century. However, knowledge has become hyper-specialised and disconnected. On reflection, should the future or human rights be conceptualised on the basis of assumptions made during the Enlightenment when our epoch is increasingly characterised by a high level of complexity? In this planetary era, when globalisation, irreversible and widespread pollution, the phenomenon of bio-accumulation and catastrophic events are affecting people's health and the environment in whole regions or worldwide, an outdated way of interpreting the concept of human rights opens the way to a progressive diminution of rights for future generations. It seems obvious that contemporary human rights law is inadequate to face the challenges of the twenty-first century. We need to deal with the complexity of the world in which we live in the way we think about human rights. In this perspective there are not several distinct generations of humans rights any more but several processes of enrichment of human rights. The application of the dialogic principle (Morin 1992, 98)[14] to the analysis of human rights for future generations makes it possible to go beyond the appearance of contradictions between recognising rights for today's humans and those of future humans; the recognition and defence of tomorrow's interests do not necessarily contradict respecting the rights of contemporary humans. There are obvious tensions (such tensions are also a characteristic of complex situations) but it is henceforth possible to avoid concluding that one necessarily excludes the other or that they must compete with each other. It becomes possible to use the complementarity lying beyond the tension of today's rights versus the rights of future people. Also, all theoretical objections raised against rights of solidarity can thus be overcome. The recognition of each generation of human rights can reveal not just a false hierarchy or a suspect dilution of the rights proclaimed; new facets can be developed, such as grafting on an ethical and temporal dimension, and the insertion of a long-term perspective can enrich all types of human rights law (Gaillard 2011). In fact, those entitled to rights of solidarity are at the same time creditors and debtors. Juridical obligation is no longer dominated by the logic of reciprocity but can work with an assumption of asymmetry in a logic of transmission. It is founded on transgenerational responsibility and the principle of temporal non-discrimination. The dialogic principle is key for bypassing many obstacles raised against the recognition of human rights for future generations. For example, the right to a healthy environment can benefit both people in the present (individually and collectively) and future generations. We also need to think about the theory of the subject in law in a more complex way (Gaillard 2012, 45). The right to health (proclaimed at the end of the Second World War, meaning in France the right to social security) could be transformed and presented as a "sustainable health human right". This right was initially drawn up in a narrow temporal perspective, but it could also be seen as a right in an intergenerational perspective. Conceptualising a right to lasting health would throw a bridge across space and time, reinstating humankind as a whole to nature from which it thought itself excluded so as to accomplish a pretentious destiny as "leader and possessor of nature".

The juridical time frame has to be opened up to be longer in scale and to integrate a concept of disaster. Voices are being raised calling attention to the major social and anthropological changes which are taking place in this era of catastrophes. According to Monsieur Lemarchand, *"a catastrophe originates in a reversal in history where the future has no future"* (Lemarchand 2007, 57). In other words, there is no resilience and no return is possible when a disaster occurs. The French philosopher J.-P. Dupuy led the way by explaining the paradox inscribed inside the concept of catastrophes and its prevention (Dupuy 2002, 13).[15] Transposed into the human rights field, this means that we have to think about "transgenerational harms" in terms of risk and disaster in order to avoid closing the horizons of the future. This requires a complex anticipatory legal framework. The precautionary principle is key for anticipating, in a dynamic way, risks of disasters (Gaillard 2014, 2015a). Various impulsions for recognising human rights for future generations now have to be put into perspective with other processes of transformation in human rights law. This is a process of convergence which often happens currently.

3.2 Processes of convergence recognising human rights for future generations

The issue of recognising human rights for future generations is far from new. It was hotly debated at the end of the 1980s internationally by civil society and some global organisations (Zanghi 1999, 1459). It was Commander Cousteau who took the initiative of awaking and mobilising the opinion of international civil society so that the *Universal Declaration of Human Rights* for future generations was adopted (Brown Weiss 1993, 339).[16] It began with only five articles and notably proclaimed the right to inherit an uncontaminated earth, the duty to steward it for future generations by preserving it from irreversible harm, the right to freedom and dignity for humankind and the obligation to watch over developing techniques so that the conditions of the life and evolution of humanity be respected (Brown Weiss 1993, 339; MacFarlane 1997). This raised questions for juridical doctrine concerning the possibility of proclaiming human rights for future generations. A Charter of Future Generations' Rights was drawn up at a college in Germany by a multidisciplinary team of researchers between 1984 and 1985

(Saladin and Zenger 1988). An Institute for Future Generations was set up at Malta University by UNESCO, and it organised several international conferences on the subject. In February 1994, the university held a meeting in Tenerife to further develop the project initiated by the Cousteau Foundation. In the opinion of the Rector of the University de la Laguna, the question of human rights for future generations is *"one of the most fascinating and simultaneously the most urgent questions of the 20th century"* (UNESCO Experts 1994, 97). On 26 February 1996, a Declaration of Humankind Rights was passed. Consisting of a preamble and 14 articles, this universal Declaration then had a double objective: *"the legal recognition of the concept of future generations . . . and the recognition of future generations as entitled to human rights understood as rights and faculties ensuring the freedom and dignity of the human person"* (UNESCO Experts 1994, 111). Even though the momentum given here was at least historic, it has not been sufficient (Mayor 1996, 36). Inside global organisations resistance persisted, for both theoretical and practical reasons, leading to real perplexity in the face of the idea of recognising human rights for future generations. In the end, the (non-compulsory) *Declaration on the Responsibilities of the Present Generations Towards Future Generations* was adopted by the UNESCO General Assembly in 1997 (Zanghi 1999, 1469).[17] In my opinion, the first objective has been achieved, for since the end of the 1990s the concept of future generations does appear as a fundamental concept of international law relating to the environment. It has continued to grow via structural concepts such as the "common heritage of humankind", the "human family" or via the phenomenon of nations rallying round shared values that are directed towards future protection; for instance current progress is being made regarding the protection of world heritage sites. As for the second objective, recognising human rights for future generations, it is gathering strength again today (Gaillard 2011, 139–220). A number of research programmes are working specifically on this theme, and often the same theoretical obstacles arise to impede researchers' thoughts on the subject. However, obstacles do not necessarily imply that progress is impossible. In 2012, the Collegium International launched an appeal for a world government of solidarity and responsibility (Collegium International 2012). At the heart of this project is the following objective: *"to reaffirm all fundamental Human rights for those now living, to extend them to future generations and to reinforce their application within necessary limits, in a world democratic society, respecting national and international public order"* (Collegium International 2012, 21–2). In June 2015, the President of the French Republic tasked Me Corinne Lepage with drawing up a declaration of rights of humankind: "that is to say the right for all inhabitants of the earth to live in a world where the future is not compromised by the irresponsibility in the present".[18] This could be a historical text which could proclaim human rights for future generations at the global level.

4   Concluding remarks

Many people are calling for the recognition of crimes against future generations, notably via recognition of ecological harm and the extinction of species

(Gaillard 2015b). At this time of a growing wave of scientific interest in the formulation of human rights for future generations, it is important to get to the heart of obstacles and possibilities and seriously consider them. Since a Charter for the Environment was added to the French Constitution in 2005, it is no longer possible to deny the constitutional validity of the right to a good and healthy environment.[19] This right, presented as part of a third generation of human rights, still remains much in need of elaboration and refinement. For some, it remains a marginal text because of the many references to the terms of "duties" which can in no way be legally enforced.[20] For others, the Charter of the Environment, contextualised in a global movement of constitutional recognition of the duty to protect the environment, is the instrument or vector of a new juridical humanism which incorporates defending the future in law (Kiss 2007, 1239), notably by recognising new kinds of juridical duties.

In this twenty-first century it is vital from now on that human fragility and finitude be inscribed in the juridical field (Delmas-Marty (1988), préf. Gaillard 2011, XVI). Ultimately, probing the challenges and opportunities of contemporary human rights with regard to human rights for future generations opens up a very large and active area of research and of debate. Intellectual engagement currently tends to revolve around Hölderlin's words: "But where danger is, salvation too is found" (Hölderlin 1802).

Notes

1 Amnesty International (2009) *Nigeria: pollution causes a human rights tragedy in the Niger Delta. Amnesty activists protesting in Luxembourg*, Available at (www.amnesty.lu/informez-vous/nouvelles/news-archive/news-archive-singleview/detail/nigeria-la-pollution-provoque-une-tragedie-des-droits-humains-dans-le-delta-du-niger-les-milita/#.Vdn5zy-hr2ww), accessed 1 September 2009.
2 In its report, Amnesty International writes that the pollution of the Niger Delta deprives tens of millions of people of their most elementary rights to food, water and health. It says that "people who live in this region have to drink polluted water and cook and do their washing in that water. They eat fish, when lucky enough to catch any, which are contaminated by petrol and other toxins."
3 Edgar Morin developed the paradigm of complexity as a new way of thinking. Taking account of the fact that everything is at one and the same time interdependent and separate, the author invites us to develop new logical modes of thought. His thesis throws light on the existence of a simplifying mode of thought which compartmentalises disciplines and prevents our thought from engaging with the complexity of the real world.
4

> The social fabric in modern society is made up of individuals: this is proof of the irreducible particularity of each human being ... but also the idea that the source of all power and the foundation of all authority reside in the consent of individuals. Thus the individual becomes the supreme reference, as much in the private as in the public domain, through the figure of the citizen.
> (Chevallier 2008, 12; translation by Sheila Brown).

5 Professor Chevallier enumerates them thus:

> The realm of Reason consists of assorted beliefs ... in the virtues of "Science", endowing man with an ever growing mastery of Nature; faith in "Progress", which

should lead to an improvement in individual well-being and social justice; the idea that "History" has a direction (historicism) and that Reason will finally impose its sway; a conviction about the 'Universalism' of models made in the West, which are called to serve, as expressions of Reason itself, as role models.

(Chevallier 2008, 12; translation by Sheila Brown)

6 According to Professor M. Delmas-Marty, the transformation from an ethical affirmation of human rights to legally binding rights, which happens when those rights become implemented in constitutional law and on a supranational level, is a real challenge for human rights law (Delmas-Marty 1988, 317).

7

The preamble to the Constitution of 1946 establishes new collective rights. However there is a discontinuity between the proclamation of principles and their concrete application. In order to proceed from one to the other, it is in fact necessary that the principles may be opposed to the State and only an independent judiciary can enable this to happen.

(Denquin 2009, 254; translation by Sheila Brown)

This epistemological shift deserves to be kept fully in mind as a stage in the evolution of human rights.

8 The *International Covenant on Civil and Political Rights* and the *International Covenant on Economic, Social and Cultural Rights* (1966).

9 This Charter was adopted in 2000, in Nice. It is composed of 54 articles and the chapters articulate the human right to dignity, freedoms, equality, solidarity, citizenship and justice.

10 Art. 37: "A high level of environmental protection and the improvement of the quality of the environment must be integrated into the policies of the Union and ensured in accordance with the principle of sustainable development", EU Charter of Fundamental Rights.

11 According to J. Rivero, those rights do not correspond to the concept of human rights as this has been worked out through centuries of philosophical and legal thinking (quoted by Amor 1986, 76).

12

Human rights cannot be conceptualised or thought about outside juridical categories, notably the category of the subject of rights: one can only think of human rights from the time one postulates that a human being is a subject of that right, endowed with the capacity to have (subjective) rights and to claim them in the face of power, that each human has a will and his or her own powers.

(Loschak 1984, 54–5; translation by Sheila Brown)

13 "By virtue of which human beings have no rights apart from intervention by positive law, when a legal system is organised in such a way that rights are protected by action in court" (Sudre 2012, 53; translation by Sheila Brown).

14 By virtue of this principle, complex associations are possible, without reasoning in terms of exclusion, and it becomes possible to make multiple reliances on what would be simply excluded by a binary logic.

15

Catastrophes are characterised by this temporality that is in some sense inverted. As an event bursting forth out of nothing, the catastrophe becomes possible only by "possibilizing" itself and that is precisely the source of our problem. For if one is to prevent catastrophe, one needs to believe in its possibility before it occurs. If, on the other hand, one succeeds in preventing it, its non-realization maintains it in the realm of the impossible, and as a result, the prevention efforts will appear useless in retrospect.

(Dupuy, 2002, 13)

16 Over-population and consequent effects of human activity will weigh heavily upon our descendants…. We demand that the rights of future generations be solemnly declared valid so that all people will inherit an uncontaminated planet where all forms of life may flourish.

J.-Y Cousteau, quoted by Brown Weiss (1993, 339)

17 Zanghi emphasises that all references to terms of "responsibility", "duty" and "rights" have been carefully expunged from the titles and dispositions (Zanghi 1999, 1469).

18 Letter dated 4 June 2015, written by President François Hollande to Me Corinne Lepage. During his presidential vows, given on 31 December 2014, he recalled, "Seventy years ago France was able to organise a large conference for universal human rights. Now we must carry the world with us so that all may join in adopting a Declaration for humanity's right to preserve our planet."

19 Article 1: "Everyone has the right to live in a balanced environment which shows due respect for health."

20 Article 2: "Everyone is under a duty to participate in preserving and enhancing the environment"; Article 3: "Everyone shall, in the conditions provided for by law, foresee and avoid the occurrence of any damage which he or she may cause to the environment or, failing that, limit the consequences of such damage"; Article 4: "Everyone shall be required, in the conditions provided for by law, to contribute to the making good of any damage he or she may have caused to the environment."

References

Amor A. (1986) "Les droits de l'homme de la 3ème generation" *Revue Tunisienne du Droit*, 13 43–83.

Brown Weiss E. (1993) *Justice pour les générations futures: droit international, patrimoine commun & équité intergénérations* Paris, UNU Press/Sang de la Terre/UNESCO.

Chevallier J. (2008) *L'Etat post-moderne* Paris, LGDJ.

Collegium International (2012) *Le Monde n'a plus de temps à perdre. Appel pour une gouvernance mondiale, solidaire et responsable [The world has no more time to lose]* Paris, LLL.

Delmas-Marty M. (1988) "Un nouvel usage des droits de l'homme" in *Éthique médicale et droits de l'homme*, Paris, Actes Sud, 313–23.

Denquin J-M. (2009) "Droits civils et politiques" in *Dictionnaire des droits de l'homme*, Paris, PUF, 254–62.

De Vel G. (2003) "Le rôle du Conseil de l'Europe en matière de bioéthique" *R.T.D.H.*, 54 347–62.

Dupuy R-J. (1984) "La notion de patrimoine commun de l'humanité appliquée aux fonds marins" in Pédone A. ed. *Droit et libertés à la fin du XXe siècle: influence des données économiques et technologiques* Études offertes à Cl-A, Paris, Colliard, 197–205.

Dupuy J.-P. (2002) *Pour un catastrophisme éclairé: quand l'impossible devient certain* Paris, Seuil.

Gaillard E. (2011) *Générations futures et droit privé. Vers un droit des generations futures* Paris, LGDJ.

Gaillard E. (2012) "Pour une approche systémique, complexe et prospective des droits de l'homme" in *Changements environnementaux globaux et droits de l'homme*, Cournil C. and Fabregoule C. eds, Brussels, Bruylant, 45–67.

Gaillard E. (2014) "Precautionary principle – French law" in *Juris-Classeur Environnement* LexisNexis, Paris in fasc. 2410.

Gaillard E. (2015a) "Precautionary principle – International and European juridical systems" in *Juris-Classeur Environnement* LexisNexis, Paris in fasc. 2415.

Gaillard E. (2015b) "Crimes against future generations" *E-publica*, 5, Available at http://
e-publica.pt/crimes-against-future-generations.html, accessed 5 July 2015.

Hölderlin Friedrich (1802) *Patmos* [no place], [no publisher].

Kiss A. (2007) "Le devoir de protéger l'environnement" in Touscoz J-A. ed., *Droit international et coopération internationale* Nice, France Europe, 1239–47.

Lemarchand F. (2007) "Catastrophe" in Dupont Y. ed., *Dictionnaire des risques*, Paris, A. Colin, 57–61.

Loschak D. (1984) "Mutation des droits de l'homme et mutation du droit" *Revue Interdisciplinaire d'Etudes Juridiques*, 13 49–88.

MacFarlane K. (1997) "Los derechos humanos de la generaciones futuras (la contribucion juridica de J.-Y. Cousteau)" [The human rights of future generations (the juridical contribution of J-Y. Cousteau)] *Ultima Década*, 8, Available at http://dialnet.unirioja.es/servlet/articulo?codigo=2256365, Accessed 1 September 2007.

Marcus-Helmons S. (2000) "La quatrième génération de droits de l'homme" in Lambert P. *et al.* eds, *Les droits de l'homme au seuil du troisième millénaire* Brussels, Bruylant, 549–59.

Mayor F. (1996) "The rights of future generations" *The UNESCO Courier* 49(3) 36–7.

Morin E. (1992) *La méthode, la connaissance de la connaissance* Paris, Seuil.

Morin E. (1994) *La complexité humaine* Paris, Flammarion.

Morin E. (1999) *Les sept savoirs nécessaires à l'éducation du futur* Paris, UNESCO.

Ost F. (2003) *La nature hors la loi* Paris, La Découverte.

Saladin P. and Zenger C.A. (1988) *Rechte zukünftiger generationen* Basel; Frankfurt, Helbing & Lichtenhan Verlag.

Sudre F. (2012) *Droit international et européen des droits de l'homme* Paris, PUF.

UNESCO Experts (1994) *Les droits de l'homme pour les générations futures* Brussels, Bruylant.

Zanghi C. (1999) "For the protection of future generations" in *Boutros Boutros-Ghali amicorum liber: paix, développement, démocratie* Brussels, Bruylant, 1459–77.

5 International human rights and duties to future generations

The role of an international constitution

Stephen Riley

1 Introduction

Can international human rights law 'frame' philosophical and legal debate on sustainability duties? Framing the debate would not be to demonstrate that human rights law offers one regulatory option among others. It would be to articulate the challenge of sustainability through the concept of human rights. And it would do this in a way that coheres with our other moral and political commitments. This chapter argues that such a framing of the debate is a viable project because duties to future generations, like international human rights themselves, are tied to the notion of an international constitution. That is, an idea of an international constitution is implied by any account of sustainability expressed in terms of intergenerational duties, and is also implied by any understanding of human rights as moral and not just legal rights.

The argument proceeds as follows. There are a number of ways in which there is 'fit' between international human rights law and the problem of duties to future generations (section 2). I argue that, more fundamentally, three specific conceptualizations of international human rights law are identifiable: humanitarian, humanistic, and constitutional (section 3). Each is defensible, but only the final, constitutional conceptualization of international human rights law implies a range of rights being, of necessity, extended to future generations (section 4). We should ask whether such a constitutional conceptualization really gives us a clear account of the structure and implications of human rights obligations (section 5). Assuming that it does, we should conclude by asking whether sustainability duties are thereby 'framed' by international human rights law (section 6).

2 The problems of future generations

The problem of sustainability duties can be treated as a cluster of practical and theoretical problems. We are concerned with climate change, biodiversity, governance and depletion of natural resources, new technologies and their actual and possible by-products, and older technologies and their by-products. These are entangled with epistemological problems concerning the calculation of risks, with normative problems such as the meaning of equity in situations of uncertainty, and with conceptual problems concerning the identity of the agents implied by concepts such as 'generation' or 'responsibility'. Above all, we are concerned with the intelligibility of the duties to and rights of future generations. It is only through positing future generations that many of our most valuable personal and political projects make sense (Slote 2003). And it is only through the language of rights and duties that questions concerning future generations gain purchase on our existing legal and political institutions (Caney 2005). However, it is clear that the legal and political norms of the international arena are poorly attuned to the long-term and transnational demands of intergenerational justice (Allott 2002; Franck 1989).

This set of interlocking issues can be summarized as follows: we are concerned simultaneously with a problem of normative harmonization, a problem of norms and risk, and a problem of the interaction of (on the one hand) knowledge and norms and (on the other) time and action. More fully, sustainability problems are transnational problems requiring concerted actions through states. However, states are poor at coordinating their actions and, due to privatization and globalization, are only one set of actors among a range of regulatory actors. Moreover, such governance takes place under circumstances of uncertainty concerning which of our resources should be conserved and which of our actions should be perceived to be risks. To leave 'as much and as good' as we ourselves received may not only be impossible but also unintelligible (Holland 1999); equally, failure to anticipate risk, or to correctly apportion risk, could itself be conceived to be a wrong even in circumstances when complete knowledge is impossible (Shue 2010). And future generations are constituted through our actions and choices; their nature, and not only the physical conditions of life, will be determined by our actions (Mulgan 2003). This, then, is the conceptually, epistemologically, and normatively unstable ground on to which the question of duties and rights arrives.

We can argue that human rights at least have a prima facie relevance in relation to these problems. Human rights are: (a) able to legally draw together national and international regulatory practices; they are also (b) non-utilitarian legal claims that can function where there is uncertainty of outcome; and can (c) lend themselves to creative development through interpretation. Linking these properties to the problems above, human rights can be said to overcome some problems of regulatory pluralism because they are both nationally and internationally significant. Human rights, as non-utilitarian legal claims, are able to express absolute negative or positive requirements on the part of the state regardless of our ability to calculate expected consequences. And, because they are dynamic and evolving, human rights are not intended to anticipate all social problems but are to be tailored to such problems. This captures some important aspects of why human rights should be pivotal in our regulatory orientation towards future generations. Morally and ideologically, human rights are important because they address the concerns and interests of humanity now and (presumably) in the future. Practically and pragmatically, human rights law is a more useful area of law for sustainability purposes than those fields of law that are tied to private interests and private disputes. In addition, under human rights law it is possible to be proactive (to bring claims prior to harm or without proof of direct harm): human rights are not dependent upon the calculation of risk, and the range of claimants is potentially wider than is permissible under tort law.[1]

We should not be too quick to assume, however, that human rights frame (let alone solve) the distinctive conceptual, normative, and epistemological problems relevant to future generations. To be able to frame debate, a theory of human rights is needed to show the necessity and coherence of human rights within our social and political practices now and in the future. And such coherence must encompass constitutive or constitutional practices that will shape and constrain the whole range of regulatory activities that we are likely to rely on in the future. More acutely, reliance on specific human rights norms or institutions is inadequate because their endurance in international law cannot be guaranteed and because existing norms and institutions alone fail to offer a decisive link with the conceptual and epistemological problems identified above. A valuable account of human rights in this context must combine the constitutive and the regulatory in such a way that our concerns for future generations remain intelligible and at least some relevant epistemological questions concerning the nature of their identity and their entitlements are answered. The following section describes three of the broadest possible theories of (international) human rights. These should be assessed in terms of what they contribute to understanding and solving such problems.

3 International human rights theories

These theories concentrate on human rights as *international* and *human* rights. We are concerned, in other words, with a set of norms that are located in international law and a set of norms that take the human to be definitive or distinctive of that group of rights. It is a paradox of modern human rights scholarship that international human rights law – the *Universal Declaration of Human Rights*, the Twin Covenants, and related human rights treaties – has become the focal example of a defensible discourse of human rights given that international law is the legal system least amenable to their maintenance. The normative limitations of the international arena, flowing from states' status as both authors and addressees of law, mean that the normative resources available to reconstruct and defend human rights are limited. Thus, the 'hard law' found in human rights treaties has been treated as containing 'manifesto rights', and the enforcement of such rights is conditioned by the short-term demands of diplomatic and political processes (Hahn 2012). Moreover, the combining of human rights and the 'humanitarian' has blurred the legal and political still further. Human rights can form part of the conditions for 'humanitarian intervention', but this is a practice that is neither squarely justified by international law nor has an obvious normative link to the substance of international human rights law treaties. On this complex legal and political stage, international human rights could be thought to have one of three possible core functions that to a greater or lesser degree transcend the accidents of present-day law and politics. In different ways these draw out the normative and conceptual distinctiveness of these rights via the notion of the human.

First, it is no coincidence that legally distinct fields of human rights law and international humanitarian law have coalesced around the language of the *humanitarian*. Both, it could be argued, are concerned with the most basic interests of humans understood as vulnerable persons entitled to have (all, but only) their basic interests fulfilled. This is intelligible but legally confused. It blurs the law of the Geneva Conventions (international humanitarian law), the law of international human rights, and the law governing the legitimate use of force (which in turn can be distinguished from humanitarian intervention). This fails to respect long-standing legal categorizations and obscures the institutional mechanisms that monitor and enforce human rights. However, the argument for seeing human rights as 'merely' a component of humanitarian political decisions has been justified by methodological commitments (variously describable as non-ideal theory, political realism, or philosophical pragmatism) that aim to faithfully reflect international legal and political practice. That is, 'human rights talk' is at its most efficacious when we are dealing with the existence of international crimes that are so transgressive of basic human interests, and so shock the conscience of humanity, that violation of sovereign inviolability can be justified (Rawls 2001). Human rights work only when carried along on a tide of political opinion.

With this model, human rights' principal constitutional role is symbolic, as they combine with the United Nations Charter to signal an alternative to the Westphalian system of state inviolability (Peters 2009). We can say that human rights reflect certain general concerns with humanity and human welfare, and that human rights imply qualification of the core regulative assumptions of international law (Rawls 2001). But with this model there are no clear means to anticipate future normative demands; human rights only allow us to coordinate our reactions to chronic problems. There is no way in which human rights form a coherent body of doctrine concerning the positive responsibilities of states; they are necessary but not sufficient conditions of states being permitted to interfere in the affairs of other states. International human rights law with this model could not *be* a constitution for an international community; these humanitarian norms are regulative and conditional, claiming no moral or political necessity beyond the amelioration of immediate suffering (Waldron 2013). In sum, this theory of human rights aspires to methodological accuracy in that it tracks some existing and stable international practices. But this tells us little about what the content of human rights norms should be beyond basic interests, and there is no reason to consider the suffering of anyone, or anything, other than our living contemporaries. Human rights are an aspect of international political practice that is reactive to the immediate needs of humans, but they do not transcend the present.

Second, and under the title of *humanism*, we would stress human rights' links with autonomy, agency, and human dignity. The human is not merely vulnerable but uniquely self-determining, and human rights law maintains the conditions of such self-determination. In contrast to the negative and prohibitive aspects of humanitarian discourse, humanism might be thought to include the positive and constructive aspects of the 'human' of human rights. This understanding of the human can be described, using Ruth Macklin's terms, as 'recognition of the inherent dignity, the basic autonomy, or the intrinsic worth of human beings [and] the totality of attributes that distinguish man from other beings, or as denoting the "essential" human quality or character' (1977, 372). According to these assumptions, the 'human person' as bearer of human rights takes on significance. The historically and biologically particular *human* and the formally equal *person* who bears a basic bundle of rights and duties are conjoined such that equal respect is demanded for each individual in their particularity and not on the basis of their socially defined roles. In other words, humanism permits a dual conception of the bearer of human rights: both the 'thin' person of law and the 'thick' human of lived reality.

Rather than emphasizing human vulnerability, human rights here concern 'the priority of the right' and concern legal protection of the self-constitution of the individual. This grants human rights political force and invites enforcement and expansion of rights through adjudication. The humanistic model can be associated with a demand for the embedding and expansion of human rights as regulatory norms and for their creative development. With a more rounded menu of social, economic, and political rights, along with a stress on litigation, this model assumes the possibility of creative expansion of human rights jurisprudence. Human rights are more than of symbolic importance because they can map ideological changes and our changing social and political concerns. However, international human rights on this model do not, conversely, entail any structural change to the international legal and political system. Extension of the field of human rights law is not the same as constitutionalization of the law or equivalent to a genuine sense of obligation that transcends national or state affiliations. Human rights are more than the amelioration of suffering and responsiveness to human vulnerability, but they are also less than a principled commitment, within a community, to projecting a certain kind of society into the future.

Finally, *constitutionalism* denotes precisely that principled commitment, within a community, to projecting a certain kind of society into the future. Here, human rights are irreducibly constitutional, and to be constitutional means to be essential to the self-constitution of a community or society (Reisman 2013). Since 1945, international human rights law has not only championed the rights of individuals but has changed the nature and limits of sovereignty. It has insisted on there being limits to 'internal' sovereignty (the powers of the government within the territory that it controls) and has changed the conditions of 'external' sovereignty (the conditions under which a state is recognized as a legitimate or viable state). The linking of internal and external

sovereignty through human rights standards is not merely a political or ideological change but a constitutional one, altering what it is to be a state and
altering the basic rules of international conduct. Put strongly, sovereignty has
been replaced by humanity as the *Grundnorm* of the international arena (Peters
2009). The consequences of this are not merely symbolic, but an expansion of
the concept of international legality beyond its traditional sources and towards
a notion of international moral responsibility.

A constitutional model of international human rights law treats human
rights as informing or dictating the creation and application of other regulations. It is also a model with a clear temporal component and a clear sense of
ownership of the norms. We are not only concerned with managing problems or
preserving the status quo, but with binding ourselves into the future in ways that
are premised on core ideas such as humanity *and* humanitarianism. And these
are commitments within a community, i.e. the international community con-
ceiving itself as having shared interests rather than a simple commitment to
non-harm and non-intervention. This community projects a certain kind of
society into the future: one that not only conserves the unity of the whole but
that continues to be characterized by principles and that seeks its own self-
improvement (Dworkin 1986). The parallels with individual obligation and
self-constitution here are not accidental. Collective constitutional commitments, like practices of personal self-constitution, are future orientated and
principled commitments and are not merely reactive and technocratic (Korsgaard 2009).

The remainder of this chapter will be a defence of this constitutional model
as the most appropriate conception of human rights, given the need to frame
our understanding of sustainability duties. However, it is appropriate at this
point to briefly reflect on what general features and implications this model
might be thought to have. There is no doubt that this is a progressive understanding of human rights that anticipates substantial changes in their content
and functioning over time. It is also in some respects a cosmopolitan model that
claims the necessity of certain kinds of norms at a transnational level. Those
norms are international constitutive norms that seek the good self-ordering of
international society now and in the future (Allott 2002). This implies, in turn,
that there is an international community or international society that is author
and beneficiary of these international legal duties. This 'modest cosmopolitanism' (Caney 2005, 116) runs counter to the basic assumptions of international
realism, with its insistence that we cannot assume any constitutive norms at all
in international law except the self-interest and security of states (Franck 1989).
In contrast, the attraction of a modest cosmopolitanism lies in *not* assuming that
the constitutional duties of states are superseded by an international constitution, but rather in assuming that an international constitution coordinates
national constitutions where the international is the most appropriate level of
regulation. This nevertheless implies that there is a nascent international
society and that this society is a condition of the future being governed by law
and not by luck or accident. To the extent that such a society can be said to

exist, it is a society committed to international human rights and not just to the self-preservation of states.

4 Rights, constitutions, and future generations

The reason for considering each of the ideal types considered above was to demonstrate that our understanding of the function of human rights depends upon how they are related to constitutions and how they are related to the human of human rights. Two questions arise from that (but will for now be deferred) concerning the subject and addressees of rights. Namely, is an international community structurally essential to international human rights and how can we delimit the class of humans to which human rights claims are applicable? We should first inquire into how and why rights are important, and this requires us to move to a closer questioning of the significance of human *rights*.

Whatever our conception of the basic nature or requirements of rights, it is easy to see that the language of rights insinuates itself between the legal and moral without allowing clear 'ownership' by either law or morality. Legal rights often look to morality for their justification; moral rights often look to legal ideas for their form. The point of expressing social demands in the form of rights is to deny that the purely legal, or the purely moral alone has enough normative weight to do the task required. What this denies, by extension, is that rights necessarily imply some kind of dialogical or dyadic form, i.e. a single right-holder plus a single duty-holder. Even if legal rights often take this form, human rights as general, moral, rights need not. Communities have rights; states have duties; individuals can have both.

For this reason, I would want to argue – and the constitutional model strongly implies – that international human rights law claims should not be seen as admitting one kind of right–duty relationship exclusively and should not be thought to imply one conception of the nature of rights. It is clearly not the case that human rights are only claims by the individual against their state, because international human rights law includes some rights existing horizontally (individual–individual, state–state) and also includes some rights possessed by groups. By extension, when we investigate 'human *rights*' we would be better attending to three characteristic aspects of human rights: the indivisibility of the moral and legal in the claim of human rights to be rights; the possibility of any agent (natural or non-natural) standing in a normative relationship with another (natural or non-natural) actor; and also how the scope of such norms can be self-limiting vis-à-vis other normative goals and practices. It is questions concerning these characteristic aspects that I will now direct towards the constitutional model.

First, the humanistic and constitutional models share a *moral* world view within which human rights are universally necessary. In other words, the notion of obligation – at the state level – is held not to be exhausted by the political rights that the state is *willing* to (voluntarily, by supererogation) grant the individual. Rather, a defensible view of obligation would include obligations that the state *must* grant. This much is shared by any moral, and not merely political or legal, understanding of international human rights. However, in the constitutional model we see the most successful integration of the moral and the legal. Not only is there a class of rights that it is obligatory for the state to acknowledge and grant, but these must be among the constitutive norms, not merely the regulative norms, of the state. Put another way, the conception of law that we find flowing from humanistic and constitutional models of human rights is not a positivistic one that reduces obligation to the validity and authority of the state's will. Rather, the very idea of law is inclusive of constitutive norms that have a moral function, namely the good self-constitution of collectives.

Accordingly, this constitutional reading that refuses to separate the moral, legal, and political is not simply pointing to a distinctive function for human rights but a particular conception of obligation that necessarily includes *a whole class of rights*. International human rights are not a menu of rights that states can pick and choose from, but a group of rights that sit alongside constitutional rights and give expression to interests rather than, say, institutional arrangements. And such a conception of obligation only makes sense against the backdrop of constitutional commitments: that is, the idea that an entire social group is to project itself into the future using a class of rights as part of this self-constitution. But this, of course, is to leave open the content of those rights (discussed below). And it is not to 'determine the future' any more than national constitutions of the past were the sole determinant of the shape of our societies today. The constitutional reading, then, is better able to make sense of the co-constitution of law and morality and, specifically, is able to make sense of our projection of human rights per se into the future, not just specific norms.

Second, it cannot be true a priori that human rights hold only between state and individual. We start from the position not of the isolated, rights-claiming individual but of the collective concerned with the future. This could equally describe the traditional nation state, regional groupings, or the society of all societies – international society. International society is the collective, composite, social entity par excellence, and we would assume that this has need of a constitution. There is nothing that precludes this society from standing in a normative relationship with particular individuals within nation states. We might say that the normative relationships we are concerned with when we are concerned with human rights are relationships that transcend individual constitutions and encompass the whole panoply of horizontal and vertical relationships.

Third, it should be stressed that if the constitutional model is to be championed, it must have something to say about the kinds of rights claims that are possible. Thresholds or other limiting conditions are not entirely extrinsic to human rights theory (Griffin 2008), and each model (excepting perhaps the humanistic one) anticipates some self-limitation to human rights with regard to other social practices and institutions. Human rights as constitutional norms are self-limited by the role they are intended to play in projecting an international society into the future. They are, then, to be associated with the basic or generic rights necessary for good self-constitution into the future. They are, negatively, not therefore to be associated with a *complete* constitutional project. We could, then, assume that international human rights (even understood as constitutional norms) are subject to a principle of subsidiarity: they are to play a constitutional role, but nevertheless political and social decisions can and should be made at the lowest possible political level provided they are compatible with international human rights law (Carozza 2003). What is important is that when scholars have considered thresholds or other limits to the scope of human rights, they have often included within such limiting conditions the rights of states to determine certain (justice-based, democratic) policies and practices. These are allowed to limit the functioning of human rights law which would otherwise intrude into every level of political life. It is, I would argue, a clear implication of the constitutional model that, given that sustainability and intergenerational justice fall clearly and conceptually within the scope and concerns of the international community, this overrides claims to subsidiarity and that environmental and sustainability decisions should be determined at an international level. The human interests that international human rights law seeks to protect are the interests shared by individuals and groups up to, and including, the international society whose responsibility it is to respond to them.

5 Evaluation

The foregoing analysis has drawn out one distinctive constitutional thread in international human rights law and theory and has, in the process, pointed to some limitations of competing models. At this point we should take stock of the implications of such an argument, whether it makes sense of duties to future generations, and whether we can make good on the promise of giving specificity to the actors and agents owning, and addressed by human rights.

First we consider *content*. Note that existing human rights principles have a decisive contribution to make to the problems of sustainability, but the impact of these principles through positive human rights laws is, at present, limited. Some human rights can be used to make environmental changes (health, life, or private life); others can be used for procedural purposes to allow better or more informed public debate about such matters (right to expression or to a legal remedy); some group rights or third generation rights (right to self-determination) contain a mixture of substantive and procedural possibilities. Moreover, some existing and potential human rights (right to clean air or right to water) clearly make a substantive contribution to articulating international standards and create grounds for individual petition and sometimes group rights. We must be able to retain these gains while being able to show the *necessity* of granting such content the status of human rights. Moreover, we must, if we are to take the constitutional model seriously, ask whether and how this can be generative of other rights attuned to the possible interests (or claims) of future generations.

We can assume that a constitutional model of international human rights does not imply selectivity within, or deflation of, existing rights and does not preclude the creation of new rights. The necessity that human rights possess is not related to the assent and the will of states, but relates to the ongoing process of the creation of an international society. This permits the defence of any number of values provided they make a claim to either the self-preservation of that society or the projection of ideals by that society. The generation of human rights' content is inseparable from immediate, practical demands, and there is much in human rights law that is therefore time-bound or even accidental. The generation of future rights and the content of those rights is only restricted, then, by being able to be part of constitutional commitments and therefore necessarily intended to be entrenched (for the foreseeable future) and generation-determining (they will inevitably determine the character of future generations that they are intended to create). On that basis, they may be duties related to justice (assuming that future persons have equal moral weight to our-selves) or they could be fiduciary duties related to guardianship (either of our children and their offspring or of the environment itself).

Second, we must ask, 'Who is this *duty-holder?*' Again, while it is paradigmat-ically the state (and its organs and representatives) that hold duties, it is intelli-gible (and there is legal precedent for this) to see human rights responsibilities stretching to business, transnational corporations and, in some instances, indi-viduals as duty-holders. However, it has been denied that a viable or relevant theory of human rights in this context must imply a strict Hohfeldian correla-tivity or perfect duties. After all, states stand in human rights relationships rel-ative to other states, and the state can have duties to progressively realize rights (i.e. failure to immediately grant the object of a right is not necessarily a human rights violation). Conversely, individuals, their offspring, or generations and the generations that they themselves produce, can each make claims upon us, or can be said to have interests. The status (even intelligibility) of these different parties is contentious, but there is no doubt that they can fulfil one or both of the criteria for a theory of rights, i.e. waivable claims that can command acts or forbearances from others or have interests that create reasons for action in others. As such, while duties to future generations are subject to certain concep-tual peculiarities, there is (formally at least) the appearance of the necessary conditions for the existence of rights.

Third, we should see international human rights law as *addressed* to the inter-national community as a whole, to individual states, and to each of us. We rightly see the development of international law, certainly after 1945, as the reaction to violence and tragedy. However, the inclusions and exclusions driving its present direction of travel are unclear. In 1945, we could easily identify the dangerous and lawless 'them' against which 'we' define ourselves through human rights law. Who are 'we' today: the society of states, the international com-munity, or coalitions of the willing? From that uncertain pluripolar regulatory perspective, we have all the more reason to demand that international human rights laws be treated as constitutional and not simply regulative norms. More specifically, when we address states we make a mistake if we address states qua domestic governments as the highest moral and political actors: our assumption should be that an international community is the product of, and governs, those states. No doubt the state is likely to remain politically and therefore normatively decisive into the future. However, conceptually inadequate understandings of the 'international community' are a problem. As indicated above, a minimal cosmo-politanism implies that a genuine international society, a society of all societies, is capable of having a constitution: a sense of self and a desire to project that self into the future. Properly understood, international human rights laws address themselves to the international community, demanding that it conceive of itself as such (Donnelly 2009).

Fourth, and finally, can we say anything about the individuals or collectives that will *claim* such rights? Assuming the existence of future generations, our actions may remove the conditions for the possibility of human rights being realized. With resource scarcity or environmental degradation in the future, it may be that no human rights could, in certain conceivable future circumstances, be afforded to some or all societies. This would be an injustice: inequitable treat-ment of one generation vis-à-vis another. It would also, arguably, be a human rights violation in itself given that human rights instruments contain provisions demanding the equitable and non-discriminatory provision of rights. Con-versely, it has been a proven temptation in human rights theory to treat the – socially and politically – possible as among the conditions for the possibility of human rights being binding. In circumstances where the object of human rights is impossible to realise, the claiming of such rights becomes meaningless (Hahn 2012). This conclusion should be resisted not only because of the moral defens-ibility of many if not most of our existing human rights laws, but also because it misunderstands our obligations of intergenerational justice. Future generations are not simply postulates or variables in our calculations. Such generations have to be constituted: we create what they are. As a consequence, the non-identity problem is treated here as disingenuous because, while it is certainly the case that what and who future generations are depends upon our actions and choices, this argument distracts us from the crucial analogy of a state constitution through which 'we, the people' project ourselves into the future. This creative and self-regulatory act is not stultified by the uncertainty of the outcome.

6 Framing the debate

Our initial and driving impulse here was to explore one possible route to framing the debate about sustainability duties. Such framing concerned 'articulation' and 'coherence'. Can we show that sustainability must be articulated in terms of human rights and, even if such an articulation is possible, is this coherent with our other moral and political commitments? By way of conclusion, we should ask whether we have achieved clarity by these standards.

Sustainability duties and duties to future generations cannot, to put it nega-tively, be successfully articulated through the basic assumptions of Westphalian international law. In this view, international law is the self-interest of states expressed through contracts; this self-interest is best understood in terms of a prisoner's dilemma, and their contracts are conditional contracts that may have general effect but are not universal. These are not adequate foundations for robust future-orientated action. Nor does international law offer resources for understanding risk (such as that which demands action in the absence of complete evidence) or for articulating how collective (self-)constitution at the international level might be obligation-generating. Against this background, trying to articulate sustainability duties through a field of international legal practice – international human rights law – seems senseless. Such norms, for all their prima facie relevance, are fundamentally conditional norms unable to transcend the system they are a product of.

However, are international human rights laws merely a 'product' of international law? This is not the case, and despite the humanitarian model showing human rights being *efficacious* in international law, there is no reason to insist that international human rights law is irreducibly conditioned by the political characteristics of international law or to insist that the only legitimate methodology in this area is a pragmatic one. On the contrary, other models bring out defensible conceptions of international human rights law centring on their conception of the human. This in turn requires that when we come to articulate sustainability duties we should be concerned with finding a conception of human rights that can treat them as a class of norms capable of categorical expression and deriving from non-statal authority. The challenge, then, is to show that this, in turn, is not reducible to a conception of the human as merely vulnerable or autonomous, but individualized. The constitutional model of human rights does this by allowing the normative grounds of human rights to be both collective and individuated. And, more to the point, this allows the *articulation* of sustainability duties through the self-projection of societies, including international society, into the future. When we articulate sustainability duties as 'duties central to the self-constitution of international society', we leave unanswered questions about the content of those rights. But we do articulate the duties in a way that is not susceptible to the contingency of state will and in a way that is consonant with the general function of all constitutions, which means that we see our collective obligations as future orientated.

The question of content does, however, press upon us, and it is here that we should be most concerned with *coherence*. We must find ways of making the content of international human rights norms coherent with other constitutional norms and with the interests of the constituencies that they are intended to serve. This is not to treat human rights law as timeless, nor is it to treat human rights law as equivalent to an overlapping (international) consensus. The 'moral' status of international human rights law can be articulated roughly as Donnelly suggests:

It is an exaggeration to say that [in the words of Weisstub] 'the conception of humanity as expressed in the Universal Declaration of Human Rights has become the only valid framework of values, norms and principles capable of structuring a meaningful and yet feasible scheme of national and international civilized life.' But this claim does contain a kernel of truth. The Universal Declaration may not be the *only* valid framework. It is, admittedly, an incomplete framework. Nonetheless, it does represent a realistically utopian cross-cultural vision of the demands and possibilities of our moral nature, a vision that has something like universal validity for us today.

(2009, 7)

However, this does not fully define human rights' constitutional role. The general content of any constitution is both substantive and institutional. Constitutions concern the kinds of basic rights we (the people) think are universal and the kinds of institutions that we think are necessary for justice. Accordingly, we should not look for clear demarcations between (international) constitutional and human rights norms. What we are looking for, in essence, is coherence between domestic or municipal constitutional norms and international constitutional norms. At every level we are concerned with universal rights and interests. But we are also, and inescapably, concerned here with concerns for international economic equity and other socio-economic commitments.

What this leaves as the background of our analysis, but which should be foregrounded, is the link between the problem(s) of sustainability. Norms, risk, actions, and uncertainty are the mixture of problems that we are seeking to frame. Have they been given the unity of a single problem? One of the ways in which an international constitution is important is in its signalling of the importance of time and space in our thinking. Constitutions concern the future and concern everyone within the relevant territory. Equally, the problems of sustainability are themselves problems that speak to the very conditions of our lives and practices; they understand our obligations as transcending time and territorial space. The essence of the foregoing arguments could, then, be summarized as the inability of existing international law to transcend generational limits but also that it contains, through human rights, the means to achieve such a transcendence.

We might say, fundamentally, that it is only through positing the existence of an international community that we can make transnational duties and future generations intelligible. An international community is, like any political community, a present grouping projecting itself into the future. And such a community needs politics in order to ensure that dynamism and law lead to justice. The antagonism of law and politics is productive of our sound governance, though it is no guarantee of peace or that things will flourish in the future. This is the paradox of constitutionalism that exists within individuals as much as it exists within the international community. Autonomy and authenticity depend upon commitment to a project of principled self-constitution that will encounter enormous challenges, including change within the entity that is seeking to constitute itself. Nonetheless, without such commitment, we will act upon norms and maxims that create nothing whatsoever.

Note

1 The most famous and successful instance of a human rights case in this context is *Minors Oposa v Secretary of the Department of Environmental and Natural Resources*, Supreme Court of the Philippines, 33 ILM 173 (1994).

References

Allott P. (2002) *The health of nations: society and law beyond the state* Cambridge, Cambridge University Press.

Caney S. (2005) *Justice beyond borders: a global political theory* Oxford, Oxford University Press.

Carozza P.G. (2003) 'Subsidiarity as a structural principle of international human rights law' *American Journal of International Law*, 97 38–79.

Donnelly J. (2009) *Human dignity and human rights* Commissioned by and prepared for the Geneva Academy of International Humanitarian Law and Human Rights in the framework of the Swiss Initiative to Commemorate the 60th Anniversary of the Universal Declaration of Human Rights, Available at www.scribd.com/doc/229433530/Human-Rights-and-Human-Dignity#scribd, accessed 27 October 2015.

Dworkin R. (1986) *Law's empire* Oxford, Hart Publishing.

Franck T.M. (1989) 'Is justice relevant to the international legal system?' *Notre Dame Review*, 64(4) 945–63.

Griffin J. (2008) *On human rights* Oxford, Oxford University Press.

Hahn H. (2012) 'Justifying feasibility constraints on human rights' *Ethical Theory and Moral Practice*, 15 143–57.

Holland A. (1999) 'Sustainability: should we start from here?' in Dobson A. ed., *Fairness and futurity: essays on environmental sustainability and social justice* Oxford, Oxford University Press, 46–68.

Korsgaard C.M. (2009) *Self-constitution* Oxford, Oxford University Press.

Macklin R. (1977) 'Moral progress' *Ethics*, 87 370–82.

Mulgan T. (2003) 'The non-identity problem' in Dyke H. ed., *Time and ethics: essays at the intersection* Netherlands, Kluwer, 219–36.

Peters A. (2009) 'Humanity: the alpha and omega of sovereignty' *The European Journal of International Law*, 20(3), 513–44.

Rawls J. (2001) *The law of peoples: with "the idea of public reason revisited"* Harvard, Harvard University Press.

Reisman W.M. (2013) *The quest for world order and human dignity in the twenty-first century: constitutive process and individual commitment* Netherlands, Brill.

Shue S. (2010) 'Deadly delays, saving opportunities: creating a more dangerous world' in Gardner et al. eds, *Climate ethics: essential readings* Oxford, Oxford University Press.

Slote M. (2003) 'Empathy, immediacy and morality' in Dyke H. ed., *Time and ethics: essays at the intersection* Netherlands, Kluwer, 179–88.

Waldron J. (2013) *Human rights: a critique of the Raz/Rawls approach* Public Law Research Paper No. 13-32, New York, NYU School of Law, Available at http://ssrn.com/abstract=2272745, accessed 12 June 2015.

Part II

Long-term responsibility and the theory of human rights

6 Human dignity and intergenerational human rights[1]

Marcus Düwell

1 Introduction

Should we think about our responsibilities with regard to future people in terms of human rights? Current human rights institutions primarily deal with existing conflicts of existing people; they are concerned with actual conflicts. Perhaps they deal with preventive measures as well, measures to avoid a conflict arising in the first place or a simmering conflict becoming violent. But primarily human rights have a focus on present human rights violations. There may be reasons for such a 'presentistic bias', reasons that already play a role within the philosophical debates. Those reasons may have to do with the fact that we don't know how the future will develop or what kind of conflicts will arise in the future and that we cannot predict how our actions will affect the future. And finally, if we understand the expression 'future people' in the sense of 'people who are not born yet', we have the problem that there is no right-holder. We can then speculate about whether there can be rights that we have to respect where we cannot identify the right-holder, a problem that becomes more complicated because we have an influence on the process of bringing future people into existence and how many of them there will be.

From another perspective, this first reaction seems to be less plausible. With regard to several ecological challenges, we can be quite certain that our present behaviour has far-reaching consequences for the life of future people. The IPCC reports (www.ipcc.ch) of the last decade clearly present evidence which shows that climate change is real (at least to a large extent as a result of human behaviour), that the extent to which the climate has changed is more drastic than we have previously thought and that it will happen much faster than we thought before. There is a variety of uncertainties regarding what the effects of these changes will be, but that makes the situation even worse because it reduces our possibilities of anticipating specific scenarios and taking appropriate measures of adaptation. To the extent that human beings can be certain about something, we can be certain that our actions, as far as the climate is concerned, have irreversible and dangerous effects on future people. This situation makes that it is impossible to avoid asking what kind of obligations we have towards future people and whether we should see those obligations as related to the rights of future people.

Why should we conceptualize those obligations within the framework of human rights? If we analyse some conceptual features of human rights, we will find that the duties with regard to future people and the obligations that result from the human rights framework cannot be neutral towards each other. Of course, we can conceptualize the human rights differently and we can also disagree about the content of human rights. But we generally assume that human rights have normative priority in some meaningful sense. We can think of rights as 'trumps' (Dworkin 1984) or as 'side-constraints' that we have to respect when realizing our own goals (Nozick 1974, 29) or we can think of them in Kantian terms as duties that correspond to rights as categorical obligations. In all these perspectives, we assume that duties which correspond to the rights of others override other practical considerations; the normative priority we ascribe to human rights forces us to evaluate our practical concerns in the light of duties that follow from the respect for human rights. Even if it is economically advantageous or will give us pleasure to torture or enslave other people, the rights of people infringed upon by these activities have normative priority. That doesn't mean that from a practical perspective we should only be concerned about human rights, but it does mean that economic, eudaemonistic and other practical considerations are legitimate only to the extent that they respect the side-constraints of human rights obligations. But it is a central feature of human rights that although they forbid cruel behaviour by human beings towards other human beings (torture, genocide, etc.), at the same time they protect human liberties and formulate an obligation on states to give human beings the support they need to exercise those liberties. This means that human rights protect the liberties of human beings to carry out the activities they want to do and in some cases even assist them to do so. Human rights protect the liberty of human beings to move, to build houses, to procreate and to use technology to make their lives easier. Those liberties are either protected directly (such as the right to procreation) or they are implications of other rights, such as the duty to enable disabled people to have equal access to transport and to engage in social activities. All these exercises of liberties do, however, to some extent result in the use of energy, the use of natural resources, the production of waste and emissions of CO_2. Exercising these liberties therefore results in the use of energy and natural resources, the production of emissions and population growth. That means the exercise of these liberties is responsible for the problems we create for future generations.

If these first, tentative considerations are correct, that is, if we have to assume that human rights have normative priority and that as a consequence of human rights liberties being exercised that have negative consequences for future people, the relationship between human rights and the duties towards future people cannot be a neutral one. Investigating how these duties relate to each other is unavoidable. In what follows, I will discuss some of the conceptual and normative presuppositions of this debate in more detail (section 2). Afterwards, I will present my own proposal as to how to respond to this problem by, first, analysing the starting points of the human rights regime (section 3) and then showing that these starting points make it necessary to extend the human rights regimes in a future-oriented perspective (section 4).

2 Some presuppositions

In the introduction I presented some first reflections on the question of why we should think about our future-oriented duties in terms of human rights. Before I present my own normative proposal, it is necessary to discuss some conceptual and normative presuppositions that have to be clarified before the discussion can get started.

First of all, we have to wonder what kind of analysis is appropriate for dealing with this question. In the current debate, ethical interpretations of human rights is often criticized and instead a 'practical approach to human rights' is proposed – most prominently by Charles Beitz (2009) – that takes its starting point from the practice of human rights. The practice refers to human rights as they are formulated in the declarations and international contracts, which form a basis for the international human rights practice of observing, criticizing and condemning states if they infringe upon those principles. This reference point is perhaps not as clear as one would hope insofar as the international human rights legislation involves principles that it expects the national legislation to incorporate, had a lot of indirect effects on national law and politics and will continue to do so.

While I agree that it makes sense to focus on human rights not just as a list of provisions but as a practice, it is less plausible to assume that such a focus would make a moral interpretation of human rights superfluous. Current human rights practice has established standards for the evaluation of governmental action and political orders. These standards claim normative priority in the sense that states cannot legitimately ignore them. There is already a widespread intuition that we ought to give these standards such a strong position because they are seen as morally important (we assume that no state may legitimately torture people because of the immorality of such behaviour). But besides this, the claimed normative priority is a feature that links human rights conceptually to morality. We can understand morality as a set of standards according to which we ought to act. Perhaps that is not the entire role of morality: perhaps morality does not just entail principles of right action but also provides us with orientation in how to live in an appropriate and successful manner. But there is at least a central part of morality that deals with permissible human behaviour. If human rights claim normative priority, then we necessarily find in human rights practice itself the claim that those standards have moral authority, and without understanding this claim it is hard to understand the human rights practice as such. That doesn't mean that the forming of the human rights regime would just be a codification of a transhistorical list of natural rights. Rather, I think that the opposition that Beitz introduces between 'naturalistic' and 'practical' approaches to human rights is a misguided way of categorizing the differences between human rights approaches. It is of course problematic to assume that the

human rights practice of the twentieth century would be a kind of direct political codification of the ideas of natural rights, which were developed in early
modernity (Tierney 1997; Tuck 1979). But in analysing human rights practices
we will find a claim on moral authority. It is hard to understand discourses about
human rights where people fight for the legal condemnation of children's rights
or where other people deny that gay marriage should be a human right if we do
not see these disputes as based on the moral views of such people. And it is hard
to understand the process of establishing human rights practice after World
War II if we do not interpret this in light of a historical development in early
modernity. It was only because people developed a conviction that a decent and
just society would be one that would give equal rights to human beings that it
was possible to establish such a practice. And when, during the preparation of
the *Universal Declaration of Human Rights* (UDHR), the Chinese representative
Peng Chun Chang argued that one would find similar concepts in the Confucian tradition, a moral interpretation was presupposed as well (for the history of
the UDHR see Morsink 2000).

We can therefore only understand discourses about human rights when the
conceptualization tries to do justice to this implicit moral claim, tries to elaborate the conceptual presuppositions under which this claim is intelligible and
tries to investigate under which conditions this claim can be defended. Even if,
factually, very obviously different and opposing attempts are made to defend the
authority of human rights, to specify their content and their role, these attempts
cannot be understood if we do not interpret them as attempts to elaborate and
justify the moral authority of human rights. This also means that the diverse
histories of moral and political thinking that could make such interpretations of
human rights intelligible will play an important role in this discourse. If this is
so, it seems problematic to disentangle international human rights practice from
the moral discourse, as follows from Beitz's proposal.

This means that a philosophical interpretation of human rights is unavoidable. Such an interpretation explains the conceptual presuppositions under
which human rights *can* be thought and aims at an evaluation of the possible
reasons we may have to subscribe to the moral authority of human rights. If it
is true that human rights claim normative priority, it is impossible to understand human rights without understanding their role in comparison to other
normative convictions we may have. Insofar as a philosophical interpretation
of the relationship between the normative duties we may have with regard to
human rights and the normative obligations we have towards the future is that
they cannot be understood independently from each other, we have to understand their relationship. In the following, I will use 'human rights duties' to
refer to those duties that we have on the basis of the human rights regime, and
I will use 'sustainability duties' to refer to those duties we may have to ensure
decent life conditions on the planet for future people. I will not specify here in
detail what these conditions may entail but I will assume that fulfilling these
duties will involve asking agents to restrict their possible courses of action
significantly.

A short remark is necessary here about whether we really have to interpret human rights as overriding other practical considerations. James Griffin (2008) has proposed seeing human rights just as the protection of a specific core of our normative conviction, namely to protect the 'normative personhood' and basic liberties of human beings and their ability to choose how they live their life (Griffin 2008, 33). But there would be other practical considerations, and we do not have to assume that human rights would always override the other normative considerations we would find important. We may also want to protect those human beings who don't have personal capacities (yet), which would not be covered in his view of human rights as the protection of 'normative personhood'. Of course, it is correct that the legal human rights regime as a project in development and under constant change is incomplete in the sense that it cannot and does not aspire to provide a comprehensive set of regulations for all areas of life for all states. In that sense, there will always be aspects where human rights provisions conflict with specific values that are not incorporated in the human rights regime. But if we assume that there may be conflicts between human rights provisions and other normative considerations, and if, in general, we assume that human rights can be infringed upon because of those concurrent normative considerations, we would need a kind of meta-framework that would allow us to determine the relationship between the human rights provisions and other legitimate normative considerations; otherwise, the authority of human rights cannot be systematically defended at all.

If it is true that human rights include *permissive* rights, rights that entitle human beings to do things they want to do (moving, using energy, reproducing, etc.), there must be reasons to restrict the exercise of these permissive rights. Some of these activities are restricted because they interfere directly with rights of other human beings. Other activities are restricted or required on the basis of the exercise of rights. Here we can think about cases in which a political body (that represents the people) has decided to use the public space in a specific way and this decision is binding for all agents, or we can think about institutions, such as the police or the tax authority, whose functioning is a necessary requirement to protect rights in the first place. But in any case, restrictions of permissive rights within the human rights regime have to be justified by provisions of the human rights regime itself; we cannot just introduce restrictive reasons that are not justified within these provisions.

On the basis of what we have said so far, only the following relationships between human rights duties and sustainability duties are possible: 1. Human rights duties and sustainability duties are not congruent and human rights duties override sustainability duties; 2. Human rights duties and sustainability duties are not congruent and sustainability duties override human rights duties; 3. Human rights duties are only a partial regime that has to be restricted by sustainability duties; and 4. Human rights duties entail sustainability duties.

In the *first* option we would have to be completely committed to the provisions of the human rights regime without taking into account what these provisions will mean for the future as long as the human rights of present-day people are not affected. The *second* option would force us to take the protection of future life options seriously but we would not assume that these duties are justified by human rights considerations and we would respect human rights only to the extent that their exercise would not endanger the life options of future people. In fact the second option would mean the end of the human rights regime. The *third* option would be in line with Griffins' proposal that sees human rights just as a part of our normative commitments. This would – as already argued – presuppose a more overarching criterion that allows us to determine under which condition a restriction of human rights is possible. The *fourth* option would be that we have duties regarding future people within and because of the commitments to human rights.

Perhaps other options are possible, but if the above options are right we cannot avoid investigating whether or not we should see ourselves as morally obliged towards future people because of the convictions we hold regarding human rights.

3 Human dignity as the basis of human rights

If the assumption I started with is correct, that is that we have to make an attempt to understand our duties regarding future people within the human rights regime, the task would now be to investigate whether the extension of it to future people would follow from the rationale of this regime.[2] Since this question affects the interpretation of the basic structure of human rights, the question would not be whether we can just add another human right or whether specific rights would apply to future people as well but whether this extension would be necessary on the basis of the starting points of the human rights regime. Therefore, we have to wonder whether an interpretation of human dignity as the foundational concept of human rights would require us to extend human rights duties to future people. Some remarks about this concept are therefore necessary.[3]

Assuming that we have normative reasons to establish an order that incorporates respect for human rights this presupposes on the one hand that human beings are in *need* of the protection and support that human rights grant and on the other hand that we are *obliged* to *respect* human beings. The first assumption can hardly be contested: human beings are vulnerable and cannot survive and develop without protection and support of others. Justifying the second assumption is more demanding. It raises all kinds of questions about *who* is obliged to fulfil *what kind* of duties on the basis of *what reasons*. In specific human rights practices there are all kind of concrete mechanisms, rules and constraints that are relevant when determining answers to these questions. Human rights are specific responses to challenges and threats human beings are confronted with, and to the extent that those challenges and threats are changing and to the extent that new actors appear that may be capable of protecting human beings against these challenges, new forms of responses may be appropriate. But in order to evaluate the appropriateness of responses we must have a systematic understanding of the reasons we have to establish such an order.

Why would we have to assume that we have to structure our social order and the state on the basis of equal respect for human beings? And why would the concept of human dignity provide us with a reason for believing that we have such an obligation? In its long history, this concept referred to a status as rational beings that would form a basis for moral duties. In this sense, Cicero thought that human beings, due to their rational nature, would have to live up to specific standards, such as controlling their emotions and desires (Cicero 1913, I.30: 105–6). The Christian tradition would assume that our specific capacities would be grounded in our creation in the image of God. We cannot go into here the complex history of this concept, but we can see that there are specific capacities of human beings that give them a specific status.

Neither the Stoic nor the early Christian or Confucian tradition would draw the conclusion that this status would be a reason to ascribe rights to human beings. But in the old idea of human dignity, human beings were already seen as self-reflexive beings capable of governing their own life. Of course, there are all kinds of natural, cultural and psychological constraints on the way we can give shape to our life, but there is a meaningful space in which self-governance is possible. It was thought that it would be important for human beings to understand themselves in a right way and that they would organize their practice according to such appropriate, practical self-understanding. A central element of this understanding of ourselves as practical beings was the assumption that we have the capacity for self-governance. For the contemporary concept of 'human dignity as a foundation of human rights' it is important that this practical capacity is not just the basis of the possibility of organizing one's own life but is also the basis of a duty to respect rational beings. In the Kantian way of thinking, respect for us as practical beings implies respect for other agents, as well as respect for our own status as rational beings. For Kant, this respect has two sides, which are reflected in the two parts of his *Metaphysics of Morals*: on the one hand, the law is thought to enforce the protection of the freedom of each individual, and on the other hand, when leading our own life we are obliged to live as virtuous beings by respecting our own status as an end in itself.[4] This means that having respect for rational beings requires establishing a legal sphere in which the freedom of the individual is protected. We cannot go into the exegetical details at this point. If we did we would then have to discuss: how Kant uses the term 'human dignity' precisely,[5]; how this term relates to the idea of respect for humanity as an end in itself; how a right in the national order relates to an international or global normative order; and to what extent Kant already has a concept of human rights in the modern sense. In response to all these questions nuanced answers would be necessary. My claim is not that the way Kant uses the term 'human dignity' would be identical with the contemporary use of it. But the relevant point in this context is that the same capacity that in the premodern concept forms the basis of duties human beings would have to live up to, forms in the Kantian way of thinking the basis for seeing human beings as obliged to respect themselves and each other, and this required respect forms the reason for establishing a legal political order that protects our freedom.

If we take this Kantian way of thinking as a kind of blueprint for the interpretation of the relationship between human dignity and human rights, such a reconstruction would have the following lines of argument: we are beings that have the capacity to govern our own life; we are able to reflect on our own life; we can ask ourselves how we lead our life, whether we could lead it in different ways, what possibilities and opportunities we have and how we want to lead our life; and we can understand what kind of maxims we are following, we can think about the appropriate means to realize our goals, we can ask whether the maxims we are following are really making us happy and we can ask ourselves whether those maxims are morally acceptable. This capacity for careful consideration may be limited in various ways but, nevertheless, it is required for all practical reflections. It confronts us with the question of how we should understand ourselves. Asking about our practical self-understanding has different dimensions. It is concerned with the question of how I can understand myself as an individual in the context of my concrete life-world and of my biography, it involves the question of how specific groups and communities can understand themselves, and it entails the question of whether there are some elements that are important for the practical self-understanding of human beings in general. To find moral obligations that may form the basis of enforceable law, it is important to investigate whether there are elements of the practical self-understanding of human beings that we cannot rationally deny. The assumption here would be that normative commitments that we find within our practical self-understanding are, on the one hand, subject-relative in the sense that they are bound to the way we see ourselves but, on the other hand, there are ways of seeing ourselves that are not arbitrary but are necessary in the sense that each rational form of self-understanding would have to take them into account.

A Kantian position would assume that human beings should have respect for beings with this basic capacity to govern their own life, and this respect involves the duty of establishing a social and political structure in which freedom is ensured. This freedom brings about the possibility of living together in ways in which individuals are not dominated by others. We can discuss where the limits of this legitimate freedom are precisely, but that would be a follow-up question. In any case, such a justification of the law would have to formulate limitations when it comes to the enforcement by political institutions and by law. These limitations are a consequence of the aim of the law. If the law is established to make the lives of individuals in freedom possible, the law must protect rights in the sense that it limits itself. The law has to enforce a legal order (otherwise it would not be law), but if it does not limit its enforcement individual freedom could not develop and therefore the aim of the law would not be reached.

What it means to enable equal freedom for all agents will probably be more demanding for the state than Kant in the eighteenth century could have thought. If it is the aim of the law to enable human beings to realize goals, to govern their own lives and to interact with each other, etc. some goods have to be available and some preconditions have to be fulfilled in order to make that possible. If our capacity for freedom is the normative ground of the law, this is the basis of rights to the necessary requirements for developing as a free being and for the realization of our goals. This requires not only negative duties to not intervene with the freedom of others; it also requires positive duties of the state to support people by providing them with those goods that are necessary for them to be able to realize their goals. In a modern society we need, for example, at least some form of education to be able to realize our goals and it would be a positive duty of the state to help people develop those skills that are required for a successful realization of important goals. This is primarily a task of the state but to some extent of individuals as well. What precisely the scope of positive duties is and how we can determine the actors that have to fulfil these duties, is an important topic of discussion but we will not go into this debate here (in this context see in particular Gewirth 1996, 31–70).

The most relevant point in the context of this chapter is the following: there are some ecological side-constraints that are implied in all fundamental rights to freedom as necessary preconditions for realizing the objects of the rights. If we, for example, have rights to freedom of expression, some conditions have to be given, as the cultural, institutional and biological side-constraints for developing opinions, to be able to express them, to find a political climate in which we may find the courage to express views on the world and to have an ecological climate which makes a life in some form of security and prosperity possible. Having a right to freedom of expression in Beijing nowadays, for example, not only requires that the government does not hinder me in speaking, but it also includes allowing me to breathe despite the smog, and this right would therefore necessitate duties of the state to reduce this smog. Gewirth speaks in this context of '*generic rights*', rights that are necessary requirements for the enjoyment of other rights (Gewirth 1978, 64–104), and in this sense those rights are implied in other rights.

If we have rights to govern our own life, and if some conditions are necessary in order to do so, we have a right to those conditions as well. If governing our own life requires the ability to breathe, it is necessary to have access to fresh air. If we now tried to justify specific rights and correlative duties in more detail, we would have to discuss how important specific potential rights would be for the realization of freedom and to what extent specific preconditions would really be necessary for their realization. But the importance of freedom and the necessity of the specific preconditions for freedom cannot be justified independently of the perspective of the agents themselves. Because if it is the task of the law to enable the realization of freedom, the justification or rights has to take the perspective of the agents themselves into account. This implies that it is not only the 'hard' dimension of the necessity that has to be discussed, e.g. whether some goods are in a biological sense necessary to realize freedom, but the cultural and psychological dimension as well. It is possible that in different cultural contexts different preconditions are necessary for realizing the self-governance of human beings.

What I have sketched out here is only the general outline in a methodological sense, not a detailed and technical justification of these assumptions. My reconstruction of the Kantian way of thinking is inspired by the justification of human rights that Alan Gewirth has presented (Gewirth 1978; Beyleveld 1992). In this context the following elements are relevant. Seeing human dignity as the basis of human rights does not mean that we take a concept of human dignity from one specific historical tradition and decide that it has to be the framework for the interpretation of human rights. Neither does it mean that we see human dignity as a specific important value and use it as an evaluative basis of all legal orders. The idea is, however, that some presuppositions are necessary to make the ascription of human rights intelligible. If we ascribe rights to all human beings, if we assume that respecting these rights deserves normative priority compared to other practical considerations, and if we assume that the legal order has to be formed according to the provisions of the human rights regime, we have to assume the concept of human dignity as sketched out above.

It follows that this human rights practice is only intelligible if we assume a specific status of human beings that makes it necessary to ascribe rights to them. Since this practice is assumed to be a global practice, it would be necessary that the rights have to be ascribed to human beings in general and not only to those of a specific culture, nation or religion, etc. Since a central aspect of human rights protection has the aim of enabling human beings to decide freely about their own course of action, it claimed that human rights are protecting the ability of humans to govern themselves. If the normative basis of human rights is to enable the self-governance of human beings, the justification for this normative basis has to be compatible with the importance of this self-governance as well. This will imply that the aspect of self-governance which provides us with a justification that it should be affirmed by each form of practical self-understanding must be a non-contingent aspect of the self-governance.

Self-governance can probably be realized in different cultures in different ways – which is not to say that all cultures will be characterized by respect for self-governance. If self-governance is so fundamentally important, it is necessary that the inner perspective of the human being affirms this importance. Only if we interpret ourselves in such a way that self-governance is important for us is there a basis for its importance, because that is something we cannot affirm in a neutral or objective way, independently of our own perspective. But at the same time this affirmation has to be necessary, not dependent on contingent wishes and desires of individuals. Rather, it has to be a necessary element of our practical self-understanding in general: we can only understand ourselves well if we assume that the possibility of self-governance is so important for us that we necessarily have to want others to respect this possibility. And this can only be extended to all human beings if we assume that human beings in general can understand themselves well if they share this assumption. In that sense, claiming that self-governance is important for human beings is not claiming that each human being reflects on this explicitly; it is rather the assumption that we can only understand ourselves well if we subscribe to this conviction explicitly or implicitly. And this is not just a dogmatic claim; it is open for contestation – an opponent would just have to show that it is possible to defend human rights without these presuppositions.

4 Human dignity and the rights of future people[6]

The aim in this context is to discuss to what extent the presuppositions of the human rights regime would provide us with a reason to extend human rights practice to future people. An appropriate, practical self-understanding of human beings would entail the conviction that we have to grant all human beings the protection and the support they need in order to realize their freedom. There are side-constraints for such an obligation that are concerned with real possibilities and feasibility considerations with regard to appropriate ways of reaching this goal. The obligation would not only imply concrete measures to protect individual rights, e.g. by installing a police force that directly enforces specific rights, but it would affect all kind of policies in various ways. Extreme forms of international human rights policies, such as condemning or even invading states because of human rights violations, are only intelligible on the basis of the more fundamental assumption that governmental power has the task of enforcing the possibility of a life in self-governance for all people. Seeing human dignity as the basis of human rights does in this sense not only affect human rights law as a 'specific' legal domain, but also affects the understanding of the national and international legal order.

How does this affect our duties towards future people? I said earlier that respect for human dignity implies that we must protect the necessary requirements for self-governance of human beings. This means that in the first place the normative relationship between rights and duties is as such not restricted to current living beings. Of course, it makes a difference that our contemporaries exist while future people do not. In that sense, there is a significant difference between the duties we have towards our contemporaries and the duties we have towards future people. But if the approach as sketched out above is correct, a commitment to human dignity would be a reason to establish an order in which the necessary conditions of self-governance for human beings are protected. With regard to future people we have to assume four things: 1. We have to assume that there will be future people. Of course there might be a catastrophe that destroys the earth, but we have no convincing reasons to believe that this will happen. Humanity's reproduction rates are now higher than ever. Therefore, we have to assume that there will be human beings in the future; 2. We know that there are some aspects that are connected to the biological and ecological conditions of human beings that are important for a self-governed life. Of course, there can be differences in terms of what is necessary, humankind can adapt and our biological nature can undergo some changes. But there are some ecological conditions that will be relevant for future people; 3. If future people will exist, they will have rights to these conditions; 4. Our current behaviour is affecting these conditions in a way that is very dangerous for future people insofar as we have the possibility of infringing upon their rights. All these considerations together mean that we have to see ourselves as obliged to change our behaviour due to the respect we owe to human dignity. Since the climate change that we are generating at the moment endangers future people in such a fundamental way, this obligation involves a high level of urgency.

It is clear that this general picture requires a much more detailed argumentation. My intention was to show that the basic assumption made about human rights practice is also a reason to see ourselves as obliged to protect decent living conditions for future people. But the nature of the challenge that climate change forms for human dignity is different from other challenges. This means that other forms of responses are appropriate. Human rights violations, such as infringements of the individual right to express one's opinion, require laws and political measures on the national level that enable the individual to express him- or herself freely. And international courts of human rights, probably even those in which individuals' complaints can be made, are subsidiary institutions for enforcement. Climate change, however, endangers humankind in general on a generic level. The instruments that are required to avoid this threat are certainly different. In this sense, specific human rights practice will change fundamentally if we see duties with regard to future generations as part of this practice. But it should be a normal procedure within human rights practice that the practice is organized in accordance with the rationale we had for establishing the practice in the first place. If we have reasons to think that this rationale is still plausible, and if this rationale forces us, under changed conditions and different forms of threats than we were confronted with in the middle of the twentieth century, to establish a new practice, it would be irrational not to do so.

Notes

1 This chapter is a follow-up to two earlier publications on this topic: Düwell (2014b) and Beyleveld, Düwell and Spahn (2016).
2 See in this context as well Hiskes (2009).
3 For a more general discussion of the philosophical dimension of human dignity see Düwell (2014a) and McCrudden (2014).
4 See, for an excellent interpretation of the *Metaphysics of Morals* (Kant 1996/1797) and the relationship between moral philosophy and philosophy of law in Kant, Steigleder (2002).
5 Sensen (2011) has argued in a very erudite study that the term 'human dignity' used in Kant's work has a meaning that is quite different from the contemporary use of the term within the human rights regime. But Sensen assumes that 'human dignity' within the human rights regime would function as a fundamental value, and he shows that such a concept would be not compatible with a Kantian framework. I would, however, claim that within the human rights framework we should understand 'human dignity' as an expression for a status and not for a value. Such a status concept is, however, much more compatible with the central role that Kant ascribes to rational beings as ends in themselves. I would, furthermore, distinguish between the question of how Kant uses the *term* 'human dignity' – which is quite underdetermined in Kant – and the question of which role the *concept* of 'human dignity', in the sense of a status that is the basis of respect, plays in his moral philosophy.
6 Also see the following: Gewirth (2001) and Steigleder (2016).

References

Beitz C. (2009) *The idea of human rights* Oxford, Oxford University Press.

Beyleveld D. (1992) *The dialectical necessity of morality. An analysis and defense of Alan Gewirth's argument for the principle of generic consistency* Chicago, University of Chicago Press.

Beyleveld D., Düwell M. and Spahn J. (2016) 'Why and how should we represent future generations in policy making?' *Jurisprudence* 6,3 (2015) 549–566.

Cicero M.T. (1913) *De officiis* ed. and trans. Miller W. Boston, Harvard University Press.

Düwell M. (2014a) 'Human dignity: concepts, discussions, philosophical perspectives' in Düwell M., Braarvig J., Brownsword R. and Mieth D. eds, *Cambridge handbook on human dignity* Cambridge, Cambridge University Press, 23–52.

Düwell M. (2014b) 'Human Dignity and Future Generations' in Düwell M., Braarvig J., Brownsword R. and Mieth D eds, *Cambridge handbook on human dignity* Cambridge, Cambridge University Press, 551–8.

Dworkin R. (1984) 'Rights as trumps' in Waldron J. ed., *Theories of rights* Oxford, Oxford University Press, 153–67.

Gewirth A. (1978) *Reason and morality* Chicago, Chicago University Press.

Gewirth A. (1996) *The community of rights* Chicago, Chicago University Press.

Gewirth A. (2001) 'Human rights and future generations' in Boylan M. ed., *Environmental ethics* Upper Saddle River, NJ, Prentice Hall, 207–12.

Griffin J. (2008) *On human rights* Oxford, Oxford University Press.

Hiskes R.P. (2009) *The human right to a green future. Environmental rights and intergenerational justice* Cambridge, Cambridge University Press.

Kant I. (1996/1797) *Metaphysics of morals* ed. and trans. Gregor M. Cambridge, Cambridge University Press.

McCrudden C. (2014) *Understanding human dignity* Oxford, Oxford University Press.

Morsink J. (2000) *The Universal Declaration of Human Rights. Origins, drafting, and intent* Philadelphia, University of Pennsylvania Press.

Nozick R. (1974) *Anarchy, state and utopia* New York, Basic Books Inc.

Sensen O. (2011) *Kant on human dignity* Berlin; Boston, Walter de Gruyter GmbH.

Steigleder K. (2002) *Kant's Moralphilosophie. Die Selbstbezüglichkeit reiner praktischer Vernunft* Stuttgart; Weimar, J.B. Metzler.

Steigleder K. (2016) 'Climate risks, climate economics, and the foundation of a rights-based ethics' *Journal of Human Rights* (in press).

Tierney B. (1997) *The idea of natural rights. Studies on natural rights, natural law, and church law 1150–1625* Grand Rapids, MI, Emroy University.

Tuck R. (1979) *Natural rights theories. Their origin and development* Cambridge, Cambridge University Press.

7 Human rights and threats concerning future people

A sufficientarian proposal

Jos Philips

1 Introduction

Can human rights incorporate future people and their interests, considering all the risks and uncertainties by which these interests are surrounded?[1] Given problems such as climate change, resource depletion and pollution, human rights cannot afford not to be able to do this if they are to remain relevant.[2] On the other hand, taking future people on board may lead to (another) multiplication of human rights claims, and this is hardly good news either. Therefore, an adequate account of how to incorporate the interests of future people into human rights is much needed. It should also tell us about the *weight* of protecting these interests compared with that of providing other human rights protections. This chapter aims to give the first outlines of such an account. I will call it *sufficientarian*, because it understands human rights as articulating a 'threshold of enough'.

To delineate the chapter's scope more clearly, consider three doubts about the ability of human rights to incorporate the claims of future people; I will be concerned only with the third. First, some authors doubt whether future people can *at all* have (future) rights that are relevant to us now.[3] However, I will leave these debates aside and simply assume that future people can, and do, have (future) rights. Second, some worry about the assumptions we should make about such uncertain things as the number, whereabouts and needs of future people. But I will assume that we can make plausible assumptions here.

Rather, my focus will, with climate change as the main example, be on *threats* to future people's interests, on possible *protections* against those threats and on uncertainties and risks involved in those threats and protections. It is clear that climate change is happening and is man-made. But it is not clear how much exactly the earth will warm up if we behave in certain ways, or what global warming of (say) 2, 4 or 6 degrees Celsius will entail in the way of extreme weather events, food and water provision and loss of biodiversity, etc. Nor is it clear exactly what measures are sufficient to limit this warming or some of its effects. It is such risks and uncertainties that this chapter will focus on.[4]

The philosophical literature is far from clear and settled on the question of how we should deal with future risks and uncertainties, such as those involved in climate change (cf. Section 3.1 below), and it has, as far as I can see, been concerned very little[5] with what will be this chapter's main aim: to propose how *human rights* could plausibly integrate the interests of future people, given such risks and uncertainties as those just explained.

The chapter will be structured as follows. Section 2 will outline my proposal and, in particular, how it could, also in the face of uncertainty, deal with a multiplicity of human rights claims. Section 3.1 defends the proposal by showing that it has some important advantages over two prominent alternatives: Stephen Gardiner's and Henry Shue's. Here, the proposal's *sufficientarian* shape, in that it thinks of human rights as articulating a *threshold* composed of particularly weighty protections, will also become fully explicit. This will help us to better understand the proposal's content as well as some of its strengths and weaknesses. Section 3.2 shows that certain objections flowing from this sufficientarian shape can be answered.

Overall, then, the argument will be that human rights can incorporate the interests of future people and that they can do this without losing their force by virtue of the sheer multiplicity of human rights claims.

2 Human rights and threats concerning future people: a proposal

This section will develop a proposal for how human rights could deal with threats concerning future people. But let me first explain the account of human rights that will be used. This account is philosophical in the sense that it is sensitive to all acceptable reasons rather than only those reasons admissible within a juridical framework. I assume, furthermore, that for a philosophical account of human rights to be acceptable, it should be possible, at least, to understand it as one interpretation of the post-World War II practice of human rights.[6] Central to this practice are, among other things, the *Universal Declaration of Human Rights* and the major human rights documents that followed in its wake (such as the two 1966 Covenants). However, the practice is not only, or even mainly, juridical, but also political and social. Among other things, human rights guide states, orient activism and help – in cases of extreme human rights violations – to legitimize forceful intervention.

For the present purposes, I simply propose one account of human rights which can, I believe, count as an interpretation of this practice while also being plausible overall.[7] This account thinks of human rights as, primarily, articulating the most important standards for living together on a global scale. As such, human rights will also offer standards for governments, and for international institutions and activism, etc. With such roles in the background, the account holds (following the arguments of Shue (1996)) that human rights are concerned with the *social protection of urgent human interests against standard threats*.[8] The interests concerned are such that they are present *among broad categories of people in all human societies.*

Some explanations are in order. 'Social protection' leaves open the question of who exactly bears the human rights duties, but does assume that important social institutions, domestic or global as the case may be, will be prominent, not least because it is essential, for there to be a right at all, that one can *count* on there being protection. Which 'interests' are to count as 'urgent'[9] requires interpretation and may depend importantly on a view of human nature, which cannot be developed here. In any case, as human rights claim universal validity, only such interests will qualify as substances for human rights that are urgent for broad categories of people everywhere and in all times.[10]

As for the weight of human rights, I take human rights to be concerned with the weightiest protections that should be socially provided, and I shall assume that providing such protections may consume a considerable part of social wealth, but by no means all of it.

Finally, for my purposes the notion of a 'standard threat' is important because, at least for Shue's and also for my account, it points to threats against which *protection* is required.[11] Shue's notion of a standard threat, as commonly understood, conveys the idea that protection is required against the most prevalent and predictable threats (cf. Beitz 2009, 109; cf. Shue 1980, 29–34). I would say, as this is more informative, that talk of standard threats is most helpfully understood as pointing out that protection is required against certain threats only, and that only certain kinds and likelihoods of protection are required. This, however, is still rather uninformative. A novel way will now be proposed of making, in two steps, the notion of a standard threat more definite. These steps will simultaneously show us how human rights, in my conception, can plausibly take threats concerning future people on board.

I

The *first step* borrows from Gardiner's (2006) and Shue's (2010) accounts (see Section 3). Regarding threats concerning the future, both rightly observe that not just any possible threat can rightly trigger precautionary action (Gardiner 2006, 51ff.; Shue 2010, 149ff.).[12] It is not plausible that any kinds of 'wild' or 'fantastic' threats should influence what we are to do now. For threats to do so, Gardiner cautiously suggests (2006, 51, n. 61) that they should not be merely logical possibilities but that there must be scientific evidence to back them up (2006, 51, n. 61). Shue elaborates further: we must, he says, understand the *mechanism* of the threat and the *conditions* for this mechanism to start *operating*, and these conditions must begin to be *fulfilled* (Shue 2010, 154).[13] All this, I would argue, is a necessary condition for a threat to be taken into account at all in considering what we should do (in general, and in what should be done as a matter of human rights in particular). Call it an *entrance condition*. Shue applies his particular entrance condition only to threats relating to climate change, but, as I will show, some similar conditions can have much wider application.

I propose, then, that this is the first step in integrating threats concerning future people into human rights: to qualify at all as a matter of human rights, protections must concern threats that meet a suitable entrance condition and are not merely logical possibilities. In fact, something like this condition is implicit in common talk and thought about human rights. Take the human right to freedom of assembly. Protection against which threats does this right call for? We know that certain actors might threaten this freedom, and we can be quite specific about the circumstances in which this is especially likely to happen. Thus, we understand the *mechanism* of the threats and the *conditions* for its *operation*. Moreover, the *fulfilment* of those conditions could, in many different societies, come about easily, and not only in social situations very different from the present ones. Something similar is true in relation to the right to food: we understand the *mechanisms* of the threat (governments and other agents can bar access to food; those who do not grow their own food may be dependent on volatile markets, etc.[14]) and, relatedly, we understand the conditions needed for these mechanisms to start *operating* and that these conditions may easily become *fulfilled* in a wide variety of societies. Thus, on reflection, it seems that *all* threats that qualify for protection under human rights plausibly have to meet an entrance condition that is very much like the one suggested for threats concerning the future.[15] This entrance condition is part of what should go into the notion of a standard threat if that notion is to tell us which protections are required as a matter human rights.

II

The articulation of what a standard threat is, is not yet complete. I turn to the *second step*, which will complete my account of how human rights could incorporate threats concerning the future. The issue is that there will be many threats that meet a suitable entrance condition. This raises the question of *just what kinds and levels of protection against them are called for*.[16] I submit that this can only be decided by considering *together* all the threats (to widely present urgent interests) that meet a suitable entrance condition. I assume that protection of widely urgent interests should, taken as a whole, have considerable social priority. It is appropriate for it to take up a considerable amount of a society's resources, but not (of course) all or even nearly all resources.[17] Then specifically what and how much ought, all things considered, to be done against particular threats to particular urgent interests depends on such things as: (a) the degree of urgency of the interest in question; (b) the degree to which the threat jeopardizes this interest; (c) how many people are concerned; (d) the (rough) likelihood of the threat occurring, more about which in a moment; and (e) the avenues and possibilities for, and impediments to, providing protection that will (with a certain likelihood) be effective,[18] where the costs involved should also be considered.

These considerations are not meant to be exhaustive. Nor is it plausible that they can defensibly be neatly combined into one framework approaching a ('mechanical') decision procedure.[19] Rather, it is a combination of general principles (such as that one ought, other things being equal, to prioritize dealing with a greater threat over dealing with a smaller one) and case-by-case judgements that could tell us which levels and kinds of protections against threats are in the end required as a matter of human rights. Some protections may fall away at this stage because, say, they are relatively less important or disproportionately costly or difficult to realize.

Let us turn specifically to threats concerning future people and begin by considering the uncertainties involved. Take the following example: a certain level of CO_2 emissions might trigger global warming of up to 4 degrees Celsius, and this might jeopardize food provision for many people in the future. There are uncertainties in at least two places here: how much warming is occasioned by a certain level of emissions; and what, precisely, are going to be the impacts on food provision for whom? Given that a suitable 'entrance condition' is met, we have respectable accounts about both, and the current emissions levels may get us close to making those accounts real. But even so, there remain uncertainties in the stories. How are we to deal with those?

The fact that an 'entrance condition' is met can, I suggest, be translated into broad (ranges of) probabilities.[20] As we are dealing with uncertainties, the probabilities are evidently not 100 per cent. But since we understand the mechanisms – how given emissions may lead to temperature rises and how these in turn may endanger food provision – it would also be very strange to assign 'very low' chances to the threat to food provision, given a certain emissions level. To avoid thinking of the threat as miniscule, we might have to think of it as having a probability of no less than 10 per cent, or a different small but substantial probability, as is suitable for the case at hand; we should not in any case think of it as having a probability higher than, say, 90 per cent – otherwise we have virtual certainty. Such a broad range may seem useless, but I do not think it is. It gives us something to work with in the account that I have proposed, and is certainly much better than discounting threats concerning the future in an arbitrary manner, as some economists would have it (cf. Stern 2010 for criticism). Furthermore, there are cases in which meeting a certain entrance condition can plausibly be translated into narrower probability ranges – these may be arrived at if we consider what it means, on reflection, for something to be 'not certain but quite likely' or 'not too likely but definitely possible'. We should never forget, of course, where these broad ranges of probabilities come from, and they should not be allowed to float free from their origins. Furthermore, ultimately uncertainties should be taken into account, not in a utilitarian, calculus-like manner, but as one factor to be considered when coming to judgements about cases – one factor among many others, such as the importance of the interests and the threats and the number of people involved.

This brings us back to the question of what action ought, all things considered, to be taken against threats concerning future people, such as the threats relating to climate change. Given what has been said, many such threats will come out as rather weighty, even taking into consideration all the other threats to urgent interests, and even considering the uncertainties involved. This is because such threats often concern very weighty interests of very many people. They are therefore likely, in the end, to call for protections of quite a few kinds at quite high levels. This will probably mean that human rights require that global warming be limited to levels that are generally deemed relatively safe – 2 degrees Celsius maximum, as the scientific consensus has it – unless this is quite excessively at the expense of other very weighty interests which also concern very many people.

This last addition already indicates that I do not think that threats concerning future people should *always* take priority over concerns of the present. This may be so on a conventional utilitarian model (cf. Heath 2013, 31), as there are potentially very many *more* future people than present people (cf. Parfit 1984, 453–4), but not on my model. However, we should proceed very carefully here lest we, the people presently alive, too easily allow ourselves to get away with doing rather little. Three broad kinds of cases can be helpfully distinguished. In each, two (sets of) human rights claims confront each other, and only one can be honoured. In the first case there is a great difference between the two claims. One concerns a few people, and a significant but not overwhelming advance in the protection of important interests (such as their right to work). The confronting claim, by contrast, concerns very many people and makes a great difference to avoiding absolute disaster for them (starvation, etc.). It is overwhelmingly likely that here the second claim will win out, even if it concerns future people and there are important uncertainties involved. The second kind of case is one in which the starvation of very many people in the present confronts the starvation of very many more people in the future. If, tragically, we really have to choose one or the other – for if at all possible we ought to attend to both causes at the expense of less weighty ones (cf. Philips 2014) – I believe that generally the present ought to get priority. Here, various uncertainties really matter, not only about whether the starvation will happen but also about whether alternative ways may be found, at some point, to avert this disaster (by contrast, such alternatives can hardly be found where the starvation is imminent). Third and finally, there are all kinds of difficult intermediate cases in between the two just outlined. Should we, for example, accept the curtailment of important freedoms in the present to avert dangerous climate change and the attendant future evils? Again, we will want to avoid the hard choice if at all possible. If this cannot be done, we may have to curtail the freedoms, in the least intrusive and most reversible way possible.

Ideally, much more should be said. However, given the disasters that climate change could entail, and given that the choices we face are typically closer to the first case, and possibly the third case, than to the second, the above suffices to show that climate change, and the related threats concerning future people, should get considerable priority within human rights.

We may wonder, however, whether there are suitable duty bearers around to protect against such threats concerning future people, now or when modest changes are made to the institutional arrangements we currently have (cf. Risse 2012). Recall that I have been assuming that human rights should consume a considerable part of social wealth but by no means all of it. The implication is that realizing human rights is not excessively costly for a society as a whole;[21] this makes it likely, but does not necessarily imply, that suitable duty bearers can be found. Relevant considerations would be a potential duty bearer's capacity to do the job and also their causal contribution to the problems at hand (as well as, perhaps, certain other special relationships). Also, it should be ruled out that an allocation of duties could, on some good ground, be considered grossly unfair. It seems that, on the basis of such criteria, certain agents (such as states or companies) would have to bear considerable duties,[22] although whether they can be made to actually carry them out is, of course, quite a different matter.

To summarize, in two steps I have developed an account of how threats concerning future people could be incorporated in human rights. First, an 'entrance condition' has been specified for a threat to qualify at all for protection against it under human rights. Second, I have contemplated how to decide which all-things-considered protections against threats are required as a matter of human rights.

3 A first defence of the proposal

Now a first defence of the above proposal will be offered. First, it will be shown that the proposal has important advantages over Stephen Gardiner's and Henry Shue's alternatives. Second, the proposal's sufficientarian shape will be made more explicit and some prominent objections against this shape will be answered.

First line of defence

Stephen Gardiner (2006) and Henry Shue (2010) have offered proposals for how threats concerning the future ought, under certain conditions, to be treated.[23] However, it will be argued that their proposals are too limited in scope and do not address many situations that need addressing. In addition, Gardiner and Shue suggest that if threats meet an appropriate entrance condition, the risks and uncertainties associated with them should be neglected. This, I will argue, is incorrect.

Gardiner's 'core precautionary principle' (inspired by Rawls (1999)) holds that under certain conditions the course of action ought to be chosen where – compared with all alternative courses – the worst possible outcome is best. This is so even if the probability of the worst possible outcome happening is not known, provided that its occurrence is not merely a logical possibility but is backed up by scientific evidence (Gardiner 2006, 51). Sufficient conditions for choosing this course of action are (my paraphrasing): (1) that we have reason to care a lot about achieving the best possible worst outcome; *and* (2) that we care relatively little about what we lose by realizing that outcome; *and* (3) that we do not have, or have reason to disregard, information about probabilities (Gardiner 2006, 47). What should we think of this proposal? To begin with, concerning the second condition, caring *relatively* little could mean we care little about the loss *compared to* how much we care about the gain, or it could mean that we do not care much about the loss anyhow. Especially if Gardiner chooses the second interpretation,[24] which I find more plausible and which seems closer to what Rawls had in mind, the scope of application of his principle is drastically limited. There may not be very many cases where we have reason to care relatively little about what we lose by realizing the best possible worst outcome.[25] In cases where we have reason to care a lot about what we lose, Gardiner's principle is inapplicable. However, we do need guidance in such cases, and the principle's scope of application is therefore infelicitously narrow. Something similar is true in Shue's account. He says that great harms ought not to be imposed (on future people), at least where this can be avoided while also duly attending to other urgent causes. This is so even if those harms are uncertain – provided only that they meet, in my terminology, a suitable entrance condition.[26] But what if we can only avoid imposing great harms by impinging on other urgent causes? Shue's principle doesn't seem to apply here, but we do need to know how to deal with such – possibly frequent – situations.[27] The proposal outlined above does address such situations, and in fact takes them to be the rule, without leading to paralysis in deciding which protections ought, all things considered, to be provided.

A second criticism of both Gardiner and Shue is that they suggest that uncertainties and risks ought sometimes to be disregarded. For Gardiner, one of the conditions for his account to be applicable is that it is appropriate to disregard probabilities (or to be exact to 'sharply discount' them, Gardiner (2006), 47). When, however, is this so?[28] This could be so when no probabilities are known; but if what has been said above (in Section 2) is correct, we already know the (broad ranges of) probabilities once a threat meets a suitable entrance condition. Ought they, then, to be disregarded? Perhaps so, if: (1) we rightly care a lot about maximizing some minimum; and (2) if we care relatively little for what we lose thereby. But then these two conditions seem to do all the work. By contrast, if we do care a lot – absolutely or perhaps in relation to what we gain – about what we lose by realizing the highest minimum, we are back to where we were before: to cases where Gardiner's account as it stands does not apply. Thus, Gardiner's condition concerning the disregarding of probabilities seems either redundant or inapplicable.

It is quite similar for Shue's account. He writes that uncertainties beyond the threshold plausibility ought to be disregarded. There are two kinds of cases. The first, which are clearly Shue's central concern, involve: (1) massive potential losses, with a threshold plausibility of those losses occurring; while (2) the costs of not imposing such losses are not excessive. Given (1) and (2), one ought, we could say, to act even in the face of uncertain losses; the uncertainty is then not disregarded but outweighed, and all the work is done – as it was in Gardiner's account – by conditions (1) and (2). In the second kind of case, condition (2) – non-excessive cost – is not met. Any suggestion that uncertainty should be disregarded here is inappropriate, and Shue's account does, as he would agree, simply not apply to such cases. By contrast, the account developed in Section 2 does have something to say about how to deal with the uncertainties here; they should be factored in as one consideration in the (non-mechanical) decision exercise. In short, compared with important alternative proposals, the above proposal seems to have a number of advantages.

Second line of defence

However, we need to consider the proposal's peculiar shape, which may be called sufficientarian and to which a number of objections could be made. The second line of defence consists in answering those objections.

Sufficientarianism as I understand it (after Shields 2012, 101) states that there are weighty reasons to provide certain goods up to a certain threshold of 'enough', while the reasons for providing more, or different goods, are less weighty, and are also likely to be of a different sort. In this particular case, the threshold is constituted by all the protections of urgent interests which ought in the end to be provided as a matter of human rights with, in the background, the idea that a considerable part of social wealth, but by no means all, ought to be spent on protecting urgent interests.

A prominent objection against sufficientarianism is that it would require bringing as many people as possible up to the threshold (Shields 2012, 103ff.). If so, we should give priority to helping people who are just below the threshold a little so that they can get to the threshold, rather than helping people far below the threshold a lot – as they are unlikely to reach the threshold anyway. This seems perverse, however; it prioritizes helping the better-off a little over helping the worse-off a lot. The response to this can be straightforward: sufficientarian accounts need not imply that as many people as possible should be brought up to the threshold.[29] They merely claim that providing goods up to a threshold is more weighty – and usually backed up by different reasons – than providing goods beyond that threshold.

A second objection concerns the particular kind of sufficientarianism proposed in Section 2. I suggested a two-step procedure. First, threats should meet a suitable entrance condition, and then second, all such threats need to be considered together to decide which protections should, all things considered, be provided as a matter of human rights. Which protections this will be will depend on such things as the urgency of the threat, the number of people affected and the possibilities of providing protection, etc. The sufficiency threshold is constituted by all those protections taken together which are, all things considered, called for, assuming that human rights should consume a considerable part of social wealth but by no means all of it. However, we may object that such a threshold is arrived at in a rather contingent way. How could such a threshold bear the weight it has to – namely that meeting the threshold is much more important than attending to what lies beyond it?

But the threshold *can* bear the weight because, even if it is determined by relatively contingent factors, it gives expression to a fundamental underlying concern, the 'protection of urgent interests'. The threshold articulates what it takes to do justice to that concern in a given situation of scarcity.

Third, it is also because of this underlying fundamental concern that the threshold can succeed in being both high enough to include everything of importance and low enough to exclude what is not sufficiently important. Some authors doubt whether sufficientarianism can hit such a mean. However, if, in my particular kind of sufficientarianism, the threshold formulates the protections of urgent interests that are, in the end, socially called for on a balance of considerations, then meeting this threshold is both considerably important and much more important than engaging with what lies beyond it.

4 Conclusion

This chapter has articulated and defended, in a first outline, a proposal for how human rights could incorporate threats concerning the interests of future people, considering the uncertainties by which such threats are surrounded. A two-step procedure has been proposed for deciding which protections ought, in the end, to be forthcoming as a matter of human rights. My proposal can be regarded as a particular kind of sufficientarianism, and it has been argued that it fares better, in some respects, than certain prominent alternatives, and can also be defended against important objections. Thus, human rights may be very well able to take on board future people.

Acknowledgement

I would like to thank Gerhard Bos, Gertrude Hirsch-Hadorn, Anne Polkamp, Henry Shue and Clive Spash, and conference participants at Graz, Soesterberg and Utrecht for their very useful comments. The text remains solely my own responsibility. The work reported on in this chapter has benefited from participation in the ESF-funded networking programme 'Rights to a Green Future'.

Notes

1 Risks refer to cases where probabilities are known, and uncertainties to cases where they are not. In cases of ignorance, which I will not consider, it is not even known what outcomes may occur.
2 I understand human rights primarily as articulating the main standards for living together on a global scale. See Section 2.
3 Especially in the wake of Parfit (1984) (cf. Gosseries 2008; Hurka 2001); Meyer 2008.
4 Of course, climate change also threatens people who are alive now. This will not be my main concern, but the proposal to be developed can accommodate it.
5 Work drawing on the Gewirthian framework, which deals in depth both with human rights and with risks/uncertainties, may be relevant.
6 Cf. Beitz (2009) but not, for example, Gewirth (1978).
7 It is beyond the scope of this chapter to defend this account, which is different from those of, for example, Gewirth (1978), Griffin (2008), Beitz (2009) and Risse (2012). I do think, however, that it can be acceptable to people from widely varying backgrounds.
8 Shue himself speaks, somewhat less appropriately I think, of a 'moral' right: 'A moral right provides the rational basis for a justified demand that the actual enjoyment of a substance be socially guaranteed against standard threats' (1996, 13; it was Shue who introduced the notion of a standard threat). There are a number of differences

between Shue's account and mine, which cannot be elaborated upon here. The text makes it clear which rights are, in my view, to be regarded as *human rights*.

9 I use this expression in the sense of weighty, important and fundamental, with no idea of an imminent threat being involved.

10 If a requirement of universality in this sense is abandoned – as it is by, for example, Beitz (2009) – human rights may be too much deflated. Three (separate) remarks need to be made about such a requirement. First, to require that interests be very urgent for *each and every* member of the species seems to ask too much. Second, democratic participation – to take just one example – could still qualify as a substance for human rights if having a social institutional structure with such participation were urgently in the interest of broad categories of people everywhere and in all times. Third, importantly, all urgent interests could qualify as substances of human rights, and this explains why human rights could and should consume a considerable part of social wealth. Urgent interests applying only to smaller categories of people (e.g. 'musical education') could qualify if subsumed under more general categories (such as 'developing one's creative abilities').

11 A human right, say the right to freedom of expression, can be articulated at two levels of generality, and the notion of a standard threat features at both. At a general level, we could say that the human right to freedom of expression protects this freedom against certain threats (prevalent and predictable ones, etc.) but not all threats. At a more specific level, we can articulate more concretely against which threats, and how, protections ought to be provided. This can vary across time (as well as perhaps place) without the universal validity of the right, which refers to its general characterization, being jeopardized. The project of Section 2, and its two-step procedure, is to reach clarity in relation to the second, specific level.

12 Here, 'precautionary' is meant in a colloquial sense. Cf. footnote 23 below.

13 See footnote 26 below for a quote.

14 Cf. Sen (1999), Ch. 7.

15 This also implies that, on reflection, almost all threats involve elements of risk and also uncertainty. In this respect, threats concerning the future do not seem so different after all. Perhaps they are thought to be different because people believe the future to be so different that a suitable entrance condition cannot plausibly be met for threats concerning the future. Of course, such threats have their peculiarities. For example, assumptions must be made about the needs, number and whereabouts of future people, and it is relevant that these are assumptions rather than certainties. Nonetheless, a suitable entrance condition often remains met.

16 Here, the notion of a standard threat might also lead us astray as it harbours many potential ambiguities (cf. Beitz and Goodin 2009). It may, for example, refer to ideal or certain non-ideal circumstances; to pro tanto or all-things-considered requirements of protection, etc. The notion's main importance, I believe, is to point out that *only certain degrees and kinds* of protection are required as a matter of rights. If we want to be more precise, we do well simply to argue which protections, more concretely, are required, and when. This is what I aim to do in the text.

17 It is beyond the scope of this chapter to consider exactly how many resources.

18 Note that an account of a protection's effectiveness will also have to meet a suitable entrance condition.

19 A (mechanical) decision procedure (Scheffler 1992, 39ff.) broadly refers to a model which, given certain inputs (how severe is the threat? or how many people are concerned?, etc.), produces the right decision for all cases, with no further judgement or context sensitivity, etc. being required.

20 This is in the spirit of the following remark by Henry Shue: 'The specification of a clear mechanism is the central contributor to our conviction that the probability is significant in spite of our not being able to calculate it' (Shue 2010, 149). However, I

certainly do not claim that Shue would agree with everything I say. Indeed, as will become clear below, I don't think he does.

21 Ought we not to spend more on fighting climate change if this is needed to avert a warming of more than 2 degrees Celsius? Not, I'd say, as a matter of human rights, although I can't argue the point here.

22 Contrary to Beitz (2009), I do not regard states as by definition the main duty bearers of human rights.

23 I take Gardiner and Shue to be concerned mainly with what the main social institutions, national and global, ought most importantly to do. This is basically the same topic as mine. Many would call their accounts *precautionary* in a technical rather than everyday sense, but nothing depends on this nomenclature and I will not rely on it.

24 But also to an extent if he chooses the first one.

25 Also, frequently, what we care about is realizing a possible worst outcome that is *good enough* rather than best (of course the two could coincide).

26 Shue considers cases with three features:

> (1) *massive loss*: the magnitude of the possible losses is massive; (2) *threshold likelihood*: the likelihood of the losses is significant, even if no precise probability can be specified, because (a) the mechanism by which the losses would occur is well understood, and (b) the conditions for the functioning of the mechanism are accumulating; and (3) *non-excessive costs*: the costs of prevention are not excessive, (a) in the light of the magnitude of the possible losses and (b) even considering the other important demands on our resources.
>
> (Shue 2010, 148)

In cases with these features, Shue says that 'one ought to try urgently to make the outcome progressively more unlikely until the marginal costs of further efforts become excessive, irrespective of the outcome's precise prior probability, which may not be known in any case' (Shue 2010, 148).

27 Or if Shue's proposal should be read as applying to such cases, it is very vague about them.

28 Rawls himself discusses this condition in relation to his Original Position, but this case is not clearly and immediately relevant here.

29 Although sometimes this is a good idea, for instance where the threshold would be in a position of 'having enough water to survive'.

References

Beitz C. (2009) *The idea of human rights* Oxford, Oxford University Press.

Beitz C. and Goodin R. eds (2009) *Global basic rights* Oxford, Oxford University Press.

Gardiner S. (2006) 'A core precautionary principle' *Journal of Political Philosophy*, 14 33–60.

Gewirth A. (1978) *Reason and morality* Chicago, University of Chicago Press.

Gosseries A. (2008) 'On future generations' future rights' *Journal of Political Philosophy*, 16 446–74.

Griffin J. (2008) *On human rights* Oxford, Oxford University Press.

Heath J. (2013) 'The structure of intergenerational cooperation' *Philosophy and Public Affairs*, 41 31–66.

Hurka T. (2001) 'Future generations' in Becker L. and Becker C. eds, *Encyclopedia of ethics* London, Routledge, 586–9.

Meyer L. (2008) 'Intergenerational justice' in Zalta E.N. ed., *Stanford encyclopedia of philosophy*, Available at http://plato.stanford.edu/entries/justice-intergenerational/, Accessed 30 October 2015.

Parfit D. (1984) *Reasons and persons* Oxford, Oxford University Press.

Philips J. (2014) 'On setting priorities among human rights' *Human Rights Review*, 15 239–57.

Rawls J. (1999) *A theory of justice*, 2nd edn Cambridge, MA, Harvard University Press.

Risse M. (2012) *Global political philosophy* New York, Palgrave Macmillan.

Scheffler S. (1992) *Human morality* Oxford, Oxford University Press.

Sen A. (1999) *Development as freedom* Oxford, Oxford University Press.

Shields L. (2012) 'The prospects for sufficientarianism' *Utilitas*, 24 101–17.

Shue H. (1996) *Basic rights*, 2nd edn Princeton, NJ, Princeton University Press.

Shue H. (2010) 'Deadly delays, saving opportunities' in Gardiner S., Caney S., Jamieson D. and Shue H. eds, *Climate ethics: essential readings* Oxford, Oxford University Press, 146–62.

Stern N. (2010) 'The economics of climate change' in Gardiner S., Caney S., Jamieson D. and Shue H. eds, *Climate ethics: essential readings* Oxford, Oxford University Press, 39–76.

8 Human rights, climate change, and sustainability

Adina Preda

1 Introduction

In an unprecedented ruling, a Dutch court has recently upheld the case brought by climate change campaigners on behalf of some Dutch citizens and has ruled that the government has a legal obligation to protect its citizens from climate change and must therefore cut greenhouse gas emissions by 25 per cent by 2020. Similar actions are being undertaken by citizens of other countries.[1] This chapter asks whether this legal obligation is backed up by a *moral* obligation that would correspond to anyone's (human) rights, and answers that question in the negative. This is not to say that we have no duties to address climate change or that the Dutch court's ruling was mistaken; I am only suggesting that it should not be understood as a recognition of pre-existing moral rights of either current or future Dutch citizens or indeed citizens of other countries. Notwithstanding this conclusion, such actions are probably the most effective way to address the issues raised by climate change.

Let me start with a few clarifications. Climate change poses three distinct types of question: a question of intergenerational justice, since it affects future generations; a question of environmental justice, because it affects the environment itself; and a question of global justice, because it also has an impact on some people who live in various parts of the world today. The first two issues are or should be central to discussions about environmental *sustainability*, which I take to refer to policies with a very long-term impact. We need sustainable policies inasmuch as we are concerned about future generations or the environment itself. Responses to global justice problems, however, do not, strictly speaking, require environmentally sustainable policies.

Now, in some views, duties of justice are (by definition) correlative to rights. That is to say, for every duty of justice that I have, someone else has a right that I perform that duty. This kind of view, namely that correlative duties and rights exhaust the domain of justice, is controversial. What is, however, largely uncontroversial is that duties correlative to rights are duties of justice, even if there may be more to justice than this. So the question I will address in this chapter is whether the three issues identified above can be framed in terms of rights, in other words, whether future generations, the environment, or distant others have rights against us that pertain to climate change.

Before answering that question, I must also explain how I will use the term human rights here. First, it may be worth stressing that what I envisage here are *moral* rather than legal rights. In other words, the question is not whether a right (that would imply sustainability duties) can be identified or inferred from legal documents but rather whether any such right can be justified through moral argument. Second, I take human rights to be simply 'general' rights, in Hart's sense, namely rights that do not arise out of any contracts, agreements, or special relationships, and that are held by everyone against everyone else (Hart 1984, 84). Thus, human rights are pre-institutional rights and are held by all (human beings) against all others. Here, I depart from the legal understanding of human rights, which sees them as rights against one's own government or state. Third, I assume that rights have correlative duties, that is, to each right corresponds (at least) one duty whose content is the same as that of the right. To be more specific, 'the duty and the right share a content that is satisfied by the performance of the duty' (Sreenivasan 2010, 465). Finally, I should say that the assumptions listed above only refer to the *concept* of human rights. I make no assumption at all about the content or grounding of human rights as this has no bearing on the question discussed here. The question is simply whether our duties to adopt sustainable policies and act in ways that protect the environment can correlate with rights. And in order to answer this question, we need to know what rights *are* or examine the *nature* of rights; in other words, we need an account of what makes a duty a correlative one.

2   Theories of rights and rights of future generations

There are two main theories that account for the concept or the nature of rights. These two theories are the Interest (or Benefit) theory and the Choice (or Will) theory. Out of the two, the Interest theory is usually regarded as the more generous one, in that it can arguably accommodate ascriptions of rights to any creature or entity that has interests, including infants, animals, groups, and future people, supposedly. One aim of this chapter is to explain that both theories face serious difficulties in ascribing rights against us to future people or the environment.

Before advancing the argument, let me clarify that the disagreement between the Choice and the Interest theorist essentially concerns the pairing of duties – legal or moral – with rights and consequently the identity of right-holders. These are not theories about the justification or the grounding of rights but only about their nature. In other words, they do not seek to explain when a right should be *granted* but rather when a right can be *ascribed* to someone given an existing (legal or moral) duty.[2] So both theories start with the assumption that not all duties correlate with rights; duties that correlate with rights must be in some sense *directed* or *owed to* someone. What being directed or owed to someone amounts to is the issue that is disputed between them, but the shared assumption is that for rights to exist there must be directed duties. It is this assumption that gives rise to problems in relation to future generations' rights.

According to the Interest theory, rights should be seen as protections of interests. Thus, a necessary – but not sufficient – condition for being a potential right-holder is having an interest. This is not a sufficient condition because there may be actions that benefit a large number of people but we would not want to say that everyone who stands to benefit in some way from the performance of these actions has a right to their performance, since this would lead to a counter-intuitive proliferation of rights and right-holders. So the Interest theorist must also find a sufficient condition for a right that would allow us to distinguish correlative from non-correlative duties. One way of distinguishing between duties that correlate with rights and duties that do not is by establishing when a breach of duty *harms* someone. If this is the test for identifying rights, the Interest theory may turn out to be less hospitable to some potential right-holders in spite of the fact that it is usually thought to be able to accommodate rights for a variety of creatures that are not moral agents or do not even exist.

The Choice theory holds that a duty correlates with someone's right if and only if that person has control over the performance of that duty. A Choice theory right-holder is, in Hart's words, a 'small scale sovereign' over a duty; what this means, more precisely, is that the right-holder is the entity that is empowered to make decisions regarding that duty. In other words, all Choice theorists claim rights come equipped with Hohfeldian powers, more specifically with powers to waive or enforce the correlative duty.[3] To be a right-holder one must, therefore, be able to exercise such powers. Given this assumption, the Choice theory has to exclude all un-empowerable creatures from the domain of rights so it is quite economical with them.

Let me now take in turn the three issues of justice I identified at the start and see whether they can be framed in terms of (human) rights. To start with the question of intergenerational justice, I am assuming that the putative rights corresponding to our sustainability duties would be ascribed to (individual members of) future generations. Here, I understand future generations as people who will exist in the future and are as yet unborn. Can these people have rights against us? It seems clear that, if we conceive of rights along the lines of the Choice theory, the answer is negative. People who do not exist cannot have powers to waive or enforce *our* duties. Inasmuch as they cannot release us from or enforce our obligations, they cannot have rights against us so our duties to protect the environment are not correlative to their Choice theory rights. The Interest theory, however, may leave room for future generations' rights, since future generations may be said to have interests. In what follows, I will argue that this is not sufficient to show that future generations can have rights *against us*. So, let us consider in more detail the question of Interest theory rights of future generations. Future generations may have interests, but can these interests initiate rights against us, in particular rights that we refrain from certain actions that harm the environment? The answer to this question has to grapple with the famous challenge of the non-identity problem.

The challenge starts from the assumption that our actions today affect the identity of those who will exist in the future. Thus, the actions that harm the environment and thus potentially harm future generations also determine who will exist in the future. So an action that is alleged to be harmful to a person is also a necessary condition for the existence of that person. But, in standard definitions of harm, establishing that there is a harm requires a comparison between the state in which X finds him/herself as a result of the allegedly harmful action and the state he/she would have been in had the action not taken place.[4] In this case, however, if the action had not taken place, this person wouldn't have existed so the comparison cannot be made (Gosseries 2012, 310). It cannot therefore be said that actions which cause the existence of some people also harm those people. What this is taken to show is that, when the conditions of the non-identity problem prevail, we cannot appeal to non-consequentialist considerations to do with rights and fairness (Woodward 1986, 804).

Now, it is helpful to make a distinction here between the non-identity *problem* and the non-identity *effect*.[5] The non-identity problem starts, as it were, from noting the non-identity effect, namely the fact that were we to adopt more sustainable policies, 'within a couple of generations, the entire population of the world would have consisted of different people' (Broome 2012, 62). The problem occurs if we assume that we wronged or harmed the person we brought into existence even though the person would not have existed had we changed our allegedly harmful course of action. In other words, the problem is only a problem because we are assuming that there is a harm or a wrong; solving this apparent paradox is what the *problem* refers to. What I was casting doubt on above was precisely the assumption that we are harming future people given the non-identity *effect*. So the non-identity *effect* should give us reason to reject the idea that future generations can have Interest theory rights correlative to our obligation to adopt environmentally sustainable policies.

James Woodward, however, puts forward an argument that aims to refute this implication. He argues that risky policies/choices do violate rights or duties owed to future people. In order to do that, he argues against what he identifies as a crucial assumption in the challenge posed by the non-identity problem. The assumption is this:

> An action A performed by X cannot wrong person P and cannot be objectionable because of the bad effects it has on P if P is not worse off as a result of A than he would be under any alternative action which could be performed by X. Nor in these circumstances can A violate an obligation owed to P, or a right possessed by P.
>
> (Woodward 1986, 809)

Woodward supports his argument with cases that are meant to illustrate some of the ideas implicit in many moral theories. The main idea that he refers to is that people have specific interests that are not reducible to some general interest. 'That an action will cause an increase in someone's overall level of well-being is not always an adequate response to the claim that such a specific interest has been violated' (Woodward 1986, 809). One example invoked to support this argument is that of a former prisoner of a Nazi concentration camp. The experience of being in the concentration camp led to this person developing certain traits of character that ultimately contributed to his having a rich and fulfilled life. But this, of course, would not lead us to deny that his rights had been violated. Another example is that of Smith, who is the victim of racial discrimination by an airline company that refuses to sell him a ticket. As it happens, the aircraft that he was meant to board crashes and his life is saved as a result of not being allowed to board it. In these examples, the conditions of the non-identity problem are met; that is, the action that causes a harm is also the cause of one's (more fulfilling) existence and yet the action wrongs the person or violates a right of theirs.

However, these examples miss the point, in my view, or rather fail to demonstrate that future generations could have rights *against us*. It is true that an interest is only one aspect of someone's well-being and that we might fail to respect or promote someone's interest even if we (accidentally) increase their well-being. But the reason why we can say that the concentration camp or the airline policy has violated a right is because they have violated a *directed* duty, a duty owed to a *specific* person. An action was performed that harmed that person in a specified respect although it may have increased his/her well-being overall. But whether such a duty exists is precisely what we have to establish in the case of future generations; the non-identity *effect* presents a challenge to the claim that our actions violate a duty owed *to someone*. It might be said that our actions damage specific interests and perhaps even that we have a duty to promote these interests but this does not show that the duty is *directed* or owed to the person whose interests are damaged since that person would not have existed had we complied with the alleged duty. The duty, if any, is owed to no one, at least with regard to the Interest theory of rights. Woodward presupposes the conclusion of his own argument when he claims that it is possible to wrong a person by violating a specific obligation owed to that person even though one's actions advantageously affect that person's other interests (Woodward 1986, 812).

Woodward appears to concede this point, but he maintains that it is 'consistent with this claim to hold that the reason why a certain course of action is wrong is that it would involve the creation of rights and obligations that would probably be violated' (Woodward 1986, 812). I have no difficulty accepting that it may be wrong to engage in this kind of action. What I am arguing is that this does not show that the rights created are rights *against us*. It may indeed be possible to say both that our actions are wrong and that certain rights are created as a result (since people are created as a result), but these two need not be connected. Our actions may even violate certain obligations but these are not obligations owed to future people. It is worth pointing out here that this case is different from one in which the existence of the person harmed is not affected by our actions, such as Parfit's landmine example. If I knowingly plant a landmine, I do violate the rights of the person who will walk on it in 100 years' time. I owe it to that specific person – or even *any* person who will exist in the future – not to harm them even if I do not know the identity of the person harmed. If I refrain from planting the landmine, there will still be a person, who is thus not harmed. But if I refrain from actions that harm the environment, the person that would have been harmed will no longer exist. Complying with the duty extinguishes the right, as it were, because it extinguishes the potential right-holder. So, although Woodward's solution to the non-identity problem may be convincing, the conclusion that we violate future generations' rights does not follow. This is because it is the non-identity *effect* that rules out the ascription of such rights.

Axel Gosseries also seeks to argue that future generations can have rights against us in spite of what he calls the 'non-existence challenge', which points out that we cannot owe anything to non-existent entities (Gosseries 2008). This may appear to be addressing the relevant question but, for Gosseries, the challenge of non-existence is that future generations do not exist *now*. The non-identity effect refers to the fact that different people will exist *in the future* if we change our behaviour. His solution relies on challenging the correlativity thesis, as he understands it. Thus, he first tries to establish that there can be duties without correlative rights. The second part of his argument claims to show that future people have rights in the future. The first part of the argument can be easily granted; it is hard to deny that there are obligations without corresponding rights, including obligations to refrain from actions that harm the environment and therefore future generations. Some might refer to these as imperfect obligations and might see them as obligations of beneficence or charity rather than justice. But this is irrelevant here since the question under consideration is whether they correlate with future generations' rights.

But Gosseries wants to argue that we have duties that correlate with future people's *future rights* because he notes that there seems to be something added by the language of rights. To that end, he claims that the Interest theorist need not be committed to the view that for correlative obligations to exist today the corresponding rights should also exist today. So what Gosseries essentially argues is that our obligations today could correlate with non-existent rights. But this is simply a misinterpretation of the notion of correlativity. It is not the case that any duty the performance of which may contribute to a situation where the object of a right can be accessed is a correlative duty, i.e. a duty owed to the right-holder. The correlation relationship is just like that of two people holding a rope, unless there is someone at the other end of the rope, there is no correlation. In the case of remote future generations, there is always only one party holding the rope, either a current duty-bearer or a future rights-holder but not both. While it is true that members of future generations will have rights when they are alive, it is not true that their rights are held against us. This is because of the non-identity effect, as explained above, rather than the non-existence challenge.

To sum up, I am not disputing here that when future people will exist they will have rights. I am also not disputing that we have certain obligations that pertain to the well-being and interests of future people. What I am disputing is that future people have rights *against us* and that we are currently violating duties owed to them. So the issue of justice *between* generations (when this means remote generations) cannot be framed in terms of rights. This need not mean that it is not a question of justice or, of course, that there are no reasons (of justice) to have policies that reduce carbon emissions and mitigate the effects of climate change. It only means that we do not owe it to future generations to consider these things.

3 Climate change as a global justice issue

What about the question of environmental justice? This question isolates the harm done to the environment itself from its effects on future or current people.[6] In other words, it asks whether damaging the environment itself is unjust if (counterfactually) this does not harm sentient beings. It seems clear to me that this issue cannot be framed in terms of rights. That is, when it comes to the damage done to the environment itself, or to the planet, the idea that the environment or the planet might have rights is a non-starter. Furthermore, it is hard to see why harming the planet itself raises any questions of *justice* at all, that is, apart from the harm that would be done to current or future generations (including animals) as a result of environmental degradation. Nevertheless, it seems to me that many arguments ultimately presuppose that an injustice would be committed if the planet ceased to exist but I cannot imagine what the argument for this conclusion would be so I will not pursue it further.

This leaves the problem of global justice. Climate change has (harmful) consequences *today* for people living in different parts of the world. Can we say that these people whose lives are (negatively) affected by it have rights that correlate with our duties to adopt and promote sustainable policies? This kind of view has its own problems. One important question is what might be the content of these rights (that is, rights related to climate change) and therefore the content of their correlative duties? The answer would presumably be that distant people have a right to a clean environment. The difficulty with this idea is that it is unclear what exactly would be the content of the duties correlative to it; that is, it would be difficult to spell out what actions are required by this kind of right.

Rights (and their correlative duties) can be positive or negative. That is, they can be duties to perform a certain action or abstain from it. This is not about how the right is formulated, in negative or positive terms, but rather about whether the duty correlative to it requires an action or an omission. If the right to a clean environment were a negative right, it would correlate with negative duties not to engage in actions that are environmentally harmful while the positive right could be interpreted as a right to be *provided with* a clean environment. Both these interpretations run into serious difficulties when it comes to specifying correlative duties of current inhabitants of the planet. Let me start with the negative right, which is supposedly easier to account for.

I take it that the duties correlative to a negative right to a clean environment would be duties to refrain from emitting greenhouse gases. But how exactly are we to understand these duties? It cannot be the case that we have a duty to refrain from *all* activities that are harmful to the environment since that includes most of our activities. The thought may then be that we must collectively refrain from exceeding a certain level of emissions, which might in turn mean that each of us would only be entitled to a share of emissions; exceeding this share would constitute a rights violation. This way of framing the climate change issue might also lend support to the proposal that each person has an equal share of emissions rights. As Simon Caney points out (Caney 2012), this proposal is not supported by any theory of justice; an application of an egalitarian principle to emissions rights is incoherent. But deriving such shares from human rights to a clean environment may escape this objection.

But this suggestion is not as straightforward as it sounds. This is mainly because the harmful effects of climate change that some people suffer *today* are the result of the actions of past generations. By the same token, our actions today, taken collectively, will only affect future generations. So it is hard to see how a duty to refrain from harmful emissions can correlate with the rights of people living around the globe today; complying with this duty will not benefit them. Thus, if the thought is that people have a right not to be harmed by the effects of climate change, this would be best understood as a right to positive action on the part of others who would thus have a duty to *mitigate* the effects of climate change caused by previous generations. There are familiar normative difficulties with this idea but I will leave them aside for now and only outline some other potential objections to the right to a clean environment as a positive right.

A serious objection to such a right would be that it cannot correlate with general duties, i.e. duties held by everyone else, so it cannot be a genuine human right. This objection echoes the criticism raised by Onora O'Neill against all positive human rights. O'Neill objects to general positive rights because they cannot be claimed (against everyone) and therefore are not genuine rights in her view. The reason why positive rights are not claimable is that the duties corresponding to them can only be imperfect duties, and these are not claimable. This argument assumes that perfect duties cannot be positive and general; 'universal perfect obligations can impose no positive tasks' (O'Neill 1996, 147). But since rights must correlate with perfect obligations, positive rights cannot be general ones. The response is often, as O'Neill remarks, that corresponding obligations could be assigned to specific agents; thus, a positive right would correlate with a 'distributed obligation' that falls on specified agents or institutions, such as states.[7] But O'Neill correctly points out that this would mean that positive rights are special rather than universal human rights. For these reasons, she concludes that the only genuine human rights are negative. This point, as she presents it, is meant to be a conceptual rather than a normative one.

But, as I have argued elsewhere, O'Neill's argument should not be taken as a conceptual one (Preda 2012). Rather, what appears to be a conceptual point is in fact a normative requirement that duties correlative to rights be clearly delineated and specified in order to avoid a charge of over-demandingness. It would be hard to justify enforcing very demanding or unclear duties, but correlative duties are, by definition, enforceable. So the thought that positive duties cannot be general is not a strong conceptual point, I maintain, and thus it does not follow that positive general rights cannot exist. It is, however, the case that in order to justify a particular positive right we must be able to identify the content and the bearer(s) of its correlative duties.

Genuine rights must indeed correlate with perfect duties. In order to identify duty-bearers and legitimately enforce their duties, the content of these duties has to be clearly specified. Why would positive rights not correlate with such duties? The assumption here is that a positive right is a right to a good, and that its correlative duty must be to provide that good. A further implicit assumption is that not every person can have a duty to provide the whole good or service to each and every other person, especially when we are talking about public goods, such as a clean environment.

But there is no reason why this good cannot be provided by all others *collectively*. To be more specific, the correlative duty could be one that is *joint and shared* so that each person would have a duty to provide a portion of the good. Elizabeth Ashford has argued that the duties correlative to socio-economic human rights can be borne by a collectivity. As I understand it, her argument is, in a nutshell, that socio-economic rights are claimable in the sense that it is possible to identify the parties responsible for their violation or non-fulfilment even though in most cases the responsible party is a group of people rather than a single individual (Ashford 2007, 216). The further thought here is that if we can attribute responsibility for a right violation, the right is claimable. Ashford's argument seems to have the following structure:

1   Many serious harms in the contemporary world are the result of complex causal claims involving many agents.
2   Such harms constitute human rights violations.

Therefore, responsibility for some human rights violations can be attributed to a group of agents acting jointly.

Ashford's argument that harm can be caused by agents acting jointly sounds particularly plausible in the case of putative environmental rights. Climate change and environmental damage *are* the result of collective action so, inasmuch as anyone had a right that the environment *not* be damaged, it would have to be claimed against a collectivity. However, we have established that such a negative right cannot be held against contemporaries and that any human rights relating to the environment are likely to be positive rights.

Now, Ashford claims that her argument establishes that there can be positive human rights because it shows that their correlative duties can be held by a collectivity, as is the case with some negative rights in her interpretation. However, although her conclusion offers a promising avenue, her argument in fact fails to establish this. In her examples, the agents *act together* and cause harm, which violates a plausible negative right. She does not establish that the duties correlative to this right are borne by a collectivity; even if she does, the duties would be duties to refrain from acting, which are perhaps less problematic. But showing that there are general positive rights would require establishing that collectives could have correlative duties *to act*. If collectives were the bearers of such duties, they would be violating the duty by *not acting*. Arguing that collectives, especially unorganised ones, have a duty to act, which they violate by an omission, is a difficult, though admittedly not impossible task. In many views, duties can only be imposed on agents, and unorganised collectives, such as the whole of humankind in this case, are unlikely to be considered agents. I would argue that this requirement can be relaxed to a great extent when it comes to perfect duties, but I cannot pursue this line of thought here. So it is possible to argue for positive rights relating to the environment that everyone would hold against everyone else taken collectively.

However, even if such human rights could be justified, it is not clear that this has any implications in terms of sustainable environmental policies since mitigating the effects of climate change to date does not require, I take it, sustainable policies. This is ultimately an issue of global distributive justice rather than a question of climate justice, and any rights that might be at work here are not rights to do with the environment but rather rights to resources that would help overcome the negative effects of climate change. The ethical issues raised by climate change per se cannot be fruitfully framed in terms of rights.

I should, however, stress once again that this should not be taken to suggest that we do not have duties to adopt sustainable policies or that these are not duties of justice. Rights may or may not exhaust the domain of justice; the argument made here does not presuppose any answer to that question. Furthermore, even if it turns out that justice does not require environmentally sustainable policies and actions, it would not follow that we do not have such moral duties. It is quite clear, to my mind, that justice does not exhaust the domain of morality. Contrary to what is sometimes assumed, it may actually be more beneficial to admit that the language of rights is inappropriate here and insist on the, perhaps weaker but more convincing, claim that contributing to climate change is 'merely' wrong.

4 Conclusion

It is increasingly accepted that the issue of climate change must be addressed and that environmentally sustainable policies must be adopted and implemented. This chapter asked whether this kind of aim can be expressed in the language of (human) rights. Environmentally sustainable policies would benefit future generations as well as the planet itself rather than current generations, but I have argued that these entities cannot have rights against us that we are bound to implement such policies. When it comes to future generations, the non-identity effect gives us reason to doubt that their rights could correlate with our duties, and not many would argue that the planet can have any rights. Current generations could have rights against harms caused by climate change but, inasmuch as they are rights against contemporaries, they are rights to certain forms of assistance that only a theory of justice can account for. I conclude that the issue of climate justice, or rather the three questions of justice that climate change raises, cannot be helpfully framed in terms of rights, but this should not lead us to conclude that we have no duties to prevent or mitigate the harmful effects of climate change

Notes

1 For very helpful comments on previous drafts of this chapter I would like to thank Rob Lawlor, Tim Meijers, and the editors of this volume, especially Gerhard Bos.
2 For a detailed explanation of the difference between a conceptual and a justificatory account, see my 'Rights: concept and justification' (Preda 2015).
3 For a full description of these powers, see H. Steiner (1998, 240).
4 Using what I take to be the standard definition – I am harmed if I am made worse off than I would have been. It is no secret that the concept of harm is difficult to define clearly and that this definition may be disputed; I will make no attempt to settle the issue here and will just assume this simple meaning. For further discussion of the notion of harm, especially in relation to the non-identity problem, see Meyer (2014).
5 I am borrowing this distinction from Rob Lawlor, who in turn borrows it from John Broome (Lawlor, forthcoming).
6 There is, of course, also a question of harm done to animals, which could potentially be framed in terms of rights. Inasmuch as animals do have rights, I assume that this question can be treated in the same way as the issue of rights of current human inhabitants of the planet, which I address further down.
7 As I said before, I take *human* rights to be rights against everyone else rather than against one's state, but even if they are seen as rights against one's state, the objection would not be answered since it is impossible for one state to provide its citizens with a clean environment unless other states do the same.

References

Ashford E. (2007) 'The duties imposed on us by the human right to basic necessities' in Pogge Thomas ed., *Freedom from poverty as a human right* Oxford, Oxford University Press, 183–218.

Broome J. (2012) *Climate matters: ethics in a warming world* New York, W.W. Norton & Company.

Caney S. (2012) 'Just emissions' *Philosophy & Public Affairs*, 40 255–300.

Gosseries A. (2008) 'On future generations' future rights' *Journal of Political Philosophy*, 16 446–74.

Gosseries A. (2012) 'Generations' in McKinnon C. ed., *Issues in political theory* Oxford, Oxford University Press, 301–23.

Hart H.L.A. (1984) 'Are there any natural rights?' in Waldron J. ed., *Theories of rights* Oxford, Oxford University Press, 70–90.

Lawlor R. (2015) 'Questioning the significance of the non-identity problem in applied ethics' *J Med Ethics*, 41 893–6. doi: 10.1136/medethics-2014-102391.

Meyer L. (2014) 'Intergenerational Justice' in Zalta E.N. ed., *The Stanford encyclopaedia of philosophy*, winter 2014 edn, Available at http://plato.stanford.edu/archives/win2014/entries/justice-intergenerational/, accessed 7 July 2015.

O'Neill O. (1996) *Towards justice and virtue* Cambridge, Cambridge University Press.

Preda A. (2012) 'A human right to health?' in Tamara Lenard P. and Straehle C. eds, *Health inequalities and global justice* Edinburgh, Edinburgh University Press, 17–33.

Preda A. (2015) 'Rights: concept and justification' *Ratio Juris*, 28 408–15.

Sreenivasan G. (2010) 'Duties and their direction' *Ethics*, 120 465–94.

Steiner H. (1998) 'Working rights' in Kramer M., Simmonds N.E., and Steiner H., A *debate over rights* Oxford, Oxford University Press, 233–303.

Woodward J. (1986) 'The non-identity problem' *Ethics*, 96 804–31.

9 A chain of status

Long-term responsibility in the context of human rights

Gerhard Bos

1 Introduction

Should long-term environmental responsibilities be accounted for as duties towards future people? This question requires a distinction to be made between anthropocentric and other accounts of environmental responsibility. For example, our long-term responsibilities may be conceived as duties to, say, ecological systems, to life or to sentient beings (cf. DesJardins 2006). Alternatively, one could assume a more anthropocentric approach, in which environmental duties are conditional on human beings, say because they have a God-given stewardship of the environment (cf. Passmore 1974, 1–42). With my use of the term, an account would be 'anthropocentric' if it reduces our environmental obligations towards duties to human beings, either to them as natural human beings or because of their distinctive characteristics. Some of these accounts might be problematically biased against others that assume a moral significance of life or ecosystems, e.g. because they are 'speciesist' (Singer 2009). Yet still others would be more neutral insofar as they justify an anthropocentric approach via a narrative that spells out rationally why obligations are owed to human agents (cf. Beyleveld 1991; Gewirth 1978). In this chapter I will focus on a specific anthropocentric approach according to which our duties correspond with the rights of human persons – whatever the rationale for the approach. One could argue that such duties include environmental obligations, to the extent that the rights of human beings cover environmental conditions. According to this approach, long-term environmental responsibilities could be modelled as duties of justice to future human persons (cf. Caney 2010; Bell 2011; Gosseries 2008a; Hiskes 2009; Meyer 2010; Partridge 1981, 1990; Sikora and Barry 1978; Shue 2014).

In view of the distinction between this rights-based anthropocentric account and other accounts, the question I wish to raise is as follows: assuming a human rights approach to environmental responsibility, should we reduce *our* long-term environmental responsibilities in terms of them being duties we have that correspond with future people's human rights? I will argue that we shouldn't. We have duties to *present* people regarding the *securability* of human rights in the future. Before outlining my argument in this chapter shortly, let me first point out why this question needs asking. As a general observation, we have difficulty accounting for, in terms of widely shared normative assumptions, enforceable long-term environmental responsibilities that are overriding. A rights-based approach seems to be a prerequisite for enforceability and overridingness, but it is hard to convincingly explain why the environment and especially its future should be protected as a matter of rights. Although animals supposedly have some rights, and ecosystems can enjoy legal protection, the logic of rights is primed towards prioritizing human interests and liberties. These interests and liberties have environmental components alongside other components that may hide, compromise or even trump the environmental ones. For example, our interests and liberties have moral, political, social, economic and personal dimensions as well. In view of these, we may legitimately wonder how these aspects should be ranked in relation to their environmental dimension, especially when it comes to addressing human threats to the environment, let alone long-term environmental threats.

The remainder of this chapter is in four parts. In the first, I will clarify the problem we have in accounting for long-term responsibilities in generational terms, and will explain why we should approach the problem first and foremost as a question of individual rights, and duties regarding these rights. In the second part, I will draw attention to several versions of both the direct and the chain arguments that advocate rights-based long-term responsibilities and their merits and shortcomings. In the third part, I will identify the status of the human rights-bearer as a relevant link between members of different generations which results in a chain of status. I will argue that in relation to human rights we uncontroversially assume a status that is overriding and enforceable and that respecting this status between contemporaries means respecting the securability of human rights in the future. In the fourth and final part, I will position the chain of status idea and mention its benefits and costs.

2   The assumption of partially overlapping lives

One absolutely vital observation in the context of long-term environmental responsibility is that our future contemporaries (explained below) will outlive us and will have future contemporaries outlive them, *and so on* (cf. Gosseries 2008b). We can distinguish at least three periods in time here:

(t1) Members of generation A exist; members of generation B do not exist; members of generation C do not exist.
(t2) Members of generation A exist; members of generation B exist; members of generation C do not exist.
(t3) Members of generation A do not exist; members of generation B exist; members of generation C exist.

In time, there is a chain between individual members of different generations based on a partial overlap of members of different generations. At t1, members of B are 'future contemporaries' of members of A, while at t2, members of C will be 'future contemporaries' of members of B. I will refer to this as the assumption of partial overlap. Members of successive generations are ecologically vulnerable to members of preceding ones, with no means to protect themselves. The worry about long-term responsibility concerns the responsibility in t1 regarding t3 and further down the line.

To fully capture the relevance of partial overlap, let me relate it to Gardiner's thesis that climate change is a perfect moral storm in which intergenerational challenges enforce and are enforced by global and theoretical challenges (Gardiner 2006, 2013). Climate change has a *global* dimension because it is caused globally as an accumulated effect of actions performed in different regions of the world. It is difficult to identify agents responsible for these effects, as it is difficult to demand self-restriction or investment for the sake of distant people when – no matter how urgent it is for them – this is not a matter of self-interest. Poorer parts of the world that have not been and are not contributing to the causes of climate change as much as the richer ones will be exposed to the effects of climate change in a way in which the richer ones will not be. We have no institutional arrangement in place to cope with these problems. The *intergenerational* challenge is equally marked by dispersion of cause and effect, indeterminate agency and institutional defect, but is now also marked in a temporal sense. The effects of climate change will be felt by future generations, not by the past and present generations whose actions caused it accumulatively. On top of that, every generation benefits from imposing costs on successive ones, especially when preceding generations did the same. Hence, generations are unlikely to invest or restrict themselves in the interests of successive generations. We have no institutional arrangement to cope with this either.

These global and intergenerational challenges reinforce each other, and this generates a specific problem of long-term responsibility. No generation will be prepared to restrict or invest itself to prevent huge costs for poor nations and future generations – especially future generations of poor nations. In view of this, there is little hope that institutions will coordinate a solution to this. This problem is deepened by the third *theoretical* challenge that Gardiner points out: we lack the theoretical tools to explain and address problems of long-term responsibility, responsibility for nature and intergenerational equality and responsibility to contingent persons. In view of this, how are we going to analyse our failure to accept long-term responsibility as a problem, let alone argue for enforceable, overriding long-term responsibility?

In my view, a crucial step in addressing these global and intergenerational problems, both independently and in relation to each other, is resisting the tendency to frame our duties as a matter of justice between a group we belong to and a group we don't. These groups could be nations or generations. To be clear, justice between nations is important, as is justice between generations. In my opinion, we should reconceive these forms of justice primarily in view of the obligations that we have individually and collectively to each other.

Gardiner is right about the global and intergenerational challenge where I take him to be identifying patterns of thinking and acting that generate a problem for which we bear responsibility. Opposing this view, Thomas Pogge convincingly argues that we would be implicated as individuals causing global poverty, at least when failing in our responsibility to urge national agents to only support international structures that do not cause poverty (Pogge 2005, 2007). In other words, in the global context, we should understand our individual and collective responsibilities to members of different nations as corresponding with their individual rights, and because of that we have to install national agents to support international agreements that respect these rights.

A similar approach is necessary for understanding and solving the question of long-term responsibility. In comparison with Pogge's argument, I would emphasize that everyone should prevent themselves from being implicated in causing the effects that climate change will have on the rights of future people at least by taking the responsibility to urge national agents to support international agreements consistent with future people's rights. This first step is crucial, because it allows us to challenge existing theoretical divisions, such as generational thinking, on the grounds that this, for example, is contributing to the problem rather than providing an adequate normative ontology that helps us address it. For example, in relation to the intergenerational challenge identified by Gardiner, it should be noted that in reality no population consists of neatly separated generations (Gardiner 2003). Generations are, in my view, best used as categories that apply to family members *rather than societies or the world population*. Moreover, the assumption of partial overlap makes discussing long-term responsibility on the premise that distinct generations exist somewhat outlandish. Gardiner is aware of the problem and explicitly recognizes it. He argues, however, that there is a crucial intergenerational problem if we define generations as groups of people between which there exists temporal asymmetry and, more importantly, also causal asymmetry and asymmetric independence of interests. I agree with Gardiner that under his definition a generation is likely to impose costs on a later one, especially if this is a matter of self-interest. At the same time, I would insist that neutralizing the intergenerational challenge in the context of climate is best done by showing that the intergenerational challenge is intractable *exactly* to the extent that we unjustifiably think and act in generational terms. Instead of thinking and acting this way from the outset we should, individually and collectively, ask ourselves what our responsibilities are in relation to the individual rights of future human persons.

Against this background, it will turn out to be better and more conducive to solving the intergenerational challenge if we reflect on the idea of human rights using the assumption that every couple of seconds a new human person will be born that we may stand in direct or indirect, simple or complex normative relation to. As a part of this, we should note that our future contemporaries will have future contemporaries themselves, who will be non-contemporaries for us, *and so on*. Thinking and acting in generational terms may be justified in some contexts for some purposes, but is inadequate and – if used exclusively – downright problematic when it comes to appreciating the normative ontology of long-term responsibility.

3 Direct approach vs chain approach

In my view, the treatment of the issue of rights-based long-term responsibility suggests a dilemma. On the one hand, one could argue that we have long-term responsibilities as a direct result of a normatively relevant feature of a future human person, e.g. their interests or will, and thereby normative equality between members of different generations is accepted. It has been argued that these interests should not be harmed, for example, in the sense of being secured at least at some threshold level (cf. Meyer 2003). However, if we argue for environmental duties to the rights of future people, we face challenges in explaining why we have long-term environmental responsibilities to future people in the first place. Why should we recognize them as having rights? On top of that, in what meaningful way could they be said to have rights against us, given their non-existence and the fact that they cannot be identified? Why would we accept that unsustainable action could harm or violate their rights, given the contingency of their identity on our actions (Gosseries 2008a, 2008b; Gosseries and Meyer 2009; Page 2007; Partridge 1981, 1990; cf. Roberts 2013)? On top of this, we face challenges when it comes to enforcing long-term environmental duties to future people, challenges relating to the institutional, practical ways of doing so. How are future rights to be incorporated or implemented in current institutions? How are they to be enforced at all, let alone result in sustainable action? By listing these questions, I do not wish to suggest that they cannot be solved. On the contrary, I think there are good solutions to all of them. However, I wish to point out that these solutions imply controversies in theory and practice which – if they can be avoided – *are* to be avoided if only for pragmatic reasons in view of the urgent need for climate policy.

On the other hand, it is possible to take a 'chain style' approach to rights-based long-term responsibility. Chain style arguments identify a normative, relevant connection between members of different overlapping generations and develop it so that contemporaries owe it to each other to take into account members of near and distant future generations. The chain style approach could avoid the above-mentioned controversies implicated by the direct approach. However, as will become clear throughout the chapter, chains are optional in a morally relevant sense, so they may not imply overriding, enforceable long-term responsibilities.

So we seem to be facing a dilemma: confronting the theoretical and practical controversies of the direct approach to the rights of future people; or settling for long-term responsibilities that are not enforceable or not overriding. Luckily, this dilemma can be avoided, or so I will argue. We could combine the strengths of both approaches, i.e. the assumption of the universal rights of the direct approach *and* the idea of normative relevant relations between members of partially overlapping generations, for the sake of identifying a non-optional chain of status that entails enforceable, overriding long-term responsibilities.

What possibilities are there for developing duties *between* contemporaries *regarding* rights of future persons? Rights to which this approach could be applied would need to be those protecting interests that – perhaps among other things – would have the same significance for future human persons. Let us introduce a first exemplar of this approach via a brief reflection on Rawls's 'just savings' principle (Wall 2003). Just savings are specified as the means for a just society that one generation should pass on to the next. For Rawls, principles of justice are to be agreed on in 'the original position', i.e. by self-interested rational agents abstracting from their knowledge about their specific position in society. When it comes to agreeing on intergenerational responsibilities, the challenge is in explaining why in *the original position* participants would *rationally* agree on self-restraint or investment for the sake of members of future generations. If there is, as Gardiner emphasizes, a causal asymmetry and an asymmetry of interest between members of different generations, considering self-interest introduces the possibility of taking benefits *even if this entails huge costs for members of future generations*. A cross-temporal gathering of different generations in the original position contradicts features of reality. Only members of the same generation can meet, discuss and agree in an original position. So why not agree to demands to exploit generations preceding and following one's own? However, one could imagine oneself taking part in every gathering of each distinct generation in the original position. Not knowing which generation one belongs to would mean that it would be rational to insist in every gathering that just savings are made for successive generations.

That said, as a criticism of this approach, it is far from trivial that each of us could imagine ourselves hopping between meetings of different generations, especially since considering the possibility that we are members of past generations or future ones may not be at all consistent with the bare constitutive elements of rational self-reflection. Even if this were coherent, wouldn't abstracting from such knowledge be over-demanding? Moreover, there are also questions to be asked relating to the temporal dispersion of cause and effect. Why should a generation agree to make up for the accumulative effects of previous generations on its successors?

At this point, I would like to turn to the question of what *other* reasons there are for contemporaries to consider future people. Rawls has suggested the following type of argument. Each member of a generation has a direct concern for his/her children, a concern that considers – among other things – their children's children, *and so on*. This constitutes a chain of concern between individuals living in different successive generations. Considering all of these chains between individual members of different generations, we find that every future person is (indirectly) cared for by members of our generation. In view of this, because individual members of our generation depend on each other for such an interest to be realizable, they may agree to recognize a concern for future people as a matter of justice.

Rawls applies this line of argumentation when he suggests that participants in the original position would adopt the just savings principle when acting in it as family heads. As such, they would agree that out of self-interest each generation should make just savings for the next. I will refer to this as the chain of concern (Page, 2007, 117; Passmore 1974, 86ff.). Without going any further into the details of this approach, one should note that from this perspective the just savings principle depends on the 'motivational assumption' about participants in the original position, i.e. that they are concerned with their children's interests (Meyer 2010). Making this assumption is problematic, however, if only because it is far from clear that one should value having children in oneself or others, when in fact some people don't want to have any. So why should this concern be a matter of justice? Furthermore, it is unclear whether somebody's concern for their own or someone else's children should include the children's concerns as a family head – let alone whether these should be concerns that take precedence. As a result of this, it is far from clear that we should, as a matter of overriding and enforceable justice, be concerned with our immediate offspring's concern for *their* immediate offspring's concern, *and so on.*

One could replace this version of the motivational assumption with an assumption about *instrumental concern* regarding members of successive generations (Page 2007, 117). For example, care for the elderly and pension schemes provide freedom and well-being to parties during the time that they are not contributing to these schemes. Conversely, those contributing to such schemes are not profiting from the schemes themselves at this time. Arguably, these schemes function only because members of younger generations are relatively free to lead their own lives and well-off by the time they are contributing; they are of course *expecting* to benefit from the same system in the future. This expectation depends on there being functioning schemes in the future, which in turn requires younger generations in the future who are relatively free and well-off when contributing to the scheme and who have the same expectation of benefiting from it in their future, *and so on.* If basic freedom, well-being or expectation fail, these schemes may collapse at the present time. Recognizing this, rational agents within a generation may agree, out of an interest in benefiting from these schemes, to be concerned with the freedom and well-being of future people in expectation of reaping benefits.

A related but different chain style argument identifies a *chain of duties* across generations. On the assumption of partial overlap, members of one generation should recognize present duties to *future* contemporaries (cf. Gosseries 2008b; Howarth 1992). These duties to future contemporaries are then claimed to be duties regarding the duties that future contemporaries will have *to their future contemporaries, and so on.* The resulting chain of duty is different from the chain of concern. It concerns the long-term implications of one generation's duty to the future rights of the next, rather than the long-term implication of one generation's concern for the future concerns of the next.

My main worry with these chain arguments is that the responsibilities they imply may be less enforceable or overriding than a long-term responsibility needs. The chain of concern is vulnerable to the contingencies and limited normative significance of such a concern, especially when the concern is for great-grandchildren. Why should this concern be a matter of justice, even if it is widely shared? Why would it trump other short-term interests, even if these undermine the environment for future people? Why would an instrumental interest in the freedom and well-being of future people include a concern for distant people? So if a younger generation was contributing to pension schemes for its own short-term interest, would this make such a concern disappear? The chain of duty argument potentially has a stronger appeal than the chain of concern argument, since it does not ground itself in a contingent, potentially unenforceable and potentially subordinate interest that members of a generation have in future people. Rather, it points out that, once future people are recognized as having future rights, the assumption of partial overlap implies that we have duties to these future rights prior to their future existence. This approach faces the same controversies of the direct approach to long-term responsibility, but may be able to cope with these much more easily as it concerns duties to not yet existing future contemporaries only. The chain of duty approach is most vulnerable, in my understanding, when it comes to the question of why duties to future rights would be about future people's duties to their future contemporaries' future rights, *and so on*. Which account of rights would imply that we have rights to fulfil our duties?

Long-term responsibilities to the rights of future human persons would have been more promising with regard to enforceability and overridingness but for the fact that accounts of such responsibilities lead to controversies we would need to avoid where possible. Therefore, in the next section I will combine the assumption of the universal rights of the direct approach and the core idea of a chain style argument to identify a 'chain of status' between all members of generations, implying enforceable and overriding long-term responsibilities regarding future people's rights.

4 Respecting the securability of human rights

Human rights are attributed universally, i.e. they are attributed to a human person in response to his being a human person. In other words, certain rights should be *secured* for a human person without further qualification. I say 'secure' because human rights imply three duties: duties to avoid depriving; duties to protect from deprivation; and duties to aid the deprived (Shue 1996, 52–3). Recognizing and fulfilling these as duties to human persons without further qualification is what the universal attribution of rights requires.

It should be noted that this is a claim about the universality of attribution, i.e. it is not a claim about universal recognition or a claim about the nature or justification of human rights. In other words, human rights institutions are committed to attributing certain rights to a human person simply because he is a person. Although human rights institutions have been almost universally recognized since the second half of the last century, their being recognized is a contingent, vulnerable achievement. Arguably, human rights were not recognized in the past, and it is an open question whether they will be recognized in the (distant) future. It has been argued that the idea of human rights is unique for a modern state and is not easily compatible with traditional cultural assumptions (Donnelly 1982, 2009). However, questions about universal recognition concern potential disagreement about human rights, including its institutions. They concern the possibility of times without human rights and without human rights institutions. This possibility is real, and one implication of my argument for a chain of status will be that unsustainability is a threat to the future of human rights, at least insofar as it undermines the securability of human rights in the future. Nevertheless, the discussion about universal recognition does not concern the question of whether, from the perspective of human rights, rights are to be attributed to human persons universally. Rather, it concerns acceptance of human rights.

Universal attribution should not only be distinguished from universal recognition, but also from the metaphysical universality of moral or natural rights. In the literature, we find Beitz and Raz emphasizing the practical nature of human rights. Human rights exist as a result of being recognized in international practice as standards for legitimate state action (Beitz 2003, 2011; Raz 2010). They may have a moral dimension, but they have to be understood primarily in terms of their function in the international practice of human rights. In other words, human rights depend for their existence and nature on their practice in the sense that we are not talking about human rights if we talk about rights that are different from what human rights are accepted to be and what they are capable of doing in practice. In arguing this way, one is objecting to the idea that human rights existed as moral, natural or metaphysical rights prior to international political agreements on human rights. The distinction between human rights as either pragmatic or moral has one important implication for the question of whether future people will have human rights. Arguably, according to the political conception, it is an open question whether human rights should be recognized for future people. If this is right, then the question of whether future people do (will) have human rights would primarily be a pragmatic matter, contingent on what is to be accepted institutionally about future persons' rights being conditional on the purposes of international law. One could insist that the political approach to human rights is fundamentally flawed and that the rights of future people should be institutionalized politically for moral reasons. Although I would be sympathetic to this approach, it would lead us into the controversies of the direct approach that I wish to avoid where possible.

My argument for the chain of status assumes universal attribution, not universal recognition or metaphysical universality. I will *assume* that existing human rights institutions – whether morally or politically justified – are essentially built on the idea that any human person should, in response to his humanity, have certain rights secured for him. This idea leaves open the question of what human rights are by nature and whether they are recognized outside human rights institutions. In my view, human rights institutions are essentially marked by an *ambition* to secure rights for any human person in view of his humanity. Given this ambition, future people do not come into the picture only if they are or should be recognized as rights-bearers by human rights institutions; they are already in the picture because of, as I will argue, an internationally recognized responsibility to secure the human rights of currently living human persons, given the assumption of partial overlap.

In the remainder of this section I will be arguing that the fact of overlap, together with the idea of the universal attribution of rights, entails a chain of status between members of one generation and members of the next into the indefinite future. The upshot of my argument is that we should not be undermining the *securability* of human rights for future human persons, both near and distant.

The idea of universal attribution can be spelled out via what I will call 'the human rights conditional': *If x is a human person, then x should have – in response to his humanity – human rights secured for him.* This conditional would be violated if x is a human person but he has no rights secured for him or they are only secured in response to conditions that are different from or in addition to his humanity. This has two significant stages, given the assumption of temporal overlap. First, the lives of currently living human rights-bearers are temporally extended and, hence, currently living individuals have a future beyond their present with regard to which their human rights should be respected. Respecting a person's human rights regarding his future requires *respecting* the human rights conditional in relation to both his present and his future. This conditional will be respected in relation to his future only if the possibility of securing rights for him *in response to his humanity* in the future is respected. This will be securable for him *in response to his humanity* in the future only if in the future rights could be secured for him in response to his humanity. This would be the case only if it were possible in the future to secure these rights for others in response to their humanity. Hence, respect for a person's human rights regarding his future includes respect for the possibility of securing rights for him and his *future* contemporaries in response to their humanity. Therefore, because of the universal attribution of human rights, respect for the future securability of his status as a subject of human rights cannot meaningfully be separated from respect for the securability of the same status for his *future* contemporaries. Secondly, respect for the securability of the same status for his *future* contemporaries cannot, by analogous reasoning, be meaningfully separated from respect for the securability of the same status for their future contemporaries, *and so on.* In other words, the human rights conditional can be respected for a member of a generation only if the future possibility of securing human rights in response to humanity is respected.

5 Costs and benefits

At this point we can return to the central question of this chapter: are all duties *regarding* future people's rights duties *to* future people's rights. The chain of status argument shows that respect for the human rights of those currently living requires respect for the securability of human rights in the future. It delivers long-term responsibilities not as duties to future people but as duties between contemporaries regarding future people. In this respect it differs from a direct approach and has the structure of a chain style argument. Like other chain arguments, essentially it builds on the assumption of temporal overlap, not on assuming duties to (distant) future people. In doing so, it allows us to avoid the controversies to which a direct approach to long-term responsibilities leads. On the other hand, the chain of status argument differs from other chain arguments in that it identifies a chain on the basis of universal rights, which are uncontroversial, overriding and enforceable. My approach is certainly compatible with the direct approach to long-term responsibility. In fact the chain of status argument builds on an assumption of universality in the context of rights that may best be rationalized in terms of an account of rights that justifies the idea of rights of future persons. From my perspective, the chain of status argument mainly points out how recognition of enforceable and overriding long-term responsibilities *is possible* without going into and solving the theoretical and practical controversies of the direct approach to long-term responsibility. The chain of status argument is compatible with other chain style approaches insofar as the relevant forms of concern or obligation can be covered by human rights. In fact the right to marry and found a family may include a chain of concern, and the right to social security may include provision for old age and membership of a legal order that is concerned with rights to fulfil duties to (future) contemporaries. However, the chain of status involves a more fundamental normative concern, as a result of which its long-term normative implications – unlike those of other chains – trump short-termism and, when necessary, require treatment on a par with short-term human rights-based requirements.

Returning to Gardiner's understanding of climate change as the perfect moral storm, I do think the chain of status provides a significant clue as to how to address the global, intergenerational and theoretical storm. It hints at why we should first think of long-distance and long-term responsibility as questions of individual and collective duties in respect of the rights of human persons. According to human rights institutions, we should, as a minimum, respect the securability of rights attributed to human persons in response to their humanity. This has a global dimension insofar as it is completely problematic to undermine this form of securability in other parts of the world. The analogous temporal dimension would involve not undermining this form of securability in near and distant times. In saying this, I leave open the question whether there is an individual or collective responsibility to promote the securability of human rights, to assist in securing human rights or to actually secure human rights. In addition, the chain of status argument adds to the theoretical dimension in explaining how an almost universally shared normative logic, i.e. the one concerning human rights, entails enforceable and overriding long-term responsibilities.

Of course, I am assuming human rights here, or at least duties to human persons in response to their humanity. That is the cost of my approach. This approach may in itself be questioned at the philosophical level for being too morally demanding in view of theories about the circumstances of justice and politics and the actual practice of them. However, for what it is worth, human rights are actually recognized at the international level as an expression of a consensus on the view that we owe certain things to each other in response to our humanity. This does imply, however, that the fundamental idea of universal attribution of rights to human persons resonates in different corners of the world. More importantly, I do think that there are better reasons for attributing rights universally than there are for not doing so (Beyleveld and Bos 2009).

6 Conclusion

This chapter addressed the issue of whether our long-term environmental responsibilities regarding future people are to be conceived as duties to future peoples' rights. It started by clarifying some central challenges in accounting for long-term environmental responsibility given the mutually enforcing global, intergenerational and theoretical challenges involved in major long-term environmental threats. Against this background, it introduced the idea of a rights approach to long-term responsibility, which incorporated the strengths of two well-known approaches to long-term environmental responsibility: the direct approach and the chain style approach. It pointed out several obstacles in the direct approach and introduced the idea of partially overlapping lives as key to understanding long-term responsibilities as duties between contemporaries. The idea of partially overlapping lives supports chain style arguments that explain how the coexistence of members of different generations is normatively relevant and implies for us duties that concern near and distant generations. Chain style argumentation combined with the universal rights assumption of the direct approach serves to identify a chain of status between members of different generations. Because this status is uncontroversial, enforceable and overriding in principle, the chain of status entails enforceable and overriding long-term responsibilities towards currently living people – therewith avoiding theoretical and practical controversies implicated by the direct approach.

References

Beitz C. (2003) 'What human rights mean' *Daedalus*, 132(1) 36–46.
Beitz C. (2011) *The idea of human rights* Oxford, Oxford University Press.
Bell D. (2011) 'Does anthropogenic climate change violate human rights?' *Critical Review of International Social and Political Philosophy*, 14(2) 99–124. doi: 10.1080/13698230.2011.529703.
Beyleveld D. (1991) *The dialectical necessity of morality: an analysis and defense of Alan Gewirth's argument to the principle of generic consistency* Chicago, University of Chicago Press.
Beyleveld D. and Bos G. (2009) 'The foundational role of the principle of instrumental reason in Gewirth's argument for the principle of generic consistency: a response to Andrew Chitty' *Kings College Law Journal*, 20(1) 1–20.

Caney S. (2010) 'Climate change, human rights, and moral thresholds' in Gardiner S., Caney S., Jamieson D. and Shue H. eds, *Climate ethics: essential readings* Oxford, Oxford University Press, 63–177.

DesJardins J.R. (2006) *Environmental ethics: an introduction to environmental philosophy* Belmont, CA, Thomson Wadworth.

Donnelly J. (1982) 'Human rights and human dignity: an analytic critique of non-Western conceptions of human rights' *The American Political Science Review*, 76(2) 303–16. doi: 10.2307/1961111.

Donnelly J. (2009) *Human dignity and human rights*, Available at www.scribd.com/doc/229433530/Human-Rights-and-Human-Dignity#scribd, accessed 21 October 2015.

Gardiner S. (2003) 'The pure intergenerational problem' *The Monist*, 86(3) 481–500.

Gardiner S. (2006) 'A perfect moral storm: climate change, intergenerational ethics and the problem of moral corruption' *Environmental Values*, 15(3) 397–413.

Gardiner S. (2013) *A perfect moral storm: the ethical tragedy of climate change* Oxford, Oxford University Press.

Gewirth A. (1978) *Reason and morality* Chicago, University of Chicago Press.

Gosseries A. (2008a) 'Theories of intergenerational justice: a synopsis' *S.A.P.I.EN.S. Surveys and Perspectives Integrating Environment and Society*, 1(1) 61–71, Available at http://sapiens.revues.org/165, accessed 10 March 2015.

Gosseries A. (2008b) 'On future generations' future rights' *The Journal of Political Philosophy*, 16(4) 446–74.

Gosseries A. and Meyer L.H. (2009) *Intergenerational justice* Oxford; New York, Oxford University Press.

Hiskes R.P. (2009) *The human right to a green future: environmental rights and intergenerational justice* Cambridge; New York, Cambridge University Press.

Howarth R.B. (1992) 'Intergenerational justice and the chain of obligation' *Environmental Values*, 1(2) 133–40.

Meyer L. (2003) 'Past and future: the case for a threshold notion of harm' in Meyer L.H., Paulson S.L., and Pogge T.W. *Rights, culture and the law* Oxford, Oxford University Press, 143–62.

Meyer L. (2010) 'Intergenerational justice' in Zalta E.N. ed., *The Stanford encyclopedia of philosophy* spring 2010 edn, Available at http://plato.stanford.edu/archives/spr2010/entries/justice-intergenerational/, accessed 9 August 2012.

Page E.A. (2007) *Climate change, justice and future generations* Cheltenham, Edward Elgar Publishing.

Partridge E. (1981) *Responsibilities to future generations: environmental ethics* Buffalo, NY, Prometheus Books.

Partridge E. (1990) 'On the rights of future generations' *Upstream/Downstream: Issues in Environmental Ethics*, 40 56–8.

Passmore J.A. (1974) *Man's responsibility for nature: ecological problems and Western traditions* New York, Scribner.

Pogge T. (2005) 'Severe poverty as a violation of negative duties' *Ethics & International Affairs*, 19(1) 55–83. doi: 10.1111/j.1747–7093.2005.tb00490.x.

Pogge T. (2007) 'Severe poverty as a human rights violation' in Pogge T. ed., *Freedom from poverty as a human right: who owes what to the very poor?* Oxford, Oxford University Press, 11–54.

Raz J. (2010) 'Human rights without foundations' in Besson S. and Tasioulas J. eds *The philosophy of international law* Oxford, Oxford University Press, 321–38.

Roberts M.A. (2013) 'The nonidentity problem' in Zalta E.N. ed., *The Stanford encyclopedia of philosophy* fall 2013 edn, Available at http://plato.stanford.edu/archives/fall2013/entries/nonidentity-problem/, accessed 26 March 2014.

Shue H. (1996) *Basic rights: subsistence, affluence, and U.S. foreign policy* Princeton, NJ, Princeton University Press.

Shue H. (2014) *Climate justice: vulnerability and protection* Oxford, Oxford University Press.

Sikora R.I. and Barry, B. (1978) *Obligations to future generations* Philadelphia, Temple University Press.

Singer P. (2009) 'Speciesism and moral status' *Metaphilosophy*, 40(3–4) 567–81. doi: 10.1 111/j.1467–9973.2009.01608.x.

Wall S. (2003) 'Just savings and the difference principle' *Philosophical Studies*, 116(1) 79–102. doi: 10.1023/B:PHIL.0000005559.77848.5d.

Part III

Human rights approaches to sustainability

10 Human rights as a normative guideline for climate policy

Michael Reder and Lukas Köhler

1 Introduction

During the UN Conference on Sustainable Development in 2012 in Rio de Janeiro, it was acknowledged that energy use, and climate change mitigation and adaptation cannot be separated from poverty reduction and other dimensions of sustainable development, such as agricultural production and food security, water availability or human health. Sustainable development[1] will only be achieved if resource use stays within acceptable environmental boundaries along all relevant dimensions. Without climate protection, a sustainable path into the future will not be possible – climate protection that is not embedded in a broader social and environmental development context will most likely fail. However, a differentiated approach towards sustainability is required. If the concept is used simply as a buzzword without a sufficient background, it will probably have only an insignificant impact on international and national policy decision making (cf. Vucetich and Nelson 2010). This chapter will explore an approach to making human rights viable for developing a normative discourse that will help to guide policymakers towards a sustainable development (cf. Scoones 2007). In the sustainability debate, ethics is needed to accompany politics, especially for complex problems such as climate change (Vucetich and Nelson 2010, 593). Moreover, the question of sustainable development and the question of the causes and consequences of climate change are not only subjects for the natural sciences, politics or economics. Debates about sustainability, and especially the impacts of climate change, necessarily exist within ethical frameworks. In our view, human rights provide a meaningful starting point for an ethical reflection on sustainability in general and climate change specifically.

Human rights will be affected by the impacts of climate change – this is an important argumentation which a lot of academics and NGOs have already emphasized on the global scale during the last decade (cf. Human Rights Council 2008, 2009, 2011), for example, "Climate change jeopardizes human rights and in particular the human rights to life, health and subsistence" (Caney 2010a, 72). Similarly, Mary Robinson, the former High Commissioner of Human Rights, argued: "Human rights law is relevant because climate change causes human rights violations" (International Council on Human Rights Policy

2008, 2). However, in a strict juridical sense the question still to be asked is how can human rights be relevant if no one is to be brought to justice?[2] One main reason is that the relation between human rights and the duty to have a sustainable climate policy is often unclear.

Like with most economic, social and cultural rights, the link between the right and the corresponding duty is blurred. Just as a violation of the right to food, health or shelter can often not be traced back to the action of a clearly identifiable duty bearer, climate effects cannot be attributed to a culprit with name and address. Who exactly should be held responsible for hunger and widespread illness? (Sachs 2008, 360)

Sachs points out that the difference between rights and corresponding duties is often entirely unclear. Specifically, when the difference needs to be identified on a global scale of interconnected action, often the duty bearer cannot be exactly determined. Still, intuitively we want to give people rights even if a duty bearer is not likely to be brought to justice.

Although it is difficult to found moral and political duties in human rights, the tradition of human rights is an important guideline on the juridical but also on the moral level.[3] Human rights understood as a comprehensive compendium of moral norms influence political processes in many ways. "The ideas of economists and political philosophers, both when they are right and when they are wrong, are more powerful than is commonly understood. Indeed the world is ruled by little else" (Keynes 1936, 383). Keynes notes something of importance here. There is a link between ideas and the shaping of the world. If human rights are violated but no duty bearers can be held accountable, then there may be another approach to dealing with what happens when those rights are harmed. There seems to be a link between ideas and actions. If nothing else, it is clear that norms, which are nothing more than ideas in the first place, influence policy decisions on a broad scale. That is true for most democratic countries, as norms are guiding factors for distinguishing political choices as well as programmes of political parties.

Norms can be shaped in various ways: in one way, the juridical practice is the centre of this shape and therefore needs to be closely looked at. This chapter will explore the influence of human rights violations and how this in turn influences moral principles. After it becomes clear which principles are harmed, the grounds for political action will be clearer and will be explored by using a different analysis. To establish these norms, it is first necessary to show that there is some form of global practice. Norms that are relevant for decision making will be constructed within this frame to grant them the required amount of potency. Using these norms, a detailed analysis of human rights violations caused by climate change will demonstrate which moral principles are harmed and, in the last step of the process, these will be confirmed.

2 Human rights as global practice: a Hegel-orientated approach

Justice and related ethical aspects of climate change have always been important items on the agenda of climate politics (cf. Page 2007). The debates about grandfathering and historic responsibility are two examples. Justice serves as the ethical norm through which conflicts of interest in the context of climate change have to be judged, e.g. distributing mission allowances (cf. Raymond 2008). However, regarding the overall discussion about justice in the context of climate change, it quickly becomes apparent that justice is being interpreted by the different stakeholders according to their interests and belief systems. The relevant interests need to be converged from a pragmatist point of view if a problem-solving mechanism is to be found. So, to reflect the ethical impacts of climate change, one should ask for an ethical point of view that does not take the interests of only one group into account. It is necessary to use an approach that evaluates the groundwork behind the various forms of justice that are used. Thus, a generally acceptable ethical concept should be developed from a philosophical perspective.

One of the main problems of ethical approaches such as utilitarianism or deontology is that they provide an abstract moral reason without connecting this reason to the practical structures of daily life. Moral norms, however, are not only accepted because of an abstract reason but because they are incorporated in social life and heterogeneous cultural practices. This is the main argument for exploring a pragmatic approach (cf. Stout 2004). The idea of pragmatic theory is that norms and policy decisions are always connected to such social and cultural beliefs. Pragmatism means looking at these practices and analysing how people realize morality from a practical standpoint. Ethical reflections should be connected closely to these practices so that moral principles will be related to social reality and therefore could claim universal validity. Of course, this does not mean that all social practices are an expression of moral norms. The way in which social practices follow accepted moral norms, or how they do not do so, always has to be critically reflected on. But this is not an argument against the connection of ethical reflections to these practices. In contrast, such a connection could guarantee that ethical reflections are well founded in social reality and not only in abstract reasons.

Of course, several social practices exist that are embedded with different moral norms. Therefore, pragmatic theories ask for complementary moral beliefs, because humans are always realizing practical coherence between different moral beliefs in their everyday life (Nida-Rümelin 1996, 183f.). This view follows that of Axel Honneth in his interpretation of Hegel. Honneth argues that our reflections on justice should always be connected to a detailed analysis of society, including the different social and normative practices. The aim of a critical analysis of society in the tradition of Hegel's philosophy of rights should be "[to analyse] the given institutions and practices ... with regard to their normative capabilities"[4] and to show how "they are of importance for the social embodiment and realization of socially legitimized values"[5] (Honneth 2008, 21, translation by the author). By analysing the given institutions and practices, Honneth argues against a clear distinction between fact and values and against a focus on abstract principles of justice. Instead, he emphasizes the concrete capability for mutual recognition in the spheres of *Sittlichkeit*. He underlines the fact that an ethical reflection on social practices does not mean that all practices must be accepted. In fact, a critical reconstruction has to analyse and discuss the "moral" potential of such practices and to ask in what way these practices could be improved in terms of their fundamental ideas (cf. Honneth 2008). An analysis like this has to focus on which practices can be determined from the viewpoint of a pragmatic approach as theoretically described here. With regard to climate change, this will be done in the next section.

Honneth focuses on societies in their national borders. But we can expand this focus to the global level and ask which social and normative practices are important in the global sphere of *Sittlichkeit*. We already have a global practice at work. There may not be a global society that is comparable with a national one, but several indications of what is needed to create a public sphere on a global level are already present. First, developments such as modern technologies have helped to establish a platform that enables a globalized community to communicate cheaply and directly. International ideas can be discussed and established via social media, the Internet and cheap communication technologies such as Voice over IP devices. Awareness of a heterogeneous global community can easily be raised when it comes to actions and their consequences in other parts of the world. Second, the concept of the nation state was founded on an "imagined community" (Anderson 1991) that, for instance, shares common values and a common language. During the last three decades this situation has changed. Today, people live in heterogeneous societies, which means that the model of a closed national society doesn't make sense any more. Of course, people as citizens are still defined by their membership to a particular state. But according to this perspective of identity politics, people communicate and debate within groups that are not defined by nationality but by shared interests or topics. Therefore, traditional borders become less important and do not limit a broad global community any more. A good example of this is the occupy movement.

Third, global challenges such as world poverty and climate change push the world community to develop common normative concepts such as sustainability. Institutions that debate and implement these ideas on a global level are already in place. The UN or multinational NGOs serve as examples.

Today, human rights provide a basis for a universal (global) morality. From a pragmatic viewpoint, they are accepted because they are incorporated in various global practices. Global discourses regarding issues such as the Millennium Development Goals or sustainable climate policy are both examples of this. The *Universal Declaration of Human Rights* (UDHR) – which the global community has already agreed upon – seeks to provide answers to the many-faceted specific experience of injustice. From this standpoint, ethical measures are determined with reference to concrete political realities.

In many political discussions about different aspects of globalization, reference is made to human rights (cf. United Nations 2000; United Nations Development Programme 2007). Ethically speaking, they are about letting all people lead a dignified life.[6] Human rights want to protect the necessary foundations for such a life. They also play a major role in political philosophy. Independent from ethical reasons in meta-ethical perspectives, human rights function as moral standards in relation to the different challenges of globalization (cf. Habermas 2010; Walzer 2005).

These observations show that human rights – understood as a global practice – play an important role as part of a global *Sittlichkeit*. By doing so, human rights could be interpreted both as a global moral standard and as a guideline for international politics. Therefore, they could also be seen as a basis for sustainability in a broader sense. Human rights have moral and political implications for the social, economic and ecological dimension of sustainability. According to this perspective, the politics of sustainability could be grounded on human rights as a fundamental global practice. This possibility can already be seen in the debate about transnational corporations and human rights (*economic* dimension of sustainability), the post-MDG agenda (*social* dimension of sustainability) or the debate about climate change and human rights (*ecological* dimension of sustainability). The advantage of a human rights-based understanding of sustainability is that it is closely connected to human rights as an important moral dimension of global *Sittlichkeit*. This means that the normative demand of sustainability will also not be grounded in an abstract reason, but in existing global values. In addition, by referring to human rights, the different political aspects of the discourse about sustainability could be integrated normatively, because in the concept of human rights the three dimensions of sustainability are always interconnected.

As the history of the origin of the *Universal Declaration of Human Rights* also shows, discourses about human rights were mostly a response to specific suffering and injustice (cf. Müller 1997, 98–120). As a reaction to experiences of injustice, individuals or certain groups have become active in advocating human rights. They aim to protect those who are disadvantaged, discriminated against or excluded from society. In this regard, human rights apply to all people, not only to the citizens of one state. They express a cosmopolitan perspective which is the theoretical background of human rights: "The same rights that apply within the state also apply at the global level" (Caney 2010b, 23). Human rights apply to all people living today, locally and globally. Implemented as a reaction to a specific suffering and injustice, human rights apply universally to all humankind. From this perspective they are also supposed to protect people from future harm, and therefore they apply not only to actual but to future people. However, human rights always need further development because of social problems and associated changes in emerging injustice. This is also true in view of new global challenges and their consequences as well as the multiple connections between climate change and poverty. Therefore, it is convincing to analyse the effects of the impacts of climate change on human rights, as Caney points out clearly: "My argument is simply that a human rights perspective has important insights and any account of the impacts of climate change which ignores its implications for people's enjoyment of human rights is fundamentally incomplete and inadequate" (Caney 2010a, 89). According to this perspective, human rights provide an ethical threshold which could be a convincing foundation for climate and development politics. "Human rights represent moral 'thresholds' below which people should not fall. They designate the most basic moral standards to which persons are entitled" (Caney 2010a, 71). Human rights can be seen as a threshold at which all people should be granted a minimum of opportunities to act in such a way as to be able to live a decent life (cf. Wallacher, Reder and Kowarsch 2009, 56ff.). As Caney states: "Persons have human rights to a decent standard of health, to economic necessities, and to subsistence" (2010b, 44). This means that satisfaction of human rights is a minimum standard and hence a necessary (though not sufficient) condition for a climate policy to be morally admissible and just. Because climate change affects this minimum standard, the impacts of climate change undermine human rights.

Human rights also play a major role today in the political discourse on climate change. In line with this perspective, impacts of climate change are interpreted as violations of human rights. In 2007, during the 13th session of the Conference of the Parties to the United Nations Framework Convention on Climate Change (COP 13) in Bali, Kyung-Wha Kang emphasized that the impacts of climate change will affect compliance with human rights:

> Marginalized groups, whether in industrialized or developing countries and across all cultures and boundaries, are particularly vulnerable to the dire consequences of climate change. The international community should consider the human rights dimension of climate change as Governments and various stakeholders gather in Bali to mount a global response to this pressing issue.
>
> (Kyung-Wha Kang 2007, 1)

Comparing different politically orientated studies, some human rights can be identified which seem to be the ones that are most affected by the impacts of climate change (for a mapping of the different treaties see United Nations 2014).

- *Right to life, liberty and security of person* (United Nations 1948, Arts. 1 and 3; United Nations 1966a, Arts. 5 and 6.1). Oxfam mentions several reasons why these rights could be violated by climate change, e.g. increasing numbers of extreme weather events or sea level rises (Oxfam 2008, 6).
- *Right of everyone to an adequate standard of living and enough nutrition* (United Nations 1966b, Art. 11). Regarding current climate models, agricultural production will decrease in Africa, Middle and South America and some regions of South Asia (cf. Edenhofer et al., 2012). In these regions, food security is already an important issue which is difficult to realize for all of the people who live there.
- *Right to subsistence* is closely connected to the rights mentioned above (United Nations 1948, Art. 25). The impacts of climate change could, for example, also affect in an extreme way the subsistence of those people

living near the coast, and the supply of water could be affected negatively (Oxfam 2008, 6).

- *Right to health* (United Nations 1966b, Art. 12). Climate change poses significant risks to this right, for example when impacts of climate change lead to a higher infant mortality (as a consequence of malnutrition) or increase the risk of diseases. "It will affect the intensity of a wide range of diseases – vector-borne, water-borne and respiratory. In the Pacific, changes in temperature and rainfall will make it harder to control dengue fever" (cf. Human Rights and Equal Opportunity Commission 2008, 6; Inthorn, Kaelin and Reder 2010, 143ff.).
- Finally, some studies mention collective rights which could be violated by climate change, e.g. the *right to development* (cf. Office of the United Nations High Commissioner for Human Rights 2008, 11ff.). "As recognised by the United Nations Development Programme (UNDP), climate change is the defining human development issue of our generation as it threatens to erode human freedoms and limit choice" (cf. Office of the United Nations High Commissioner for Human Rights 2008, 12).

Thus, some human rights are identified which could be violated by the impacts of climate change that will happen in the future. The rights of people who today are already the most vulnerable in relation to social, economic and political issues will be especially affected by the impacts of climate change, as will the rights of those who will be born in a world where these violations will occur. Those people who live or will live below the poverty line, women, children and indigenous groups in particular, will be affected most.

3 Moral principles of human rights: freedom, equality, solidarity and participation

The (causal) relations between climate impacts and human rights abuses are often ambiguous because of several other political, economic or cultural factors which also influence these relations. From a political point of view, it is very difficult, if not impossible, to assess whether climate policies lead to a violation of specific human rights. But this does not mean that human rights could not provide a political basis for climate and development policy. Simon Caney points out that human rights focus on the duties of institutions in order not to risk the rights of those people who could be affected: "Actors should not pursue a course of action which runs a non-negligible risk of violating the human rights of others when they can pursue alternative courses of action without compromising their or other people's human rights" (Caney 2010b, 38). From a political perspective, it is not only relevant to protect human rights, but it is also necessary to construct institutions which are able to prevent human rights violations. Hence, human rights could further guide political strategies that are trying to deal with climate change and global poverty. To understand in detail what orientation they could give, it is important to ask which universal ethical principles they imply. Therefore, in the following sections these general moral principles will be extracted from the catalogue of human rights; these principles could be guidelines for climate policy in the future. The most important norm-ative impacts of human rights which will be reflected on are freedom, equality, solidarity and participation.[7]

3.1 Freedom

Human rights are based on the assumption that all people want to live in freedom and therefore want to have the same opportunities to be able to do so (Brieskorn 1997, 131). Hence, a first central ethical aspect of human rights is freedom. The human rights approach emphasizes freedom as a fundamental con-dition for a life in dignity.

In order to live freely and independently, people must have choices. Therefore, freedom is connected to several surrounding conditions, which have to be secured. These conditions change greatly because of climate change when people no longer have access to clean drinking water or when the means to feed themselves are threatened. The consequences of climate change are therefore particularly prob-lematic ethically where a life with human dignity is limited or even impossible.

3.2 Equality

Equality is closely connected to freedom (cf. Bielefeldt 1998, 92f.). This con-nection is already expressed in Article 1 of the Universal Declaration of Human Rights: "All human beings are born free and equal in dignity and rights" (United Nations 1948, Art. 1). This means that human rights are based on the premise of a decent life for *all* people. The aim of human rights is that all people should be enabled to live a decent life, whatever their race, colour, sex, language, reli-gion or nationality. Therefore, each law should be based on this premise of equality, according to the reasoning of Article 7 of the Universal Declaration of Human Rights (United Nations 1948, Art. 7).

Human rights demand recognition of each human being as equal. Hence, freedom and equality are mutually interdependent. This means, ethically, that no person may choose to do or not to do what he or she wants without showing respect for other human beings. In addition, all people have to consider the consequences of each of their actions upon other human beings. The effects of climate change are particularly problematic in this respect where the equal entitlement of all to live with dignity is limited or endangered.

Freedom and equality, as ethical foundations of a human rights approach, are not to be understood as purely individual concepts, as is sometimes the case in Western culture. Rather, both rights are based on manifold social conditions, e.g. freedom can only exist within a community. Therefore, freedom is always related to and dependent upon community. This is why the several declarations of human rights emphasize the social and cultural aspects of being human (cf. United Nations 1966b).

3.3 Solidarity

All human beings live together on the same planet. Whether they can conduct their lives in a dignified manner is dependent on the actions of others, such as their immediate community (family, local community) and right up to the state and to the global community beyond. The human rights approach points out that global problems can only be solved if all people recognize that they are in the same position. To enact solidarity means to recognize the interconnectedness of people to one another as the main starting point of political action.

At the same time, the UDHR encompasses a second element of solidarity. Namely, it always refers to an addressee who recognizes human rights and understands them as a demand in relation to his own behaviour. Human rights are not only addressed to national states that have accepted the obligation to protect human rights, but to all people. Acknowledging this claim means that there must be a willingness to reflect on just structures and to make them politically possible. Solidarity is therefore an important basis for justice. Solidarity is an ethical dimension of human rights which means that the world community needs to support adaptation measures in areas where people do not have enough financial or technical opportunities to do so (Adger *et al.*, 2006). Although governments have a major role in these processes (cf. International Council on Human Rights Policy 2008, 12ff.), solidarity as a moral principle is an important guideline for all stakeholders, for example civil society or the economy (Oxfam 2008, 21ff.).

3.4 Participation

Human rights require political institutions, and procedures which guarantee and, in case of conflict, enforce them; at the same time human rights aim to provide orientation. This is equally true of local and state institutions as well as international and supranational ones. It also applies to those institutions which are fighting climate change and attempting to support development at the same time.

The concepts of participation and human rights are interdependent on and support one another. A lot of articles express this relation, e.g. the right to freedom of peaceful assembly and association (United Nations 1948, Art. 20) or Art. 21 (United Nations 1948), which says that the will of the people shall be the basis of the authority of government. That is to say, human rights require verifiable participation of all those concerned, with respect to the institutions needed to solve social problems. According to the cosmopolitan approach, which was explored by Simon Caney (cf. Caney 2010b), the normative claim of human rights is not only the participation of people on local and national levels, but also on the global level – especially those who are facing global challenges such as poverty and the impacts of climate change. This requires reform of the international order (system) rather than only making changes in the field of climate and development politics. This reform should be based on the model of transparent participation in order to respond in a politically appropriate manner to human rights violations caused by climate change. In particular, excluded or less powerful countries and groups should be strengthened in order to permit them to negotiate with influential countries on a more equal basis. Only in this way can their concerns attract an appropriate level of attention:

> Countries with populations at greatest risk – such as the least-developed countries (LDCs), small-island developing states, and those in sub-Saharan Africa – must be allowed to participate fully and have effective voice in international negotiations on mitigation. Organizations representing indigenous people, women, and children, must also be able to participate effectively, nationally and internationally.
>
> (Oxfam 2008, 12)

Institutional climate policy, which is based on the ethical terms of human rights, focuses primarily on vulnerable groups and will protect their rights as they face climate change. Participation and international cooperation are necessary elements of such a human rights-based climate policy.

All four principles can be seen as guidelines for a politics of sustainability. As an integral concept, human rights promote a life in dignity for all people, which means that societies should develop social, economic and ecological guidelines for future political concepts that respect people's lives. From this perspective, freedom, equality, solidarity and participation could function as a normative foundation of sustainable politics.

4 Conclusion: human rights as a normative guideline

The four general principles (freedom, equality, solidarity and participation) that have been identified are the normative foundation of human rights. The history of human rights shows that there have always been conflicts between these principles concerning various social challenges. They might also yield arguments for opposing policy options. To resolve such conflicts, it is important to point out that the idea of a decent life for all humans is the centre of the normative foundation of human rights. In case of conflict, this principle takes priority over the other principles.

From this perspective, climate policy could be aimed at the practice of human rights. "First, human rights language can add considerable normative tradition to arguments in favour of strong mitigation and adaptation policies" (Oxfam 2008, 20). Human rights are a normative guideline which functions as a moral threshold: "Human rights represent moral thresholds below which people should not fall. They designate the most basic moral standards to which persons are entitled" (Caney 2010, 71). This means that climate politics could be conceptualized in a normative perspective focusing on the four normative dimensions of human rights. In addition, this chapter shows that because of the relevance of human rights there is more to climate change than the cases that come before a court.

The global community is able to adapt to the moral requirement that is provided by human rights and the threshold that they indicate. This can be more powerful for enabling change than a hearing before a court of justice.

Human rights provide a meaningful starting point for ethical considerations about sustainability in general and climate politics specifically. In global politics, they are already a key ethical yardstick that is used in the resolution of global challenges. Taking human rights as a starting point, the politics of sustainability will focus on the satisfaction of basic needs and the aspiration towards equal opportunities and fair processes. These three interrelated demands, which could be grounded in the moral principles of human rights, provide an orientation for political action towards the necessary global cooperation and towards the implementation of climate change mitigation and adaptation measures on a national level.

Sustainable policies grounded in human rights are not just a technical problem. They can only be dealt with if key aspects of equitability are taken into consideration. Therefore, it is essential to have an equitable policy framework which permits developing and newly industrializing countries to play an active part in climate change mitigation without relinquishing their rightful entitlements to broad-based development. The industrialized countries have a special responsibility in this regard, because they have the financial, economic and technical capacities and the necessary political influence that are vital in order to solve these problems. And, according to human rights practice, different fields of sustainable politics have to be developed, e.g. mitigation and adaptation, the promotion and transfer of sustainable technologies and international support for development policy (cf. Edenhofer *et al.* 2012). The fundamental prerequisite for these measures is cooperation in a spirit of partnership between industrialized, newly industrializing and developing countries.

Notes

1 As defined in the Brundtland Report, "Sustainable development is development that meets the needs of the present without compromising the ability of future generations to meet their own needs (World Commission on Environment and Development 1987)." This means that sustainability deals with questions of needs in a political perspective. In addition, sustainability as a political framework focuses on the long-term effects of human action. In this sense, sustainability will always link intra- with inter-generational justice, viewing development as a dynamic political process rather than a static policy question.
2 Cf. United Nations (2014) *Mapping human rights obligations relating to the enjoyment of a safe, clean, healthy and sustainable environment* Focus report on human rights and climate change. Prepared for the Independent Expert on the issue of human rights obligations relating to the enjoyment of a safe, clean, healthy, and sustainable environment. New York, United Nations, Office of the United Nations High Commissioner for Human Rights, Available at http://srenvironment.org/2014/08/08/report-on-climate-change-and-human-rights/, Accessed 29 June 2015. The report summarizes this issue.
3 Human rights could be interpreted as a political, normative and legal practice that the global community has already agreed upon, which seeks to provide answers to the many-faceted experience of injustice. From this standpoint, ethical measures for the

future of global governance are determined with reference to concrete political and legal practices. Cf. Reder, Michael, "Menschenrechte und Pragmatismus. Menschenrechtspraxis und nachhaltige Entwicklung im Anschluss an John Dewey" (Reder 2015, 49f.).
4 "Die gegebene Institutionen und Praktiken ... auf ihre normativen Leistungen hin [zu analysieren]" (Honneth 2008, 21, translation by the author).
5 "sie für die soziale Verkörperung und Verwirklichung der gesellschaftlich legitimierten Werte von Bedeutung sind" (Honneth 2008, 21, translation by the author).
6 "Dignified life", if used as a premise for an argument, is dependent on a concept of dignity. There is a broad debate about how dignity can be understood and defined (cf. Böhr 2013; Howard and Donnelly 1986; Sensen 2011). In this chapter a "dignified life" is simply understood as the foundation for human rights in its broadest sense as pointed out in Article 1 of the *Universal Declaration of Human Rights*.
7 As pointed out before, human rights apply to future people as well as to present people. In this regard, a change in climate policy needs to address violations of human rights regardless of whether they will harm actual or future people.

References

Adger, N.W., Paavola, J., Huq, S., and Mace, M.J. eds (2006) *Fairness in adaptation to climate change* Cambridge, MIT Press.
Anderson B.R. (1991) *Imagined communities. Reflections on the origin and spread of nationalism* London, Verso.
Bielefeldt H. (1998) *Philosophie der menschenrechte. Grundlagen eines weltweiten freiheitsethos* Darmstadt, Wissenschaftliche Buchgesellschaft.
Brieskorn N. (1997) *Menschenrechte. Eine historisch–philosophische grundlegung* Stuttgart, Kohlhammer.
Böhr C. (2013) "Überlegungen zur begründung der unantastbarkeit menschlicher würde" *Erwägen Wissen Ethik*, 24(2) 187–90.
Caney S. (2010a) "Climate change, human rights and moral thresholds" in Humphreys S. ed., *Human rights and climate change* Cambridge, Cambridge University Press, 69–90.
Caney S. (2010b) "Human rights and global climate change" in Pierik R. and Werner W. eds, *Cosmopolitanism in context: perspectives from international law and political theory* Cambridge, Cambridge University Press, 19–44.
Edenhofer O., Wallacher J., Lotze-Campen H., Reder M., Knopf B. and Müller J. eds (2012) *Climate change, justice and sustainability. Linking climate and development policy* New York; London, Springer International.
Honneth A. (2008) "Gerechtigkeitstheorie als gesellschaftsanalyse. Überlegungen im anschluss an Hegel" in Menke C. and Rebentisch J. eds, *Gerechtigkeit und gesellschaft* Berlin, Berliner Wissenschafts-Verlag, 11–24.
Howard R.E. and Donnelly J. (1986) "Human dignity, human rights, and political regimes" *The American Political Science Review*, 80(3) 801–81.
Human Rights Council (2008) *Human rights and climate change*, Resolution 7/23, Available at http://ap.ohchr.org/documents/E/HRC/resolutions/A_HRC_RES_7_23.pdf, accessed 29 June 2015.
Human Rights Council (2009) *Human rights and climate change*, Resolution 10/4, Available at http://ap.ohchr.org/documents/E/HRC/resolutions/A_HRC_RES_10_4.pdf, accessed 29 June 2015.
Human Rights Council (2011) *Human rights and climate change*, Resolution 18/22, Available at www.ohchr.org/Documents/Issues/ClimateChange/A.HRC.RES.18.22.pdf, accessed 29 June 2015.

Human Rights and Equal Opportunity Commission (2008) *Human rights and climate change* Sydney, Human Rights and Equal Opportunity Commission, Available at www.humanrights.gov.au/pdf/about/media/chapters/hrandclimate_change.pdf., accessed 29 June 2015.

International Council on Human Rights Policy (2008) *Climate change and human rights. A rough guide* Versoix, Switzerland, International Council on Human Rights Policy

Inthorn J., Kaelin L. and Reder. M. (2010) *Gesundheit und gerechtigkeit. Ein interkultureller vergleich* Wien; New York, Springer Wissenschaftsverlag.

Kang K. (2007) *Climate change and human rights* address at the Conference of the Parties to the United Nations Framework Convention on Climate Change and its Kyoto Protocol 3–14 December, Bali, Indonesia, Available at www.ohchr.org/EN/News Events/Pages/DisplayNews.aspx?NewsID=200&LangID=E., accessed 29 June 2015.

Keynes J.M. (1936) *The general theory of employment, interest and money* London, Macmillan.

Müller J. (1997) *Entwicklungspolitik als globale herausforderung. Methodische und ethische* Stuttgart, Grundlegung.

Nida-Rümelin J. (1996) "Ethik des risikos" in Nida-Rümelin J. ed., *Angewandte ethik. Die bereichsethiken und ihre theoretische fundierung. Ein handbuch* Stuttgart, Kröner, 806–30.

Office of the United Nations High Commissioner for Human Rights (2008) *Human rights and climate change study* submission of New South Wales Young Lawyers, Sydney, Office of the United Nations High Commissioner for Human Rights.

Oxfam (2008) *Climate wrongs and human rights* Oxfam Briefing Paper No. 117, Available at www.oxfam.org/policy/bp117-climate-wrongs-and-human-rights, accessed 8 June 2010.

Page E.A. (2007) *Climate change, justice and future generations* Cheltenham, Elgar.

Raymond L. (2008) "Allocating the global commons: theory and practice" in Vanderheiden S. ed., *Political theory and global climate change* Cambridge, MA, MIT Press, 3–24.

Reder M. (2010) "Globale konflikte und die heterogenität des rechts. Rechtsphilosophische anmerkungen zur kantischen und hegelschen tradition" *Archiv für Sozial- und Rechtsphilosophie*, 125 131–48.

Reder M. (2015) "Menschenrechte und pragmatismus. Menschenrechtspraxis und achhaltige entwicklung im anschluss an John Dewey" in Reder M. and Cojocaru M eds, *Zur Praxis der Menschenrechte* Stuttgart, Kohlhammer, 43–66.

Sachs W. (2008) "Climate change and human Rights" *Development*, 51(3), 322–77.

Scoones I. (2007) "Sustainability" *Development in Practice* 17 4/5 589–96.

Sensen O. (2011) "Human dignity in historical perspective: the contemporary and traditional paradigms" *European Journal of Political Theory*, 10(1) 71–91.

Stout J. (2004) *Democracy and tradition* Princeton, NJ, Princeton University Press.

United Nations (1948) *Universal Declaration of Human Rights* New York, UN.

United Nations (1966a) *International Covenant on Civil and Political Rights* New York, UN.

United Nations (1966b) *International Covenant on Economic, Social and Political Rights* New York, UN.

United Nations (2000) "Millennium development goals of the United Nations", Available at www.un.org.vn/en/what-we-do-mainmenu-203/mdgs.html, accessed 26 October 2015.

United Nations (2014) *Mapping human rights obligations relating to the enjoyment of a safe, clean, healthy and sustainable environment* Focus report on human rights and climate change. Prepared for the Independent Expert on the issue of human rights obligations relating to the enjoyment of a safe, clean, healthy, and sustainable environment. New York, United Nations, Office of the United Nations High Commissioner for Human Rights, Available at http://srenvironment.org/2014/08/08/report-on-climate-change-and-human-rights/, accessed 29 June 2015.

United Nations Development Programme (2007) *Fighting climate change: human solidarity in a divided world* Human Development Report 2007/2008, New York, UNDP.

Vucetich J.A. and Nelson M.P. (2010) "Sustainability: virtuous or vulgar?" *BioScience*, 60(7) 539–44.

Wallacher J., Reder M. and Kowarsch M. (2009) "Klimawandel, weltweite armut und gerechtigkeit. Begründung und gestaltung einer integrierten klima- und entwicklungspolitik" *Zeitschrift für Umweltpsychologie*, 13/1 52–67.

World Commission on Environment and Development (1987) *Report of the World Commission on Environment and Development: our common future*, Available at www.un-documents.net/wced-ocf.htm, accessed 29 June 2015.

11 The duties we have to future generations

A Gewirthian approach

Deryck Beyleveld

1 Introduction

Current population growth, use of natural resources, carbon emissions and the like threaten to produce much poorer living conditions for future generations (agents who do not yet exist and will not exist during our lifetimes) unless we alter our actions radically. Avoidably inflicting such conditions on our contemporaries would violate their rights. But do we have duties not to inflict these conditions on future generations? The claim that we do is open to challenge on a number of grounds.

For example, it is not certain that future generations will share our view about what they have rights to because we cannot reliably predict the preferences they will have or the interests they will consider important enough to merit rights protection. This may be called the "challenge from epistemic uncertainty".

More fundamentally, is it even coherent to think that future generations *can* have rights against us on account of the "non-identity problem" (e.g. Parfit 1987)? In order for an agent (Agnes) to violate the rights of another agent (Brian) by doing X, Agnes's action must harm Brian by violating a duty she owes *to Brian*. So, because "ought" implies "can", for Agnes to have a duty not to do X, she must be able to do something else (Y) that will not harm *Brian*. Those who invoke the non-identity problem claim that *where Brian is a future agent and Agnes is a current agent*, it is impossible for Agnes to do anything *to Brian* that will not harm him in this way. Suppose that, because Agnes does X, Brian will be harmed in such a way that Agnes may not harm Cynthia (a contemporary of Agnes). Suppose that Agnes can and does do Y instead of X, with the result that no future agents will be harmed in the way that Brian will be harmed by Agnes doing X. The objection (on grounds considered in Section 4 paragraph IV below) is that if Agnes does anything other than X, Brian will not exist. Therefore, Agnes cannot do anything that results in Brian existing and not being harmed by Agnes. Consequently, Agnes cannot have a duty *to Brian* to do Y rather than X. So Brian cannot have a right that requires Agnes to do Y.

My general aim is to elucidate why, using Alan Gewirth's Principle of Generic Consistency (PGC) (see Gewirth 1978), we must recognize duties to future generations on account of the rights they will have.

Section 2 outlines what the PGC prescribes. Section 3 outlines two arguments for using the PGC to address practical issues in general, but will not defend these arguments in any detail as that has been done elsewhere (see, especially, Beyleveld 1991, 2011; also, for example, Beyleveld 2013a, 2013b; Beyleveld and Bos 2009). Section 4 discusses the application of the PGC to the issue of duties to future generations. It also explains how the PGC counters, inter alia, the challenge posed by epistemic uncertainty and the non-identity problem.

2 The PGC

The PGC grants "generic rights" (GRs) to "agents", and only to agents. Agents are characterized by having the capacity and disposition to do things in order to achieve purposes they have chosen, which they regard as reasons for their behaviour. The GRs are rights to generic conditions of agency (GCAs). GCAs are conditions agents need in order to be able to pursue any purposes whatsoever or to pursue them with any general chances of success. Thus, being deprived of a GCA will have at least some negative impact (either immediately or if the deprivation continues) on the ability of an agent (e.g. Albert) to act at all or to act successfully *regardless of the purposes that Albert is pursuing or might pursue*. GCAs are essential or categorical *instrumental* requirements of action, needs shared by all agents regardless of their circumstances (i.e. needs for action that Albert has simply by virtue of being an agent). Life itself, mental equilibrium sufficient to permit Albert to move from merely wanting to achieve something to doing something to achieve it, health, food, clothing, shelter, and the means to these, freedom of action, the possession of accurate information, and the keeping of promises made to one by others, are all examples of GCAs (see Gewirth 1978, 53–5).

Because Albert needs assistance to defend his possession of the GCAs when he cannot do so by his own unaided efforts as much as he needs non-interference with his possession, the GRs are both positive and negative. Because the GCAs are means for Albert to pursue/achieve his purposes, he is required to defend having them only for those purposes he chooses to pursue. For this reason, the GRs are rights under the "will" conception of rights, which is to say that they are rights to possess the objects of the rights (the GCAs) *in accordance with the right-holder's will*. The PGC does not require Albert to value his having the GCAs as an end in itself, but only as essential means for him to act/act successfully. In other words, *in* any action or intention to act, Albert categorically ought to defend his having the GCAs; but he is not categorically bound to defend continuing to be able to act outside of the context of currently acting or intending to act. The GRs are also ordered according to how needful they are for agency (see Gewirth 1978, 338–54, esp. 343–50), measured by how drastic the negative generic effects of being deprived of them are on Albert's ability to act at all/act successfully. Gewirth distinguishes between basic rights (to the conditions needed to act at all, like life), non-subtractive rights (to the conditions needed to maintain an ability to act successfully, like accurate information), and additive rights (to the conditions needed to improve Albert's ability to act successfully, like further education) (see Gewirth 1978, 53–5). Within these categories, GRs can also be ranked according to how extensive or immediate the negative generic effect of deprivation of the GCA would be on action/successful action. Gewirth generally refers to the GCAs under the headings of "freedom and well-being" (see Gewirth 1978, *passim*). But the argument for the PGC is best conducted in terms of the wholly abstract idea of a GCA, with concrete specification of the GCAs and how they are ordered being left to the application of the principle. *In concreto*, what constitutes a GCA can vary according to the contingent circumstances and characteristics of the agent. So, if aquatic agents exist, air will not be a GCA for them as it is for us. Also, what can impact on an agent's GCAs can vary. So, for example, a tall agent might not need a ladder to reach food, whereas a shorter agent might. Energy for the body (food) is a GCA for all agents, but how possession of this GCA is affected can vary from one agent to another in a number of different ways and for a number of different reasons. Judging the importance of a GCA according to the hierarchy of needfulness for agency is also attended by numerous complexities, which are beyond the scope of this chapter to deal with comprehensively (but see, further, Beyleveld 2011).

3 Why use the PGC?

Gewirth himself argues that the PGC is categorically binding on agents because it is "dialectically necessary" for them to accept it. "It is dialectically necessary for Albert to accept the PGC" *means* "If Albert denies that he ought to act in accord with the PGC, he fails to understand what it is for him to be an agent, and by implication denies that he is an agent." In effect, Gewirth tries to show that Albert cannot think coherently of himself as *an* agent if he thinks that he may act in ways that are inconsistent with the PGC.[1] As well as supporting this argument (see, especially, Beyleveld 1991, 2013a; Beyleveld and Bos 2009), I have also argued that anyone who considers that all agents must be treated impartially (i.e. with equal concern and respect for their agency), which includes anyone who accepts that there are human rights as these are conceived by the 1948 *Universal Declaration of Human Rights* (UDHR) and international legal instruments that are designed to give effect to the UDHR, must accept the PGC as categorically binding (see, especially, Beyleveld 2011). The first argument is more ambitious because, if valid, it renders it dialectically necessary for agents to accept the impartiality premise contained within the idea of human rights, which the second argument cannot do, and does not purport to do, as it presumes impartiality. However, if the second argument is sound, any system or theory of norms that incorporates the impartiality premise must be construed as governed by the PGC. The second argument, thus, purports to establish that there is a rationally required convergence over a prescriptive content that all normative theories and systems incorporating the impartiality premise must accept, even though they might vary over the epistemic status they grant to this content. In other words, the first argument is directed at showing that the PGC is the supreme principle of practical reason generally, whereas the second is directed at showing that it is the supreme principle of morality (defined as a set of categorically binding impartial requirements on action) as well as the supreme principle of human rights.

3.1 First argument

The PGC is dialectically necessary for agents if three propositions are necessarily true:

1   It is dialectically necessary for Albert to accept the Principle of Hypothetical Imperatives or Instrumental Reason (PHI), "If doing Z (or having P) is necessary to pursue or achieve Albert's chosen purpose E, then Albert ought to do Z (or act to secure P) or give up trying to pursue or achieve E."
2   There are GCAs.
3   Dialectically necessary principles are universal (i.e. "objective" or "impartial" principles).

From 1 and 2 it follows that

4   It is dialectically necessary for Albert to accept, "I (Albert) categorically ought to defend *instrumentally* my having the GCAs", which is equivalent to it being dialectically necessary for Albert to accept "I (Albert) ought to defend my having the GCAs, *unless I am willing to accept generic damage to my ability to act.*"

From 3 and 4 it follows that

5   It is dialectically necessary for Albert to accept "I (Albert) ought to respect Brenda (any other agent) having the GCAs unless she is willing to accept generic damage to her ability to act", which is equivalent to it being dialectically necessary for Albert to grant Brenda the GRs under the "will" conception of rights, which is for Albert to accept the PGC.

Since Albert stands for any agent, it follows that the PGC is dialectically necessary for all agents.

Proposition 3 is the most (and very highly) contested of the three key propositions, but also the only one that many philosophers would wish to contest. Establishing its validity rests on establishing that if it is dialectically necessary for Albert to accept that he ought to do Z or have P then it is dialectically necessary for Albert to accept that the sufficient reason why he ought to do Z or have P is that he is an agent, from which it follows logically that Albert must hold that Brenda ought to do Z or have P, where "Brenda ought to do Z or have P" has the same normative force for Albert as it does for Brenda, because what makes Brenda an agent is the same as what makes Albert an agent.[2]

3.2 Second argument

This argument rests on the necessary truth of propositions 1 and 2 of the first argument, but does not attempt to establish the truth of proposition 3. It argues that, given the truth of 1 and 2, anyone who accepts that agents ought to be treated with equal concern and respect for their agency must accept the PGC, on pain of giving up this impartiality premise. This is clearly the case, because if Brian holds that he ought to act out of respect for Brenda's need for the GCAs as much as he is required to act out of respect for his own need for the GCAs, then he must grant her the GRs.

From this it follows that any theory, such as utilitarianism, contractualism, or discourse theory, that incorporates such impartiality must either accept the PGC's commands or disassociate itself from this impartiality. This does not, of course, mean that these theories must hold that the PGC is dialectically necessary. The required commitment to the PGC secured by this argument is only as strong as the justification offered for the impartiality assumption. But, *given a commitment to the impartiality assumption*, commitment to the PGC cannot be resisted coherently if it is dialectically necessary for Albert to accept the PHI and there are GCAs.

This has implications for those who hold that there are human rights as currently conceived in international law. This is because the Preamble of the UDHR specifies that all "members of the human family", all "human beings", and all "human persons" are equal in inherent dignity and inalienable rights, and Article 1 of the UDHR proclaims that "All human beings are born free and equal in dignity and rights. They are endowed with reason and conscience and should act towards one another in a spirit of brotherhood."

If all human beings are equal in dignity and rights then all human *agents* (those humans endowed with reason and conscience) are equal in dignity and rights. Since the GCAs are necessary to do anything, they are also necessary to exercise any human right. So a grant of a human right to do anything can only be sincere if it involves a grant of a human right to possess the GCAs. Given the dialectical necessity of the PHI, since human agents are to act towards one another in a spirit of brotherhood, they must accept not only that they categorically ought to defend their own possession of the GCAs unless they are willing to accept generic damage to their ability to act, but also that they categorically ought to respect the possession of the GCAs by every other human agent (unless the other human agent is willing to accept generic damage to his or her ability to act). *Therefore*, they must act in accordance with the GRs of all human agents as understood by the PGC. It follows, *on pain of denying that all human beings are equal in dignity and inalienable rights*, that those who accept and implement the UDHR categorically ought to consider that all permissible action must be consistent with the requirements of the PGC. Ergo, all agents purporting to interpret and implement the UDHR, *and all legal instruments purporting to give effect to the UDHR*, must do so in accordance with the PGC. Even though the UDHR is not itself a legally binding instrument, legally binding instruments such as the *International Covenant on Civil and Political Rights* and the *European Convention on Human Rights* make it clear in their preambles that they exist to give effect to the UDHR. They can only do so on the understanding that it is the rights of the UDHR *as conceived by the UDHR* that they are giving effect to. In this sense, the dialectical necessity of the PHI entails that the PGC is the supreme principle of human rights.[3]

4 Rights of future generations

The following considerations/principles, some of which have already been mentioned, are important when applying the PGC to the question of rights of future agents.

I.   *All agents have the GRs equally in a strictly distributive rather than in an aggregative manner.* Thus, the strength of a right claim is unaffected by the number of current agents compared with the number of future agents. Certain forms of utilitarianism imply that there is more utility or disutility when there are more agents than when there are fewer agents and that the aggregated utility or disutility of a larger group counts for more than that of a smaller group, from which it follows that if there are more agents in the future than there are now then their claims to a particular GCA will outweigh our own. No such claims can be made under the PGC.

At the individual level, conflicts between the GRs of agents are to be dealt with by using the criterion of needfulness for action. Although numbers do not matter in this per se, they can have a distributive effect. So, for example, I might (depending on my wealth and the value of the euro in relation to it) be duty bound to give up €5 to help a starving man. But I cannot give up €5 to more than a very limited number of starving people without ending up starving myself. But the PGC requires me to give the same weight to my need for the GCAs as to others' need for the GCAs. It does not, therefore, require me to starve myself for others, though it will let me do so voluntarily (unless my doing so negatively impacts on the possession of the GCAs of yet other agents against their will). For this reason, application at the group level imposes duties on states and other groups rather than on individuals (see Gewirth 1978, 312–17). This will classically be the case with the problems with which the rights of future generations are concerned.

II.   *Agents have positive duties, not merely negative ones, to other agents.* However, because assisting others to protect their GRs can impose a burden on one's ability to protect one's own GCAs in a way that merely refraining from interfering with the GCAs of others does not, these burdens will often require collective action, and cannot be imposed on all individuals equally.

III.   *Because the GCAs must be valued categorically only instrumentally, agents have no intrinsic duty to preserve their own existence.* Consequently, Albert can only have duties to preserve his own existence if the required actions are instrumental to carrying out his duties to other agents. So, if he is a father with responsibilities to support members of his family, he may not commit suicide if this will result in them suffering serious damage to their GCAs against their will.

When applying this aspect of the PGC, it is important to appreciate that the fact that the GRs are rights under the "will" or "choice" conception of a right is not contradicted by the fact that they are rights to specific interests (the GCAs). What is characteristic of the will conception, as against an interest conception, is that the right-holder's right imposes a duty on other agents to respect what the right-holder has a right to in accordance with the right-holder's will. While the *content* of the GRs is provided by the GCAs, the *form* of these rights (their nature *as rights*), is determined by the way in which the claim to the GRs is justified, and this (via the dialectical necessity of the PHI) places action in accordance with the right-holder's interests under the control of the right-holder's will.

It follows, because Albert has a duty to treat Brenda in the same way in which it is *dialectically necessary* for him to wish to be treated himself, and so has no intrinsic duty to maintain his own existence (the PGC not supporting, or resting on, the claim that agents categorically ought to exist or be brought into existence),[4] that agents (like Agnes) do not have duties to bring other agents (like Brian) into existence unless this is necessary to maintain the GRs of other existing agents (like Cynthia) in accordance with their will.

Regarding our duties to future generations, this has an important consequence: other considerations notwithstanding, current generations must ensure that they do not act now so as to leave future generations worse off in relation to the GCAs than they themselves are or act to ensure that there are no future generations.[5]

But other considerations cannot be ignored. For example, there is continuity between current generations and future generations because future generations need to be brought up by previous generations. Also, members of the current generation were not born, and are not expected to all die, at the same time. Consequently, it is not possible to make decisions about the existence of future generations that do not impact on the rights of members of the current generation.

This suggests an argument for the existence of duties to protect the GCAs of future generations. Agnes must grant Cynthia (who, let us suppose, is younger than Agnes and will survive her) the GRs. Cynthia, similarly, must grant the GRs to Brian, who (let us suppose) will be born while Cynthia is alive but after Agnes dies. Consequently, Cynthia will have duties to respect Brian's possession of the GCAs that only Brian can release Cynthia from. Now, if Agnes acts so as to leave Brian in a position that impairs his ability to enjoy the GCAs, she will interfere with Cynthia's ability to comply with Cynthia's PGC-derived duties to protect Brian's GRs (which the PGC imposes on Cynthia because she is an agent). It follows that Agnes must accept a duty to respect Brian's possession of the GCAs. Otherwise he will fail to respect Cynthia as an agent in the way that the PGC requires.[6]

IV.   *What about the non-identity problem?* The argument just given is, essentially, to the effect that we must accept duties to future generations in order to respect the rights of those members of society who are/will be both our contemporaries and the contemporaries of (what to us are) future generations. As such, it might be said, it does not address the non-identity problem if this is restricted to the claim that we cannot have duties that are owed directly to future generations for their own sakes. Perhaps, but there are problems with the non-identity problem.

To begin with, this problem only arises if we have good reason to suppose that if Agnes does not do X (doing X being something that will place Brian in a GCA-disadvantaged position) then Brian will necessarily not exist. This is highly questionable. This presumption derives from thinking that reasoning which applies in "wrongful life" scenarios can be generally applied. A classic wrongful life scenario is one where a child has inherited a severe genetic condition from his or her parents, which could have been avoided by the mother having an abortion, and he or she now wishes to claim damages against the mother. Here, the premise of the non-identity problem clearly applies. The mother could not have prevented the child from having this condition unless she had ensured that the child would not be born. The premise also has some plausibility if extended to the case of a child raising a complaint against her mother for being damaged by the drinking or smoking habits of her mother during pregnancy. The union of a particular sperm and egg has an extremely low probability and is sensitive to very tiny changes in circumstance. Hence, it is not implausible to think that if the mother had changed her drinking and smoking habits so as to bring it about that any child she conceived would not be damaged in the way that her son or daughter is complaining about, her son or daughter would not have been conceived at all. But, for this reasoning to apply to the question of rights of members of future generations, we must accept the claim that if Agnes does anything other than X then Brian will never exist even if Brian is not a descendant of Agnes. At the very least, we must suppose that if sufficient people alter their behaviour so as bring about better life and social conditions for future generations then all the members of future generations will be different from those who will exist if current generations do not alter their behaviour. This is very implausible and it needs to be a necessary truth to render *incoherent* the idea of rights of future generations held against us.

However, the PGC framework does not need to rely on such speculative counter-arguments or caveats. From the perspective of the PGC, the non-identity problem rests on a fundamental misconception about what a GR or a human right is, and in particular about what the conditions are for Brian to hold a right against Agnes (or any other agent). Under the PGC, Brian is not granted the GRs because he is *Brian*. He is granted the GRs simply because he is an agent, and what makes him an agent is just what makes any and every agent an agent. Because the GRs are to be accorded on the basis of possession of agency, the agency of every agent is to be respected as the ground of the GRs. If "dignity" refers to the ground of the GRs, then to damage the agency of one agent against that agent's will is an affront to the dignity of every agent. This is so whether the PGC is justified on the basis of the wholly dialectically necessary argument or merely on the argument operating on the assumption that there are human rights. Given the dialectical necessity of the PHI, holding that human agents have rights simply by virtue of being human also leads to the conclusion that agency is the ground of human rights (hence, that in which human dignity resides). It is, consequently, simply irrelevant whether Agnes's actions will result in Brian existing or some other agent existing instead. Actions of Agnes that foreseeably threaten possession of the GCAs of any agents who will exist in the future more than alternative actions she can perform threaten the GRs of future agents even if not performing these actions will mean that the population of future agents will be a completely different one. On the factual assumptions generating the non-identity problem, Agnes has a choice between GCA-threatening outcomes for Brian and GCA-respecting outcomes for, say, Margaret (who will exist instead of Brian), but not between GCA-threatening outcomes for Brian and GCA-respecting outcomes for Brian. But this is irrelevant, *even if it were necessarily true*. What matters is that Agnes, in choosing what will be a GCA-threatening outcome for Brian, has chosen what she knows or should anticipate will be a GCA-threatening result for *an* agent. She has acted contrary to the dignity (the moral status) that agency confers.

V. *What of the challenge from epistemic uncertainty?* Allegedly, we cannot grant rights to agents who do not yet exist because we cannot know how they will wish to be treated and what they will regard as important, *and so on*. But for this to be relevant it must be the case that GRs must be granted as a function of the contingent preferences and choices, etc. that agents make. But the GRs are functions of interests (the GCAs) that agents have simply by being agents. The GCAs are invariant. We know that an agent will need the GCAs just because the agent is an agent. So, regardless of the contingent preferences that the agent will have, or the contingent circumstances in which the agent will exist, an agent must be accorded the GRs as soon as the agent comes into being.[7]

VI. *GRs are unaffected by an inability to enforce them.* Any idea that Brian cannot have a right against Agnes because he cannot enforce his claim against her (because he will not exist while Agnes is alive) is alien to the PGC framework, which operates with a strictly normative as against a positive conception of a right, which is to say that it distinguishes between the conditions for having a right and the conditions for enforcing a right.[8] Again, this is due to the fact that agents have the GRs simply because they are agents.

Consequently, the fact that Agnes cannot now be in contact with Brian can no more affect that Brian holds the GRs against Agnes than the fact that Brenda and Albert (contemporaries) are not currently in contact with each other can affect that Brenda holds the GRs against Albert. That *an* agent will foreseeably be the recipient of my actions is all that matters. It does not have to be some particular agent, because under the PGC any agent stands for all agents when what is at stake is possession of the GCAs.

So, if I am Robinson Crusoe and there is no one else around on my island, this does not mean that I do not have duties to other agents simply because they are not around for me to interact with. If and when they (e.g. Friday) arrive on the island, I will have to respect their GRs. This will not be because their appearance on the island created these rights: Friday will have had these rights all along, which are rights to have his need for the GCAs respected if and when he becomes a recipient of my actions, which is to say when my actions impact on his GCAs.

But, to apply this to future generations, we need to imagine that while Friday is not present, Robinson is anticipating his *invited* arrival. Indeed, to make it closer still, we should imagine that Robinson will have left the island before Friday arrives and will not be able to come back. The question to be asked is, "Must Robinson ameliorate his behaviour to ensure that (if/when) Friday arrives, Friday will be able to enjoy his GCAs?"

In general terms, the answer must be in the affirmative. If Robinson is not going to keep the island in a condition that enables Friday to have the GCAs, he should not have invited him there, or (if possible) should at least have warned him about the condition that the island will be in when he arrives. The latter cannot, however, apply to future generations because they do not have a choice about whether they will be brought into existence or not.

VII.   *Inequality between present and future generations must, in principle, be treated just like inequality within generations.* Again, this is because agents have the GRs simply because they are agents.

However, this does not mean that there are no differences between the ways in which we may act towards current and future generations. For one thing, if I have a generic need now, I have a prima facie right to attend to it. That I suspect that this will damage the GCAs of future generations does not mean that I may not attend to it. If it is not implausible that science will find ways to ameliorate the effects of an overuse of relevant resources by the time that Brian comes into being, Agnes might be able to justify using current resources in a way that would leave Brian worse off than herself on the happenstance that *such innovation does not occur.* In other words, there are limits to the precautionary measures that we need to take to protect future generations. But we must be careful here. The situation is very different when we are talking about using resources to meet our basic needs from when we are talking about using them to meet merely non-subtractive, let alone merely additive needs. It is one thing for Brazilians to chop down the Amazon rain forest *when and if they need to do so to make a living.* It is another for wealthy persons, already enjoying a lifestyle that fully satisfies basic needs (and more), to engage in activities that threaten basic GCAs in order to further enhance their own quality of life.

VIII.   *Wealthy current societies bear more responsibilities to future generations than do poorer societies.* This is for exactly the same reasons and in the same ways that they bear greater responsibilities to poorer current societies. The responsibilities go in two directions. They go in the direction of having an inhibition against further improving their own conditions (unless such improvement is not merely necessary but will be used to improve the lot of the less well-off more than simply trying to redistribute existing resources more equally). John Rawls's Maximin Principle is in line with this. They also go in the direction of the wealthier having a duty to contribute more to any redistribution of resources that is required.

However, this does not mean that poorer societies have no responsibilities to future generations. For example, in some poorer/traditional cultures, having many children is seen as a necessary means to ensure a decent level of existence in one's old age. This has come about because of the very high mortality rates that are historically a feature of such societies. Advances in medicine and the like have, however, led to a higher proportion of children surviving, thus putting greater burdens on resources. This renders the custom of having many children very counterproductive, and also illustrates that the application of the PGC cannot be reduced to a set of simple rules as against principles for consideration under the rubric of the PGC.

IX.   *Agents have duties to respect the generic interests of apparent non-agents, even though the PGC grants the GRs only to agents*, these generic interests being the interests of apparent non-agents that agents can take account of, which apparent non-agents would have rights to if they were agents, with the strength of these interests being proportional to how closely an apparent non-agent approaches being an apparent agent (see, for example, Beyleveld and Pattinson 2000, 2010). While this has no direct bearing on the rights of future generations, any duties to the environment that can be generated by such considerations impose duties on the current generation. These duties require behaviour that reduces the likelihood of actions that will impact negatively on future generations (cf. Gewirth 2001; Düwell 2014).

5 Concluding remarks

In this chapter I have tried to explain the PGC and I have also sketched middle-order principles and the general lines of thinking that come into play when trying to apply the PGC to the question of the rights of future generations. To flesh this out fully requires detailed case studies and scenarios for application, and I have not put any of these forward for consideration.

I readily acknowledge that the arguments presented against objections to the idea of rights of future generations are not uniquely available to Gewirthians. They can and should be deployed by all moral theories that operate with the idea that there are rights that are possessed simply by virtue of being human or being an agent.

Indeed, arguments that are not incompatible are presented against the non-identity problem by, for example, Baier (1981) and Bell (2011) in the specific context of anthropogenic climate change, while others have claimed, more broadly, that rights-based accounts assist with countering different versions of non-identity problems (e.g. Elliot 1989; Elliot 1997; Feinberg 1981; Partridge 1990; Woodward 1986).[9]

However, the Gewirthian approach is special because it is grounded in the strict rational necessity for agents of the PHI. This basis, whether or not it is extended to establish the PGC as dialectically necessary, or involves the additional presumption of impartiality inherent in the idea of a human right as currently conceived in international law (without arguing that it is strictly rationally necessary to accept that there are such human rights), provides a sufficient solution to the non-identity problem, even if the highly contestable factual premises driving this challenge are true. This is because such a grounding abstracts from all person-specific, individualistic aspects that give rise to the non-identity problem, while nevertheless starting from an agential perspective. Consequently, it retains the idea that immoral acts are acts that harm agents without relying on the notion of "harming" in the sense of comparative harm or making a particular person/agent worse off. Similarly, it defuses the challenge from epistemic uncertainty by focusing the content of rights on GCAs that are interests necessarily held by all agents. This is because, at its root, it sees a right not as the product of contingent choices made but as a logical consequence of the dialectical necessity of the PHI for agents.

Additionally, the PGC framework, through the GCAs being the content of fundamental rights, provides a rational procedure for adjudicating between conflicting rights that have the stringency of justification enjoyed by the PHI itself. And this can be applied within any theory of duties or rights.

Notes

1 This interprets Kant's claim that a categorical imperative is one "connected (completely a priori) with the concept of the will of a rational being as such" (1785, 4: 426) (see Beyleveld 2013b).
2 See, in particular, Beyleveld 2013a.
3 See, further, Beyleveld 2011.
4 The PGC does not require agents to treat others as *they wish* to be treated themselves, which would permit a sadomasochist to torture others against their will. The dialectical necessity of the PHI (the PGC being the universalization of the PHI, given recognition of the existence of GCAs) requires Albert to treat Brenda as Brenda *must wish* herself to be treated, which is to have her possession of the GCAs disposed of in accordance with her own will.
5 However, because it will be impossible in practice to reach agreement on a decision not to have any children in the future, the latter option is not a realistic strategy to avoid responsibility for our actions in relation to future generations. The fact that the Gewirthian approach also operates with the "will" conception does not create difficulties for its application to future generations on account of the fact that Agnes does not know whether Brian is prepared to suffer generic damage to his ability to act on account of her actions. Or, rather, the difficulty is no different from that faced by a doctor who is presented with an unconscious agent patient who needs life-saving treatment for which the doctor ideally needs the patient's consent because the operation will affect the patient's GCAs. The rational solution is to presume that the patient wishes to be treated unless there is explicit evidence to the contrary (like an advance directive), not merely on the grounds that most agents would wish to have treatment, but because (all things being equal) on the scale of degree of needfulness it is worse to fail to treat a patient who wishes to have life-saving treatment (because the result is

irreversible) than to treat a patient who does not wish to have life-saving treatment (the result is not necessarily irreversible: the patient could regain consciousness and refuse continued treatment).

6 Compare the treatment of Gosseries (2008) of this kind of scenario. I am grateful to Gerhard Bos of Utrecht University for reference to this scenario, although he has a slightly different viewpoint that is presented in Chapter 9 "A chain of status" in this volume.

7 However, although agents do not have a GR to their non-generic interests (their particular occurrent interests) as such, they do have a GR to pursue their particular occurrent interests to the extent that this pursuit does not interfere with the GCAs of other agents. But interference with the particular occurrent interests of other agents is inevitable in social life. To deal with such conflicts, the PGC prescribes that agents must be given the right to have their views on the pursuit of their particular occurrent interests represented and decided upon in a democratic way. This raises questions about *how* future, not yet existing agents can be granted this right (which must be separated from the question of *whether* they must be granted this right), since we do not know what their particular occurrent interests and choices will be. This issue is addressed in Beyleveld, Düwell and Spahn (2015).

8 It must, however, be recognized, as a point of fact, not as a normative principle, that the prospects of getting the current generation to honour its duties to future generations are even worse than those of getting it to comply with its intra-generational duties. To put it cynically, this is simply because future generations are not in any position to fight back. Disadvantaged members of the current generation may be at a disadvantage in fighting their cause, but they are not powerless. Members of future generations have absolutely no power to affect the actions of the current generation by their own actions, simply because they do not already exist. Future generations will just be stuck with what we leave them with and will not be able to hold us to account. For this reason, contractualism, particularly of the kind advocated by David Gauthier (1986), is in a very poor position to render itself consistent with the PGC.

9 There is also a rich literature on the wrongful life case of Parfit's non-identity problem, which discusses the moral and legal aspects of cases of children with diseases such as Huntington's disease or hereditary deafness (e.g. Harris 1990; Shiffrin 1999; Steinbock 2011).

References

Baier A. (1981) "The rights of past and future persons" in Partridge E. ed., *Responsibilities to future generations: environmental ethics* New York, Prometheus, 171–86.

Bell D. (2011) "Does anthropogenic climate change violate human rights?" *Critical Review of International Social and Political Philosophy*, 14 99–124.

Beyleveld D. (1991) *The dialectical necessity of morality: an analysis and defense of Alan Gewirth's principle of generic consistency* Chicago, University of Chicago Press.

Beyleveld D. (2011) "The PGC as the supreme principle of human rights" *Human Rights Review*, 13 1–18.

Beyleveld D. (2013a) "Williams' false dilemma: how to give categorically binding impartial reasons to real agents" *Journal of Moral Philosophy*, 10 204–26.

Beyleveld D. (2013b) "Korsgaard v. Gewirth on universalization: why Gewirthians are Kantians and Kantians ought to be Gewirthians" *Journal of Moral Philosophy*, Advance article 19 June 2013. doi: 10.1163/17455243–4681026.

Beyleveld D. and Bos G. (2009) "The foundational role of the principle of instrumental reason in Gewirth's argument for the principle of generic consistency: a response to Andrew Chitty" *King's Law Journal*, 20 1–20.

Beyleveld D. and Pattinson S.D. (2000) "Precautionary reason as a link to moral action" in Boylan M. ed., *Medical ethics* Upper Saddle River, NJ, Prentice Hall, 39–53.

Beyleveld D. and Pattinson S.D. (2010) "Defending moral precaution as a solution to the problem of other minds: a reply to Holm and Coggon" *Ratio Juris*, 23 258–73.

Beyleveld D., Düwell M. and Spahn A. (2015) "Why and how should we represent future generations in policy making?" *Jurisprudence* (forthcoming).

Düwell M. (2014) "Human dignity and future generations" in Düwell M., Braarvig J., Brownsword R. and Mieth D. eds, *The Cambridge handbook on human dignity* Cambridge, Cambridge University Press.

Elliot R. (1989) "The rights of future people" *Journal of Applied Philosophy*, 6 159–69.

Elliot R. (1997) "Contingency, community and intergenerational justice" in Fotion N. and Heller J. eds, *Contingent future persons* Dordrecht, Kluwer, 157–70.

Feinberg J. (1981) "The rights of animals and unborn generations" in Partridge E. ed., *Responsibilities to future generations: environmental ethics* New York, Prometheus, 139–50.

Gauthier D. (1986) *Morals by agreement* Oxford, The Clarendon Press.

Gewirth A. (1978) *Reason and morality* Chicago, University of Chicago Press.

Gewirth A. (2001) "Human rights and future generations" in Boylan M. ed., *Environmental ethics* Upper Saddle River, NJ, Prentice Hall, 207–12.

Gosseries A. (2008) "On future generations' future rights" *Journal of Political Philosophy*, 16 446–74.

Harris J. (1990) "The wrong of wrongful life" *Journal of Law and Society*, 17 90–105.

Kant I. (1785) *Groundwork of the metaphysics of morals* Gregor M ed. and trans., Cambridge, Cambridge University Press (1998).

Parfit D. (1987) *Reasons and persons* Oxford, The Clarendon Press.

Partridge E. (1990) "On the rights of future generations" in Scherer D. ed., *Upstream/downstream: issues in environmental ethics* Philadelphia, PA, Temple University Press, 40–60.

Shiffrin S. (1999) "Wrongful life, procreative responsibility, and the significance of harm" *Legal Theory*, 5 117–48.

Steinbock B. (2011) "The logical case for 'wrongful life'" *The Hastings Center Report*, 16 15–20.

Woodward J. (1986) "The non-identity problem" *Ethics*, 96 804–31.

12 Ecological rights of future generations

A capability approach

Rutger Claassen

1 Introduction

One of the central questions of our time is how to think about the environmental consequences of our activities for future generations.[1] There have been relatively few attempts to think about this question from the perspective of the capability approach. I will ask what a capability theory of justice should say about the question of ecological obligations to future generations. This investigation lies at the intersection between ecological and intergenerational justice. Ecological justice is about obligations to the human use of natural resources for production and consumption. Some environmental problems may be restricted to contemporaries (e.g. pollution from which only those people currently living suffer), while others will (also) have significance for future generations. Intergenerational justice encompasses but is broader than a narrow focus on environmental resources that present generations should leave behind for future generations (intergenerational justice also raises questions about pensions and education systems, etc.). The inquiry here concentrates on the area of overlap between ecological and intergenerational justice.

A capability theory of justice (hereafter CTJ) will answer the question by drawing upon two core features: a *CTJ is (1) a rights-based moral theory with (2) capabilities as the content of these rights*. It proposes to conceive of justice as a matter of protecting a set of rights to basic human capabilities. I will not say anything about the justification of rights to future generations here. Much work has been done about this elsewhere, and I presume that a CTJ can profit from this work to show why, if present generations have a right to basic capabilities, future generations can lay the same claim to such capabilities (for an overview of objections against this extension of rights into the future, and a refutation of these objections, see Bell 2011). Instead, this chapter focuses on the content of these rights.

First, I argue that we can extend capability protection to future generations by ascribing to them the same capabilities that current generations have, but this leaves open the question of which resources such a CTJ is to leave to future generations (section 2). The influential views of Rawls and Solow are that these resources should be conceived in terms of 'total capital' (section 3). I argue that a capability approach cannot accept the assumption of substitutability between natural and human-made capital in these approaches (section 4). I propose that a CTJ best fits with a combination of two ecological approaches focusing on the preservation of specific forms of natural capital: the ecological space approach and Daly's resource rules (section 5).

2 Capabilities and resources

The adoption of a capability metric does not dictate one specific way of conceptualizing ecological obligations. At least three different approaches can be distinguished. One can extend moral consideration to the same set of basic capabilities of future generations, introduce a new capability which protects future generations' environmental interests or introduce capabilities beyond humans to other species and ecosystems.

The first approach is defended by Amartya Sen.[2] He proposes that the capability metric should take the place of the concept of needs in the famous Brundtland definition of sustainable development. It then requires of us 'the preservation, and when possible expansion, of the substantive freedoms and capabilities of people today "without compromising the capability of future generations" to have similar – or more – freedom' (Sen 2009, 251–2). His defence of the capability metric in the intergenerational context implies a rejection of both the utilitarian criterion of 'maximizing the sum total of welfare of different generations' (Anand and Sen 2000, 2034) and the resourcist approach of preserving specific resources (Anand and Sen 2000, 2037). Instead, we need to preserve a generalized standard of living, or capacity for well-being. Edward Page's defence of the capability metric in the field of intergenerational justice similarly positions the capability approach as superior to resourcist and welfarist rivals (Page 2007, 464).

A second option is to create a special ecological capability. Breena Holland introduces 'sustainable ecological capacity' as a 'meta-capability'. She defines this capability as 'being able to live one's life in the context of ecological conditions that can provide environmental resources and services that enable the current generations' range of capabilities; to have these conditions now and in the future' (Holland 2008, 324). This capability is meant to support the realization of the *other* capabilities on a list like Nussbaum's (Nussbaum 2006). Her ecological capability is meant to apply to both current and future generations. The second option is therefore structurally analogous to the first one, in that current and future generations have the same capability set; the difference is that the ecological sphere is the object of a special self-standing capability in Holland's approach, but not in Sen's.

A third option is to introduce non-human capabilities. Here, nature itself becomes the bearer of a capability instead of a means to sustaining human capabilities. Given their capacities to function and flourish in species-specific ways, Nussbaum argues that animals are entitled to capabilities to their animal-specific functionings, just like humans (Nussbaum 2006). David Schlosberg objects that this implies an overly individualistic approach to animal flourishing (Schlosberg 2007, 147–52). He argues that we should ascribe capabilities to entire species and ecosystems:

> In applying the capabilities approach to nature, we do not need to have a particular animal or ecosystem express a desire for a particular functioning; rather, we need to recognize a different type of agency – a potential, a process, or a form of life illustrated by its history, ecology, way of being, and nonreason-based forms of communication.
>
> (Schlosberg 2007, 153)

This proposal, like Nussbaum's, in going beyond human capabilities, raises specific problems about the relation between human, animal and ecosystem capabilities (Cripps 2010). Because of the metaphysically demanding nature of these proposals, I will not consider them here and will remain agnostic about their potential.

The difference between the first two options is that the creation of an ecological capability makes enjoyment of necessary ecological conditions itself a matter of capability (and therefore of rights) protection. Which of these conceptualizations one chooses does not matter as much as one may be inclined to think at first glance. If the preservation of a resource is necessary for future generations to enjoy the same basic capabilities as current generations, then present generations are required to preserve it, whether or not this preservation is itself elevated to the status of a basic capability. If a goal is morally required, necessary means to achieve that goal are required as well. The level of environmental protection for future generations would therefore remain the same under both proposals. Because Holland specifies that the ecological meta-capability is about the conditions for the enjoyment of other basic capabilities, it adds nothing substantively to these other capabilities. The main function of introducing a separate capability seems to be to attract attention to the importance of ecological sustainability. It remains the case that ecological conditions are conditions for a list of basic capabilities, which does not itself include those conditions as a capability. In the interest of not inflating our list of basic capabilities unnecessarily, it seems better to me to follow Sen's strategy of founding a concern for sustainability on the (non-ecological) capabilities of future generations.

The next step is more important than this theoretical decision about the introduction of a separate ecological capability. Regardless of whether one introduces such a new capability or not, capability-related ecological obligations to future generations must ultimately be specified or translated in terms of *resources* (I use this term broadly to include ecosystem services). We can only affect the capabilities of future generations by bequeathing certain environmental resources (and institutions) to them. Logically, since we do not live at the same time as future generations (except for the overlap with the next generation), the only link between them and us is indirect, in the world that we leave behind. This means that even if capabilities are the best metric for expressing claims of justice, the intergenerational context requires us to go beyond capabilities and consider which resources will best realize their capabilities. It is up to future generations to use these resources in such a way that each member of these generations gets an equitable level of capabilities (this includes capability theories' stress on taking account of interpersonal differences in rates of conversion of resources to capabilities – we cannot do much about that since these individuals do not yet exist). We can only bequeath a resources package as a whole.

This turn to a resource metric may seem to be a radical break with the intragenerational context, in which the capability metric does seem to be appropriate (at least for those who accept the general arguments in its favour). However, the difference is less stark than one might suspect. Even in the intragenerational context, we need to specify what it means to protect a capability in terms of the resource inputs necessary to realize that capability. For example, realization of the capability to ride a bike or the capability to be well nourished requires resources (a bike and food, respectively). More comprehensively, the realization of most capabilities is a matter of combining at least three factors: personal skills (abilities/dispositions), resources and non-resource requirements (such as institutions and laws). One doesn't only need a bike; one also needs to know how to ride a bike and how to obey traffic regulations. All of these three factors require the specification of resources. Enhancing a person's skills requires training, which requires teachers that need to be paid a wage, and training equipment, etc. The capability approach can only be made useful for political purposes once we are willing to specify which resources are needed to realize a certain capability. Capabilities and resources are both necessary for a full specification of what needs to be done, as ends and means.

Systematic discussion about the linkages between resources and functionings are largely absent from the literature. There may be two explanations for this. First, for some capabilities it may be rather obvious which resources are needed to realize them (such as the capability to ride a bike). All critical attention then goes to the issue of determining adequate individual resource inputs given differences in conversion rates (pregnant women needing a different diet, physically disabled persons an adjusted bike, etc.). Second, much of the specification of the appropriate resources will be context-dependent (a matter of 'local specification', as Nussbaum says). Even though being well nourished is a basic capability everywhere, there are marked cultural differences regarding the kinds of food that are judged appropriate. Both of these factors are absent in the intergenerational context. It is not obvious which resources need to be preserved for future generations. As we will see hereafter, there are several distinct and competing theoretical possibilities. Moreover, by definition, we lack knowledge about future generations' preferences for context-dependent specification. In these circumstances, leaving the resource question unspecified is unsatisfying both theoretically and practically.[3] *How much of which* resources should present generations preserve for future generations?

3 Total capital approaches

In this section I will discuss two very influential proposals to answer the resource question: Robert Solow's view of sustainability and John Rawls' just savings principle. Solow's view is discussed here because it is the standard view among economists. Rawls' principle has been widely influential among political philosophers. I will argue that a CTJ cannot accept either view, for the same reason: they both disregard specific human functionings and their resource requirements.

Solow starts from the following definition of sustainability: we should 'leave to the future the option or the capacity to be as well off as we are' (Solow 1993, 181), also formulated as a 'generalized capacity to create well-being, not any particular thing or any particular natural resource' (Solow 1993, 182). His argument for defining sustainability this way is that we do not know future people's preferences. Thus, while the ultimate normative goal is future generations' satisfaction of their preferences, the goal of sustainability can only be stated in terms of a generalized capacity. It is up to future people to decide what to do with this capacity. The second step is that the means to satisfy this goal is the preservation of a stock of undifferentiated capital. This presupposes that resources are substitutable. Solow stresses that we 'do not owe to the future any particular thing' (Solow 1993, 181) because of the possibilities for substitution. If one form of capital (such as natural resources) is depleted, it can always be replaced by another form of capital (such as man-made capital) to sustain a given output level. The generalized capacity for well-being can be realized by compensating for current consumption (of any sort) by investing in future assets (of any sort). Let's call this Solow's 'constant capital principle' (my term):

> *The Constant Capital Principle*: the currently available stock of capital should at least be preserved at a constant (non-declining) level.

A third feature of Solow's view is that he presumes there is something special about today's level of the generalized capacity. This is what is to be preserved. I add 'at least' because we can decide to leave the future more capital than we have inherited from our ancestors. The obligation of sustainability, however, only demands a constant level starting from today.

Rawls defended a just savings principle for future generations. It may be summed up as follows:

> *The Just Savings Principle*: a) real capital should be accumulated up to the point at which just institutions are established (accumulation stage); b) after this point no further savings are required (steady-state stage).

The belief in substitution is the common denominator between Solow's and Rawls' view. The object of savings, for Rawls, is 'real capital', which he argues can take 'various forms from net investment in machinery and other means of production to investment in learning and education' (Rawls 1999, 252). Rawls does not explicitly discuss natural capital; indeed, he does not discuss sustainability or ecological concerns at all. His use of the concept of real capital implies, as the just savings principle stands, that natural capital would have been subsumed in this category of real capital. His use of an aggregate, undifferentiated concept of capital is exactly the same as Solow's.[4] One difference is that for Rawls the leading normative criterion is the establishment of just institutions (his first principle of justice). For Solow the guiding normative criterion is utilitarian: to preserve a generalized capacity for well-being among future generations. This reflects a deep difference in theoretical commitments: Rawls is interested in the realization of a just society, while Solow is interested in levels of well-being. Another difference is that Solow implies there is something morally privileged about current levels of capital, so that it is obligatory to make sure that future generations are at least no worse off than we are. This requirement of constancy comes back in Rawls' steady-state stage, but it is distinctive of Rawls' view that the preservation of the current level only becomes normatively relevant when just institutions are established. This necessitates a separate accumulation phase as long as this goal has not been reached. What is really important, then, is the requirement to establish just institutions, and the normative relevance of the present level of capital is contingent on that requirement.

Should a CTJ adopt any of these principles? It is clear that a CTJ will be on Rawls' side with respect to the two points in which he differs from Solow. First, like Rawls, a CTJ reasons about the obligations to future generations from a perspective of justice. Whatever we ultimately conclude about the level and composition of capital (resources) to leave to future generations, the aim is to provide the conditions for a just society in the future. For Rawls, this is a society in which the basic liberties are preserved, while a CTJ spells this out in the (closely related) terms of a list of basic capability rights. Second, like Rawls, a CTJ cannot accept a normatively privileged position for current levels of capital. Whether remaining at a constant level is normatively required depends on whether basic capabilities are currently realized or not by that capital level and on whether that level is itself sustainable for the future population. Whether this requires an accumulation stage is something that I will discuss in section 5. Let's focus first on the main point of contention: Solow's and Rawls' belief in the substitutability of different forms of capital.

4 Substitutability and the capability approach

Convictions about substitutability provide a watershed in thinking about sustainability. Theories of sustainability are often divided into theories of 'weak sustainability' and 'strong sustainability' (Dobson 1998; Holland 1999; Norton 1999). Theories of weak sustainability allow for substitution between natural and man-made capital. These theories are standard in economics (Beckerman 1994, 1995). Theories of strong substitutability are sceptical about the possibilities for compensating one sort of capital with another. These theories are more popular among ecologists (Daly 1995, 1996). As we have seen when discussing Solow's view, the economist's reason for not differentiating between man-made and natural capital is that both are taken to be infinitely substitutable. We can compensate for a decline in natural capital by additions in man-made capital. Ecologists, on the other hand, argue that any form of economic output relies on some physical input (natural capital). We can substitute computers for type-writers, and typewriters for pencil and paper, but we cannot write without any physical substrate. Each of these options requires some natural capital, albeit that in each the combination of man-made (technology) and natural capital is different. These two forms of capital are complementary, not substitutes.

On both sides of this dispute, people argue about the *functions* that any piece of economic output is supposed to fulfil. This leads to two different questions, as Axel Gosseries has rightly argued:

> There is a sense in which every object is unique (token-uniqueness) and therefore unsubstitutable. But if *we agree that what matters in a good is the function it fulfills*, we can phrase the problem as follows. If a good, be it human-made (e.g. Brussels' Grand-Place or Van Gogh's sunflowers) or natural (the Mont Blanc or an endangered species of butterfly), is con-sidered as the only one to be able to fulfill a function, we then need to see if other functions are not more important. We could argue, for example, that flooding a unique forest to build a dam would help reduce greenhouse effects to the benefits of future generations. Can good g-2 be substituted for good g-1 to fulfill the same function f-1, and can function f-2 be substituted for function f-1?
>
> (Gosseries 2001, 343–4) (my italics)

These two questions are often conflated in the dispute about substitutability. The substitutability of two goods to fulfil the same function is a matter of fact: either good g-2 (Van Gogh's sunflowers) can or cannot fulfil the same function f-1 (aesthetic experience) as well as good g-1 (Rembrandt's *The Night Watch*) can. Let's call this 'factual substitutability'.

The substitutability of f-2 for f-1 is a different, normative question: do we want to abandon the availability of function f-1 (aesthetic experience) in our societies and have it replaced with function f-2 (physical exercising)? There is no possible fact of the matter that can answer that question. Let's consider Solow's point of view from this angle:

> The correct principle ... when we use up something that is irreplaceable, whether it is minerals or a fish species, or an environmental amenity, then we should be thinking about providing a substitute of equal value, and the vagueness comes in the notion of value. The something that we provide in exchange could be knowledge, could be technology. It needn't even be a physical object.
>
> (Solow 1993, 184)

There is an important ambiguity in this passage. For how can we substitute something of 'equal value' if the original thing was 'irreplaceable'? Solow must have dropped the requirement that the replacement investment is a substitute for the exhausted resource, at least in the factual sense mentioned above. He presupposes that it does not matter which concrete functions can be fulfilled, as long as there is a constant level of 'potential to fulfil functions'. Only one function, the abstract 'function-fulfilment', understood as the capacity to produce abstract levels of preference satisfaction, seems to do the work. Under this definition, we can always make sure that people are able to reach an equal level of preference satisfaction, even if some specific preferences can no longer be fulfilled because the goods necessary to fulfil them have been exhausted. We simply make sure that we bring the person to the same level of preference satisfaction by satisfying some of his/her other preferences.

From a capability perspective, this cannot be accepted. The capability theorist's position on substitutability is to accept factual substitutability but reject normative substitutability. The distinction is vital, and the fact that it is overlooked by those who have thought about substitutability from a capability perspective means that their positions do not give a sufficiently clear account of the issue (Holland 2008, 329; Page 2007, 457; Scholtes 2011, 16). This is striking, since, as we see from the quote by Gosseries, obtaining more clarity on substitutability *presupposes introducing the language of functionings*. While not explicitly endorsing a capability theory himself, Gosseries shows us something that cannot be understood in utilitarian or resourcist terms, but requires thinking in terms of what resources do for human functionings.

First, a capability theory can accept factual substitutability. Future generations should have access to the same capabilities to function as current generations do. To the extent that different goods can give them the same capabilities to function, their substitutability is morally unobjectionable. We can thus agree with Solow's argument that a full belief in non-substitutability is absurd, because this would mean that nothing in the world could be touched or used (Solow 1993, 180). We are allowed to develop and replace resources as long as we can fulfil the same functions. Whether we can do so is a factual dispute (Holland 1999, 52). It may be hard to judge whether a given replacement resource is really sufficiently available to replace an exhausted resource. It may be a matter of interpretation as to whether the two resources really fulfil the same function. But, given a list of functions, the questions should be answerable. Note that this requires decisions about the level of specificity at which we define functionings. The function of 'eating fish' cannot survive the exhaustion of all fishery resources, while the function of 'being adequately nourished' can. Questions about factual substitutability require a prior answer to the issue of which functions we think are normatively required.[5]

This problem becomes highly relevant when we consider the following objection to accepting factual substitution: we value many species, ecosystems, landscapes and natural sites because of their aesthetic or expressive value to us. If so, then these ecological goods can by definition never be replaced. Note that this objection does not rely on the controversial ascription of 'intrinsic value' to (parts of) nature. The value of the ecological good is still a value to us, in terms of our functioning. We can confine ourselves to an anthropocentric framework and still think that there is no substitute for our enjoyment of a specific unspoiled forest or coastline (Birnbacher 2002, 193). Non-substitutability here is an artefact of defining the functioning in terms of the resource, i.e. 'enjoying the Grand Canyon' instead of 'enjoying some piece of unspoiled nature'. The distinction between resource and function then collapses. In response, we should say that it is hard to see how 'enjoying the Grand Canyon' could ever be constitutive of human flourishing or dignity. Many people have lived perfectly fine lives without seeing the Grand Canyon. Basic human functions therefore have to be formulated at a higher level.

Second, normative substitutability between basic functionings must be rejected. This reflects a core commitment of a CTJ to the separate importance of each basic capability, which should not be sacrificed for one or more other capabilities. A capability theory is different from utilitarian theories in dealing with uncertainty about future preferences. The preferences of future generations are by definition unknown. If we – following Solow – substitute man-made capital for natural capital because it provides the same level of capacity for well-being, then we necessarily rely on *current* experiences of human well-being and the relation between resources and well-being. Good A typically provides the average current person with 10 units of well-being, while good B provides that person with 20 units of well-being. However, given the malleability of preferences, this might be different in the future. The utilitarian argument therefore illegitimately extends current experiences to future ones when calculating which resources are necessary (or if it does not, the theory must remain vacuous). By using current experiences to determine the mix of man-made and natural capital that we will leave behind, we are imposing our preferences on the future (Scholtes 2011, 16).

By contrast, a capability theory considers basic human functionings to be stable over time. Future generations will need nourishment, health care, shelter and physical security, etc. just like we do. This is a secure bet. Of course we cannot preclude the possibility that human beings will transform radically in the future into some other kind of species with very different types of basic functionings. But this possibility is so remote and speculative that it is unproductive in relation to thinking about our obligations to the future. Anyhow, in practical terms we can only bequeath resources to the *next* generation, not to the far future. If humans change radically, this will probably be a long-term process which may lead intermediate generations to adapt the mix of man-made and natural capital to respond to these changes.

A more serious problem is that we do not know which resources may fulfil these stable human functions in the future. Even if we know that future people may require health care, we do not know which plants we need to preserve to tackle future diseases (think of new diseases, or the development of technology to extract medicines from plants). We provide for our basic functionings with a highly specific mix of resources, which is itself variable both diachronically (changes over time due to innovations) and synchronically (subject to cultural differences between societies). We always and necessarily impose on the future a specific mix of man-made and natural capital. The only thing we can safely say is that a society which determines its mix on the basis of its own preferred way of realizing (current and future) basic functions leaves to the future the possibility of basic functions being satisfied in that very same way. Our actions should not completely foreclose future possibilities of finding *other* goods to fulfil the same functions. It is open to future generations to try to do so. However, they will have to do so within the confines of what they have received from previous generations – our actions unavoidably create a path dependency, both in man-made capital (our laws and institutions, the state of technology and our cultural values, etc.) and in natural capital (what we conserve and how). Even if we could avoid this, it is unclear whether a mandate would be required. We normally judge it legitimate for parents to acquaint their children with all kinds of ideas, habits and values, so long as they leave them to lead their own lives once they are grown up. In the same way, we may try to convince future generations that we have found valuable ways (capital mixes) to satisfy our basic functions – on condition that we leave it open to them to find other ways to satisfy theirs.

This discussion of substitutability leads us to the conclusion that man-made capital may be substituted for natural capital only to the extent that the substitute is equally well able to satisfy future generations' basic human functions. Given the specificity of these functions and the specificity of the natural capital that we now use to satisfy our basic functions, sustainability in a CTJ can be expressed as follows:

> *Capability Principle*: the stock of natural capital (either the current stock or an equivalent one) that is necessary to satisfy the set of basic human functions needs to be preserved.

5 Ecological approaches

The capability principle is still quite abstract; how can it be further specified? In this section I will present two of the best-known ecological approaches to sustainability, which both have in common a focus on the preservation of specified amounts or types of natural capital (in contrast to Solow's and Rawls' theories). These are the ecological space approach and Daly's resource rules. I will argue that a capability theory must endorse a modified and combined version of these approaches. Some present these resourcist approaches as rival metrics to the capability metric (Page 2007; Vanderheiden 2008, 452). Instead, I argue that they are the best expression of its normative commitments.

The aim of the ecological space approach is to make sure that the aggregate level of ecological space available on earth is not exceeded. The guiding thought is to consider the ecological burden that production and consumption impose upon the earth's ecosystems. When that burden becomes too heavy, this will cause damage to future generations by way of ecological degradation and natural disasters, etc. The prevailing way of thinking about climate change is one example of this approach. The available ecological space for carbon emissions can be defined in terms of a maximum number of (yearly) emissions that the earth's atmosphere can absorb, given predictions that exceeding this maximum will presumably cause dangerous temperature rises which will lead to harms to future generations. Converting all ecological pressures on earth to a common denominator and aggregating them gives us a maximum ecological burden that man can put on the planet before this will have severe detrimental effects upon the planet's ability to sustain human and animal life. The ecological footprint is the best-known aggregate indicator which expresses all ecological activities in terms of acres of land use. Using this indicator, we can derive the following 'ecological ceiling principle':

> *The Ecological Ceiling Principle*: (a) the maximum ecological space (acres per year) available on earth should not be exceeded; and (b) faced with previous violations of (a), ecological space should be underused to the extent necessary to compensate for these violations.

Three remarks are in order. First, ecological space is defined in terms of a spatio-temporal indicator. Human interactions with the environment can be split into two parts: inputs and outflows. Economic processes use natural resources as input and dump waste or pollution as output in natural sinks. Nature renews resources and absorbs pollution at certain rates. Not overusing the available ecological space means not using resources and sinks at a higher rate than nature can compensate for. Violation of this prescription results in a situation of ecological *overshoot*: economic activity overburdens the ecological space, with potentially harmful consequences for future generations.[6] Second, a (prolonged) situation of historical overshoot will have to be compensated for by using less than the available ecological space, up to the point at which ecological equilibrium is restored (see (b) above). This can be compared to a situation in which a person aims to have a certain level of savings in his/her account (say, €10,000) as a buffer in year one, spends €5,000 in year two and then saves €5,000 in year three to get back to the target level. Third, this says nothing about the distribution of ecological space among the current population. Tim Hayward and Steve Vanderheiden have used the concept of ecological space in several publications as an alternative to standard metrics for discussing the distribution of ecological burdens among contemporaries (Hayward 2006, 2007; Vanderheiden 2008, 2009). I remain agnostic about this question. For simplicity, the global society is treated as one unit which must not overshoot ecological boundaries.

A second ecological approach to sustainability is given in ecological economist Herman Daly's guidelines for resource management. His rules prescribe how every single resource or sink on earth should be treated. He formulates them as follows:

Output rule: waste outputs are within the natural absorptive capacities of the environment (nondepletion of the sink services of natural capital).

Input rules: (a) For renewable inputs, harvest rates should not exceed regeneration rates (nondepletion of the source services of natural capital); (b) For nonrenewable inputs the rate of depletion should be equal to the rate at which renewable substitutes can be developed.

(Daly 1995, 50)

Let's refer to these as Daly's 'constant resource principles'. These resource principles disaggregate different forms of natural capital, whereas the ecological space approach is an aggregate indicator. This key difference explains why we need to combine both of them from the perspective of a CTJ. The constant resource principles are necessary because a capability theory's focus on preserving specific functions requires the preservation of those *specific* resources which are necessary for that goal. Under the ecological space approach, we would be allowed to overuse resource A if we compensate for this by underusing resource B so that we stay within the prescribed maximum resource use. Such trade-offs are not allowed under Daly's resource principles: each resource is to be preserved separately. This is why the ecological space approach cannot be sufficient on its own. Resource A might be vital to a prescribed functioning. We therefore need a focus on specific resources that are necessary to realize basic functions. The resource principles make room for such a focus.

However, we need to modify the formulation of these principles slightly, for in their present formulation they pertain to all resources indiscriminately, while a CTJ is only concerned with resources whose preservation is necessary from the standpoint of its own capability-oriented prescriptions. Therefore, we have to add to the (non-)renewable inputs the qualifier 'necessary to realize basic functions'. The consequence is that natural resources (if there are any) that are not necessary for this goal may be used unsustainably. Similarly, we need to add to waste outputs the qualifier 'in so far as their depletion threatens basic human functions'. These modifications are in line with the spirit of Daly's principles. The demand for substitution of non-renewable resources in Daly's second input principle clearly presupposes a concern with preserving specific functions. The additions remain necessary, however, for the underlying function may or may not be necessary from the perspective of justice.

A second qualifier is the element of constancy. Daly's principles are similar to the economic constant capital principle in that they prescribe that currently available stocks of natural capital should be preserved at constant (non-declining) levels. There is no concern with the absolute level of each of these resources or with whether that level is enough for (current and/or) future generations to meet their basic capabilities. We saw how Rawls' principle recognized this problem. Similarly, a CTJ needs to adapt Daly's resource principles. If, due to historical overuse, a present stock of resources is insufficient to meet current and future capabilities, then rates of current use (depletion and/or pollution) need to be more stringent than the ones which only keep the resource at current levels. This addition functions as a rectification of past injustices.

With these modifications in place, the resource principles are the first component of a CTJ's operationalization of duties to future generations. They need to be complemented, however, with the ecological ceiling principle, because the resource principles on their own may not be enough. This can be seen when we reflect on the distinction between the source side and the sink side of our relations with the natural environment. On the source side, adherence to the input principles for each resource taken separately automatically leads to an aggregate situation which remains within the global ceiling. On the sink side, however, we can imagine a situation in which a global sink (such as the atmosphere, or the oceans) is overpolluted, despite the fact that this sink would be able to absorb pollution from each form of waste output taken separately. In other words, the acceptable rate of pollution for each form of waste output needs to be adjusted depending on the existence of other forms of waste for the same sink. If this is not done, then we might face a situation of global overshoot despite the resource principles being honoured on the micro-level.

Thus, a combination of Daly's resource principles for resource management, and a global ecological space approach is the most promising as an operationalization of the abstract idea of justice for future generations in terms of a set of basic capabilities. These principles give content to its abstract requirement of sustainability: we have to preserve a stock of natural capital (either the current stock or an equivalent one) that is necessary to satisfy a set of basic human functions.

6 Conclusion

In this chapter I have considered what a capability approach to justice would say about the problem of ecological obligations to the future. The capability approach differs from standard Rawlsian and economic approaches to sustainability mainly because of its commitment to normative, in contrast to factual non-substitutability. An important insight here is that rejecting full substitutability implies a commitment to something like a concept of human functionings, which is the core of the capability approach. I have shown how a capability approach would endorse a combination of macro- and micro-ecological approaches to sustainable resource management. This does not solve concrete policy issues concerning ecological sustainability, but hopefully gives a clear sense of the direction in which a capability approach would point for approaching those issues.

Notes

1 I would like to thank Gerhard Bos, Tim Meijers and Lieske Voget-Kleschin for written comments. Thanks are due also to audiences at the Societas Ethica Annual Conference (August 2013) and the 'Human Rights and a Green Environment for Future Generations' ESF workshop at Soesterberg (October 2013). The work received funding under a VENI grant 'The Political Theory of Market Regulation' from the Dutch National Science Foundation (NWO).

2 I do not consider Nussbaum's theory. She merely states that Rawls' theory provides an adequate answer for the intergenerational context (Nussbaum 2006, 23). For the inadequacy of that position, see Watene (2013).
3 This is equally true for other non-resourcist theories, e.g. utilitarians can no more maximize well-being or the preference satisfaction of future generations directly than capability theorists can realize their capabilities.
4 Here, I interpret Rawls as not differentiating between different types of capital. This leaves open whether his approach, and the just savings principle, are compatible with such a differentiation. One might then argue that Rawls is unclear about the matter, but such a differentiation is not necessarily 'un-Rawlsian'.
5 Note that there may be limits to factual substitutability in the economic approach as well. This is because at some point substitution of natural capital by man-made capital may no longer be able to preserve the same level of well-being. This limit may allow for more sacrifice of natural capital than any limits dictated by preserving a range of specific functions, but it is still a limit.
6 One could also formulate the principle as a threshold (instead of ceiling) concept: we have a situation of overshoot when on the aggregate there is too *little* natural capital available. This seems to fit better with the other sustainability indicators: it is about having a sufficient level of natural capital (the threshold concept brings out the sufficientarian nature of the principle).

References

Anand S. and Sen A. (2000) 'Human development and economic sustainability' *World Development*, 28(12) 2029–49.
Beckerman W. (1994) '"Sustainable development": is it a useful concept?' *Environmental Values*, 3 191–209.
Beckerman W. (1995) 'How would you like your "sustainability", sir? Weak or strong? A reply to my critics' *Environmental Values*, 4 169–79.
Bell D. (2011) 'Does anthropogenic climate change violate human rights?' *Critical Review of International Social and Political Philosophy*, 14(2) 99–124.
Birnbacher D. (2002) 'Limits to substitutability in nature conservation' in Oksanen M. and Pietarinen J. ed., *Philosophy and Biodiversity* Cambridge, Cambridge University Press, 180–96.
Cripps E. (2010) 'Saving the polar bear, saving the world: can the capabilities approach do justice to humans, animals and ecosystems?' *Res Publica*, 16 1–22.
Daly H. (1995) 'On Wilfred Beckerman's critique of sustainable development' *Environmental Values*, 4 49–55.
Daly H. (1996) *Beyond growth* Boston, MA, Beacon Press.
Dobson A. (1998) *Justice and the environment. Conceptions of environmental sustainability and theories of distributive justice* Oxford, Oxford University Press.
Gosseries A. (2001) 'What do we owe the next generation(s)?' *Loyola of Los Angeles Law Review*, 35 293–355.
Hayward T. (2006) 'Global justice and the distribution of natural resources' *Political Studies*, 54(2) 349–69.
Hayward T. (2007) 'Human rights versus emissions rights: climate justice and the equitable distribution of ecological space' *Ethics & International Affairs*, 21(4) 431–50.
Holland A. (1999) 'Sustainability: should we start from here?' in Dobson A. ed., *Fairness and futurity. Essays on environmental sustainability and social justice* Oxford, Oxford University Press, 46–68.

Holland B. (2008) 'Justice and the environment in Nussbaum's "capabilities approach": why sustainable ecological capacity is a meta-capability' *Political Research Quarterly*, 61(2) 319–32.

Norton B. (1999) 'Ecology and opportunity: intergenerational equity and sustainable option' in Dobson A. ed., *Fairness and futurity. Essays on environmental sustainability and social justice* Oxford, Oxford University Press, 118–50.

Nussbaum M. (2006) *Frontiers of justice* Cambridge, MA, The Belknap Press.

Page E. (2007) 'Intergenerational justice of what: welfare, resources or capabilities?' *Environmental Politics*, 16(3) 453–69.

Rawls J. (1999) *A theory of justice* (rev. edn) Oxford, Oxford University Press.

Schlosberg D. (2007) *Defining environmental justice: theories, movements, and nature* Oxford, Oxford University Press.

Scholtes F. (2011) *Environmental sustainability in a perspective of the human development and capability approach* Background paper for the Human Development Report 2011 "Sustainability and equity: a better future for all".

Sen A. (2009) *The idea of justice* Cambridge, MA, The Belknap Press.

Solow R. (1993) 'Sustainability: an economist's perspective' in Dorfman R. and Dorfman N. eds, *Economics of the Environment*, 3rd edn New York, Norton, 179–87.

Vanderheiden S. (2008) 'Two conceptions of sustainability' *Political Studies*, 56 435–55.

Vanderheiden S. (2009) 'Allocating ecological space' *Journal of Social Philosophy*, 40(2) 257–75.

Watene K. (2013) 'Nussbaum's capability approach and future generations' *Journal of Human Development and Capabilities*, 14(1) 21–39.

Part IV

Implications and implementation

13 On current food consumption and future generations

Is there a moral need to change our food consumption in order to safeguard the human rights of future generations?

Franck L.B. Meijboom

1 Introduction

Food is essential to live a decent life. This has been recognized in the 1948 *Universal Declaration of Human Rights* (UDHR). The Declaration acknowledges food as an essential part of an adequate standard of living and speaks about a right to food. This right is often translated in terms of the right to food security, i.e. the right to have access to sufficient, safe and nutritious food. Making this right operational has turned out to be quite complicated in the last five decades (e.g. Food and Agriculture Organization of the UN 2003). Wars, corruption and natural disasters, for instance, still result in serious food security problems. In addition, the current discussion on the right to food is further complicated by three related developments. First, the growing world population is estimated to total nine billion people in 2050. This change in global demography means that the level of food security is less self-evident for the affluent world too. For instance, in Europe there is renewed attention on food security. The European Commission acknowledges that Europe will be challenged by 'increased competition for limited and finite natural resources' (Commission of the European Communities 2011). With this claim, Europe and other continents are – in spite of all their differences – in a similar position: they need to think about how they can guarantee food security in the future. Second, food security is influenced by questions about the ecological sustainability of food production and consumption (Food and Agriculture Organization of the UN 2011). This has resulted in a search for innovative ways to produce food and debates on how to deal with related basic securities such as water, energy and other natural resources, but also in debates on food consumption. As Lang and Barling point out, 'The discourse about future consumption patterns is now inexorably being drawn into a debate about whether Western patterns are replicable globally, let alone damaging the West' (2012, 319). In other words, the debates on food security are no longer just about *what* to produce and consume now, but also about *how* we should consume and produce food. These debates are further complicated by a third development: the trend of defining the right to food in a broader way than in terms of mere access to nutrition and simply as a right of the current generation. In 2003, the Food and Agriculture Organization of the UN (FAO) had already defined how food security 'exists when all people, at all times, have physical, social and economic access to sufficient, safe and nutritious food which meets their dietary needs and food preferences for an active and healthy life' (Food and Agriculture Organization of the UN 2003, 29). This definition deliberately includes many more aspects than the claim that one has a right to a minimum amount of nutrients to survive. Furthermore, the link between sustainability, and food production and consumption leads to debates about duties vis-à-vis future generations.

Given this changing context, I aim to focus in this chapter on the question of whether the right to food and the related basic rights of future generations can be moral imperatives that will make us change our current food consumption patterns. This question implies: (a) that we can legitimately speak about a right to food that corresponds with duties; and (b) that future generations have rights in a way that can result in claims on our current actions. Since the latter claim has been discussed elsewhere in this book, I will now turn first to the question of whether we can speak about a human right to food.

2 Real food, but also real rights?

As mentioned above, the UDHR (1948) explicitly mentions the right to food. Nonetheless, there is still an ongoing debate on the standing of the right to food. The reason for questioning the position of this right is not limited to this specific right, but holds equally for any other social and cultural human right that is listed in the UDHR and in the 1966 *International Covenant on Economic, Social and Cultural Rights* (ICESCR). The debate focuses on the questions of: (a) to what extent it is possible to identify the holders of the moral duties that correspond to rights and the extent to which such duties are enforceable; and (b) whether these social rights manage to satisfy the proviso of practical feasibility (cf. Hahn 2012).

Let me start with the latter problem. Shue distinguishes a set of three correlative duties that are assumed by basic rights: duties to avoid depriving; duties to protect from deprivation; and duties to aid the deprived (1996, 52). In practice, the duties to *protect* from deprivation in particular lead to questions about feasibility in relation to the right to food. As a consequence, O'Neill argues that

> it is plausible to think that rights not to be killed or to speak freely are matched by and require universal obligations not to kill or not to obstruct free speech; but a universal right to food cannot be simply matched by a universal obligation to provide an aliquot morsel of food.
>
> (2000, 135)

The lack of such an obligation implies, according to O'Neill, that 'no claim to rights has the faintest chance of making a real difference' (2002). In other words, social rights run the risk of being unfeasible to fulfil and consequently they can easily remain empty. Thus, it has been argued that for a theory of human rights it would be better to focus on 'human rights proper'. This includes rights to life, personal liberty, personal property and equal treatment under the law (Rawls 1999, 78–80). In relation to these rights, it is possible to define clear duties and identify what one should do. This is not to deny that it can be relevant in a political or social context to refer to rights to food or shelter. However, these are – in O'Neill's words – 'manifesto rights', i.e. the result of rhetoric that may start from genuine and admirable intentions rather than a reference to claimable rights (cf. Feinberg and Narveson 1970, 254–5).

Moreover, O'Neill emphasizes that the first problem mentioned above, the lack of clarity about the identification of the holders of the duties that correspond to rights, is also related to the right to food. She claims that

> unless the obligation to provide food to each claimant is actually allocated to specified agents and agencies, this 'right' will provide meagre pickings. The hungry know that they have a problem. What would change their prospects would be to know that it was others' problem too, and that specified others have an obligation to provide them with food. Unless obligations to feed the hungry are a matter of allocated justice rather than indeterminate beneficence, a so-called 'right to food', and the other 'rights' of the poor, will only be 'manifesto' rights.
>
> (O'Neill 1986, 101)

The combination of the problem of the identification of the duty holder and the feasibility problem results in a tension between, on the one hand, a shared understanding of food as essential for daily life and, on the other hand, the problem that a right to food seems neither claimable nor effective.

One way to address this tension is to stress that the 'duty holder identification' problem is not exclusive to food. Heilinger, for instance follows this line when he stresses that 'no one has claimed that it would be a simple task to precisely identify the matching obligation of a given right' (2011, 191). Furthermore, especially in the case of food, the problem does not seem to be so evident. It is generally accepted that the right to food implies that the set of three correlative duties results in state obligations to respect and protect its citizens (cf. Economic and Social Council 1999). National states, but also supranational organizations such as the FAO, consider themselves to be responsible for taking positive measures towards ensuring the provision of adequate food. From this perspective, the notion of a right to food is action-guiding and duty holders seem to be identified. Nonetheless, these arguments still result in two problems. First, they seem to leave the problem of enforceability unanswered, i.e. even if an international organization is identified as a duty holder, can that organization be forced to acknowledge and fulfil its duty? If we look at the specific case of the right to food, the answer – at least in theory – seems to be positive. Since the right to food is included in the ICESCR, and since this covenant is a treaty, the rights that are part of that treaty are legally enforceable. In practice, it is a complicated route that is under judicial review by the UN. Nonetheless, we can claim that the right to food has clear duty holders and is enforceable. This, however, still leaves us with the second problem: the argument that, with the help of institutional constructs, it is possible to allocate duties and to give content to the duties raises the question of whether we can still speak about individual duty holders (cf. Heilinger 2011, 192f.). This is relevant, given the question of whether the rights claims of future generations can result in moral reasons for individuals to change their consumption behaviour.

3 A real right, but also real individual duties?

The fact that food security is on the public agenda means in practice that institutions in particular, such as governments and NGOs, are working on this issue. The assumption is that if a human rights violation takes place, 'the responsibility to act lies with an official institution' (Heilinger 2011, 192). This raises the question of whether the right to food should be dealt with on an institutional level, because this is the most appropriate infrastructure to deal with individual duties, or that we choose an institutional approach because a right to food only functions if and only if we establish an institutional setting in which duties are allocated. If the latter is the case, i.e. that only institutions can be duty holders regarding the right to food, then speaking about duties on the level of the individual is highly complicated. This does not mean that there is no moral demand at the level of the individual to care about the food security of others; yet such a demand would be an imperfect obligation with no direct corresponding right.

In my opinion, such an either-or presentation is not helpful in answering the main question of whether individuals have a moral reason to change their consumption behaviour because of future generations. On the one hand, I agree with those who claim that making the choice to deal with the right to food is not a merely pragmatic choice. Dealing with the right to food on an individual level only results in a number of feasibility problems. Food production, processing and consumption are global by nature and are so complex that if we considered individuals as the only duty holders of the right to food, then this would result in a variety of feasibility problems. In many cases, it is both practically and physically impossible for individuals to secure a food supply and, since ought implies can, rights based on duties that cannot be fulfilled are problematic. However, there is more to say about duties. We can distinguish between direct and indirect duties. Even if we agree on the implausibility of an individual duty to provide food, we can speak about indirect duties to secure the right to food. Because it is possible to allocate duties to institutions that – on behalf of individuals – are able to deal with the right to food, an individual may have a duty to demand that the institution takes its direct duty seriously. Therefore, it is possible to speak about the right to food in a way that does not leave the individual completely out of the picture. Like Pogge, we can argue that 'each member of society, according to his or her means, is to help bring about and sustain a social and economic order within which all have secure access to basic necessities' (2002, 69). Thus, while acknowledging the need for and the importance of institutions that can make the right to food feasible and make it a claimable right, it is still possible to speak about individual duties to contribute – within the limits of one's abilities to secure the right to food. From this perspective, it is still possible that the rights claims of future generations may restrict our current food consumption.

In summary, the right to food is a genuine human right that: (a) is linked to the basic needs of humans; and (b) meets the proviso of practical feasibility in the sense that we can identify duty holders and that the duty is enforceable. We also identified some problems in relation to the role that individuals play. Nonetheless, it is legitimate to argue that – even if institutions appear to be the most appropriate duty holders – individuals can have indirect duties and consequently may play an active role. However, before we can jump to the question of possible duties towards future generations, this discussion is further complicated by the notion of food.

4 Which right is at stake?

In order to get a better grip on the feasibility of the right to food and the related question of whether this has implications for our current consumption patterns, it is important to look more carefully at the definition of the right to food. The Committee on Economic, Social and Cultural Rights of the UN Economic and Social Council defines this right as follows:

> the right to adequate food is realized when every man, woman and child, alone and in community with others, has physical and economic access at all times to adequate food or means for its procurement.
> (Economic and Social Council 1999, General Comment 12/6)

This definition shows two important aspects. On the one hand, it specifies the right to food by the reference to adequacy. It is not a claim for food as such, but for adequate food. Thus, people are entitled to have food that enables them to live in a way that is in accordance with the inherent dignity of the human person and with the fulfilment of other human rights (Economic and Social Council 1999, General Comment 12/4).

On the other hand, food seems to be defined in a rather restricted way. Food is mainly defined in terms of its nutritional value. Although the value of food is more than its nutritional value (Caplan 1997; Gofton 1996), the definitions of the right to food mainly focus on its dietary and health aspects. They do not explicitly take the cultural, social or identity-related aspects of food into consideration despite these being constitutive elements of food. This implies that, from this perspective, we should speak about the *right to adequate nutrition* rather than the right to food.

However, the former UN Special Rapporteur on the Right to Food, Jean Ziegler, uses a broader view on food. He stresses the context of food and includes the cultural and social dimensions. He argues that the right to food implies:

the right to have regular, permanent and unrestricted access,..., to quanti-
tatively and qualitatively adequate and sufficient food corresponding to the
cultural traditions of the people to which the consumer belongs, and which
ensures a physical and mental, individual and collective, fulfilling and dignified life free of fear.

His reference to food 'corresponding to the cultural traditions' better addresses
the variety of dimensions important to how we value food. However, it also has
direct implications for the feasibility of the right to food, especially if this is
applied to the specific question raised in this chapter regarding possible duties
towards future generations. The inclusion of the cultural and traditional component easily runs into the question of whether in 2050 the Italians will have a
right to have pasta dishes, the Germans a right to eat their sausages and the
Chinese a right to eat rice.

Thus, it seems as if we end up either with a feasible but rather abstract right
to adequate nutrition that does not do justice to the broader dimensions of food
or with a quite specific right to food that takes the cultural and social dimensions of food into account but that entails duties that are characterized by over-
demandingness. With respect to the latter position, it is easy to ridicule the
possible consequences as completely unfeasible. However, I agree with Hahn's
view that human rights are often understood as claims that do not depend on
what is actually realizable, but on what is principally achievable (2012, 148).
And in principle, it is possible to take the cultural dimensions of food into
account.

A more profound point refers to Rawls' idea of 'human rights proper'. Apart
from the questions of achievability and the feasibility of identifying duty
holders, he argues for a restricted number of human rights that are essential to
any 'common good idea of justice' (Rawls 1999, 78–80). This implies that
human rights should be neutral and should not depend on lifestyle aspects. Consequently, a reference to the cultural aspects of food goes beyond a neutral
liberal perspective. From a Rawlsian perspective, however, the right to adequate
nutrition is already rather complicated, since Rawls does not list nutrition
among the list of primary goods, in contrast to, for instance, health care and
education (Rawls 1993). From his perspective, the relevance of food does not
need independent attention and can be covered by other rights. It is beyond the
scope of this chapter to discuss the relation between liberalism and food (e.g.
Korthals 2004), yet Rawls' account shows that if the cultural or identity-related
aspects are separated from the notion of food, we can focus better on rights
related to health.

Therefore, the above-mentioned proposal to define the right to food in terms
of the right to adequate nutrition is flawed. If we define the right to food merely in
terms of adequate nutrition, we either end up with a situation in which the right
is considered to be superfluous, because it can be covered by other rights that can
safeguard human health, or we are faced with a right that is not specific enough
and therefore will not do justice to the claims people have. Consequently, I prefer

a definition of the right to food that deals with the cultural and identity-related dimensions of food. However, what does this imply for the rights claims of future generations?

5 Future food and current consumption

In spite of the ongoing discussion, I think there are convincing arguments that can be used to start a discussion from the perspective that future generations can have legitimate claims vis-à-vis present generations (cf. Meyer 2008; see also in this volume Chapter 6 by Düwell, Chapter 9 by Bos and Chapter 11 by Beyleveld). More specific to the issue of food, we can reasonably assume that future generations have an interest in food, in the sense that they will need food for daily life too. However, this general interest still leaves room for discussion of at least two aspects: food security and safety, on the one hand, and the question of food quality and identity, on the other.

The first discussion focuses on the question of how much food is needed. Starvation is obviously something that has to be prevented for future generations too. However, to enable future people to live in accordance with their dignity, the threshold of decency should be higher than mere biological survival. In this case, the above-mentioned definition – which refers to the right to 'free and general access to adequate food' – is equally applicable.

The second aspect is more complicated. Do future generations have a right to certain types of food that fit with traditional backgrounds or personal identity? One could argue that these have changed and will change over time. Consumption patterns in, for instance, the Netherlands have changed quite dramatically over the last 50 years. And this may keep changing during the next 50 years. Therefore, this aspect can hardly be included in the concept of a right to food for future generations. Nonetheless, it would be too easy to conclude from this dynamic that we can reduce the discussion to the elements of food security and safety. This would exclude one important aspect: the value of food choice that is intrinsically related to autonomy. Only in relation to those whom we consider not to be fully autonomous persons yet (e.g. children) or no longer competent to act autonomously (e.g. people suffering from severe psychological disorders) do other persons decide what they will eat (Meijboom 2010; Meijboom, Verweij and Brom 2003). Therefore, the right to food should also include the ability to choose the food that is adequate from both a health and a social perspective.

In practice, this implies that future people have a legitimate claim (a) to have sufficient safe food to lead a decent life and (b) to have food that has a level of quality that enables people to make autonomous food choices.

The final step is to determine what such a right would imply vis-à-vis the food consumption of currently living people. Is our present food consumption to be constrained by the rights of future generations? My answer is positive, but I do not think that such constraints should be understood as direct and perfect duties. To support this answer, I have three arguments. First, there is the argument of uncertainty. The relation between a specific change in food consumption and the fulfilment of claims of future people is often characterized by uncertainty. There are no simple causal relationships between one's food pattern and addressing rights problems. To begin with, a food pattern consists of many – mostly both sustainable and unsustainable – elements. This makes it complex to define whether a consumption pattern should be changed given the claims of future generations. Furthermore, even in those cases where there are clear links between aspects of one's consumption pattern and sustainability, they still raise a question about whether one should change one's consumption behaviour. For instance, food transportation has a clear impact on CO_2 emissions and therefore on the available resources for future generations. Nonetheless, in some cases, producing food in only a few areas in the world in a sustainable way and distributing the products around the world could turn out to be more sustainable than producing it locally. Furthermore, it has been argued that, by using technology and innovation to help in a smart way, we have not yet reached the limits of food production. It is beyond the scope of this article to check and analyse these claims. However, it can be seen that it is not easy to prove that a lack of constraints on current consumption will directly endanger the legitimate rights claims of future people.

Second, there is the argument about complexity: this refers to the above-mentioned problem that the food chain is global and complex by nature. As noted, this is the reason why (supra)national governmental organizations in particular take the lead regarding the right to food. They can create the infrastructure and the level playing field that is needed to guarantee food security. For the legitimacy of the right to food this is no real problem, but for the discussion about constraints it is a serious hurdle. These governmental bodies do not consume. Therefore, that aspect has to be delegated to individual consumers. This leads to two problems. To begin with, it might result in a demand that is imposed by the government rather than an individual duty that directly follows from the rights claims of future people. This is problematic, as it becomes unclear what the real moral driver is with respect to the right to food. Furthermore, given the lifestyle aspect of food, it raises a moral problem if a government intervenes in food choices that follow specific conceptions of the good life. In addition, I referred above to Pogge to show that delegating duties to an institutional level does not imply that individuals no longer have a duty. However, even in the case of duties towards current generations, the argument is that one needs to help bring about and sustain an order that secures access to basic necessities 'according to his or her means' (2002, 69). And that condition especially leads back again to the first problem of uncertainty.

Finally, there is the argument that starts from the classification of food consumption in the private sphere. The choice of a certain type of food or a certain lifestyle is – in a liberal tradition, understood as a personal choice that should only be influenced if there are very strong reasons at stake (cf. Beekman 2008; Rippe 2000). There are differences in this line of argument, for instance in relation to the way in which obesity should be addressed. However, in this example the public health aspect or the need to protect vulnerable citizens (e.g. children) is often mentioned in order to justify any interference at the level of food consumption.

Does this imply that the right to food of future generations does not have any effects on our current food consumption? I think that would be too strong a conclusion. In spite of the above arguments, it can definitely have an impact on our current food consumption. To trace this normative impact, we have to look again at the above-mentioned arguments. To start with the final one, even if we grant that food consumption is primarily a private issue, it does not rule out governmental intervention. Intervention to guarantee the (basic) rights of future generations does not necessarily imply that the government is taking a stance in the debate on the basic conceptions of the good life, but this *can* be considered as a way to make the 'harm' principle operational. Consequently, a government can limit the freedom (of choice) of individuals. Furthermore, the impact that food consumption has on others, that is, those who are currently living and those who will exist in the future, is a strong factor to stress in advocating that food consumption is no longer a strictly private issue.

This also links to the first two arguments on uncertainty and complexity. Even though it is difficult to trace what makes a specific consumption pattern sustainable, the general imperative to strive for sustainability is still valid. Therefore, I agree with Berry *et al.* that 'without integrating sustainability as an explicit ... dimension of food security, today's policies and programmes could become the very cause of increased food insecurity in the future' (2015). Consequently, individuals can also explicitly take into consideration how their food use in everyday life may either 'facilitate or hamper environmentally, socially and culturally sustainable paths of development' (Terragni *et al.*, 2009). As mentioned previously, this focus on sustainability in the light of future generations' rights should not be understood as the moral basis for direct and perfect duties, but it can serve as the moral ideal from which individual consumption choices can be assessed (cf. Meijboom and Brom 2012). This implies that the constraints on food consumption do not and cannot have the form of complete bans that are issued by governments. Given the uncertainty, complexity and individual freedom of the current generation mentioned earlier, the rights of future generations do not result in a moral ground that can be used to enforce a ban on the consumption of, for instance, meat or on the global transportation of food products. However, we can have reasonable expectations of individual consumers that they take into account the sustainability of their food choices and the rights of future generations. Taking this one step further, the rights of future generations can be a compelling reason to start debating with those who deliberately do not take sustainability into account in their food choices. However, at this point, institutions come into the picture again. Both companies and public organizations have a duty to enable and support individuals to make these decisions. This should be improved, because 'most European consumers are not offered clear and trustworthy choices, nor is there widespread consensus on consumer responsibility and agency' (Kjaernes 2012, 158). This may – at least partly – explain the problem of 'the value-action gap'. This is not only a problem in the light of the 'ought implies can' condition of duties, but is also a way to pay due respect to current consumers to enable them to take the interests and rights of future generations into account, in spite of the complexity and uncertainty at stake.

Finally, I can identify one aspect of current food consumption that has a direct implication for future food security and food choice and does not suffer – or at least suffers less – from the problems of uncertainty and complexity: food wastage. The FAO calculated that 1.3 billion tons of food, which is one-third of all food, is wasted (Food and Agriculture Organization of the UN 2013). In some developing countries this is the result of inefficient farming; however, in the Western world it is mostly the consequence of buying too much food. From the claim of future generations there follows a duty to put constraints on this problem of food wastage. Of course, making this operational will not be easy, but this is at least one constraint that: (a) follows from the rights claims of future generations; (b) has the individual as the duty holder; and (c) is feasible to fulfil for the individual consumer without having a direct impact on their lifestyle.

6 Conclusion

In this chapter, I showed that we can speak about a genuine human right to food that is directly linked to the basic needs of humans and can comply with the proviso of practical feasibility. Furthermore, I argued that we can reasonably assume that future generations will have an interest in food, in the sense that they will need food for daily life. Furthermore, this argument entails that a genuine human right to food implies that we should have the ability to make autonomous food choices. Safeguarding this right has a direct influence on our current food consumption. Even though we cannot speak about a direct and perfect duty of the individual or about the possibilities on a public level of banning specific food consumption patterns or choices, it is possible to identify three duties regarding the rights of future generations. First, there is the duty to consume less and waste less food. This barely influences current food choices, but has a direct influence on the ability of future generations to enjoy food. Second, there is a general duty to strive for sustainability, i.e. to assess individual consumption choices from the perspective of their impact on the potential of future generations. Finally, we can identify a duty to establish and maintain competent and committed institutions that are able to deal with the collective and global dimensions of the right to food. They will carry out their remits in such a way that they will guarantee future generations sufficient safe food in order to lead a decent life and food of a level of quality that will enable them to make autonomous food choices.

References

Beekman V. (2008) 'Consumer rights to food ethical traceability' in Coff C. et al. eds, *Ethical traceability and communicating food* The international library of environmental, agricultural and food ethics, vol. 15 235–49.

Berry E.M., Dernini S., Burlingame B., Meybeck A. and Conforti P. (2015) 'Food security and sustainability: can one exist without the other?' *Public Health Nutrition*, 18(13) 1–10. doi:10.1017/S136898001500021X.

Caplan P. ed. (1997) *Food, health and identity* London, Routledge.

Commission of the European Communities (2011) *Proposal for a council decision, establishing the Specific Programme Implementing Horizon 2020 – The Framework Programme for Research and Innovation (2014–2020)*, Brussels, 30 November 2011, COM (2011) 811 final, 2011/0402 (CNS).

Economic and Social Council (1999) *The right to adequate food (art. 12)* Substantive issues arising in the implementation of the international covenant on economic, social and cultural rights, General Comment 12, Geneva, United Nations, Available at www.unhchr.ch/tbs/doc.nsf/0/3d02758c707031d58025677f003b73b9, accessed June 2015.

Feinberg J. and Narveson J. (1970) 'The nature and value of rights' *The Journal of Value Inquiry*, 4(4) 243–60.

Food and Agriculture Organization of the UN (2003) *Trade reforms and food security: conceptualizing the linkages* Rome, FAO.

Food and Agriculture Organization of the UN (2011) *Report of the Panel of Eminent Experts on Ethics in Food and Agriculture*, fourth session, 26–28 November 2007, Rome, Publishing Policy and Support Branch, Office of Knowledge Exchange, Research and Extension, FAO.

Food and Agriculture Organization of the UN (2013) *Food wastage footprint. Impact on natural resources* Rome, FAO.

Gofton L. (1996) 'Bread to biotechnology: cultural aspects of food ethics' in Mepham B. ed., *Food Ethics* London, Routledge, 120–37.

Hahn H. (2012) 'Justifying feasibility constraints on human rights' *Ethical Theory and Moral Practice*, 15 143–57.

Heilinger J.-Chr. (2011) 'The moral demandingness of socioeconomic human rights' in Ernst G. and Helinger J.-Chr. eds, *The philosophy of human rights contemporary controversies* Berlin, De Gruyter, 185–210.

Kjaernes U. (2012) 'Ethics and action: a relational perspective on consumer choice in the European politics of food' *Journal of Agricultural and Environmental Ethics*, 25(2) 145–62.

Korthals M. (2004) *Before dinner: philosophy and ethics of food* Dordrecht, Springer.

Lang T. and Barling D. (2012) "Food security and food sustainability: reformulating the debate' *The Geographical Journal*, 178(4), 313–26.

Meijboom F.L.B. (2010) 'Voedsel en identiteit: vertrouwen of betrouwbaarheid' in de Tavenier J. ed., *Ons dagelijks brood. Over oude en nieuwe spijswetten* Leuven, Acco, 243–60.

Meijboom F.L.B. and Brom F.W.A. (2012) 'Ethics and sustainability: guest or guide? On sustainability as a moral ideal' *Journal of Agricultural and Environmental Ethics*, 25(2) 117–21.

Meijboom F.L.B., Verweij M.F. and Brom F.W.A. (2003) 'You eat what you are. Moral dimensions of diets tailored to one's genes' *Journal of Agricultural and Environmental Ethics*, 16(6) 557–68.

Meyer L. (2008) 'Intergenerational justice' in Zalta E.N. ed., *The Stanford encyclopedia of philosophy*, Available at http://plato.stanford.edu/entries/justice-intergenerational/, accessed June 2015.

O'Neill O. (1986) *Faces of hunger* London, Allen and Unwin.

O'Neill O. (2000) *Bounds of justice* Cambridge, Cambridge University Press.

O'Neill O. (2002) *A question of trust. The BBC Reith lectures* Cambridge, Cambridge University Press.

Pogge T. (2002) *World poverty and human rights* Cambridge, Polity.

Rawls J. (1993) *Political liberalism* New York, Columbia University Press.

Rawls J. (1999) *The law of peoples* Cambridge, MA, Harvard University Press.

Rippe K.P. (2000) 'Novel foods and consumer rights: concerning food policy in a liberal state' *Journal of Agricultural and Environmental Ethics*, 12(1) 71–80.

Shue H. (1996) *Basic Rights*, 2nd edn Princeton, Princeton University Press.

Terragni L., Boström M., Halkier B. and Mäkelä J. eds (2009) 'Can consumers save the world? Everyday food consumption and dilemmas of sustainability' *Anthropology of Food*, Special Issue S5.

14 Climate change and the right to one child

Tim Meijers

1 Introduction[1]

Our planet currently houses over seven billion people, and the projections say that this will rise to 10 or 11 billion in 2100.[2] This raises a worry: are these demographic developments compatible with sustainability-related obligations to future generations? This chapter asks when (if ever) the right to procreate may be limited for sustainability reasons. People have a 'right to procreate' if the interest they have in procreating and having their capacity to procreate protected is morally weighty enough to trump many competing – less important – claims. Making human behaviour sustainable for intergenerational reasons raises questions of intra-generational justice: how should the obligations that come with restricting humankind's impact to sustainable levels be distributed and, what sacrifices can we ask for from whom? In the literature on the allocation of emissions rights, two questions are key: (1) how much can a generation emit; and (2) how should emissions rights be distributed? The same questions can be asked about population: how many children can a generation have, and how should procreative rights be distributed?

The question under consideration in this chapter is narrowed down in three important ways. First, it focuses on reasons stemming from a concern for sustainability, not on other possible grounds for limitations on procreative freedom (e.g. wrongful life). Second, although population matters for other sustainability questions too, I focus on CO_2 emissions here. Third, I will assume that population size matters insofar as it has an impact on how well (future and present) people's lives go: a world with seven billion people living sustainably is not better or worse than a world with 10 billion people leading equally good lives sustainably.

This chapter argues that there are good intergenerational reasons to critically examine the right to procreate, but it will be cautious about proposing (legal or policy) means to restrict it. Two distinctions have to be kept in mind. First, arguments about demographic *goals* and the *means* that can be permissibly used to reach them are distinct (one can agree about a certain goal but disagree about how to reach it), but they are often conflated in public debate because arguments favouring a certain demographic development are frequently taken to imply support for coercive policies. A second, related, distinction is between moral and legal norms: *limits* on the right to procreate discussed here are *moral* limits, not (necessarily) legally enforceable ones.

This chapter will proceed as follows. Section 2 will focus on the link between population size and emissions. Section 3 argues against an unlimited interpretation of the right to procreate, while section 4 defends a limited right to procreate. Before concluding in section 6, section 5 discusses reasons to exempt the globally least well-off from restricting their fertility levels.

2 Population size and climate change

The current environmental impact of humanity cannot be sustained: reserves of non-renewable resources are being exhausted; renewable resources are consumed at unsustainable rates; emissions cause climate change; and biodiversity is plummeting. Climate change affects many people's lives negatively, leading to clear rights violations and casualties (e.g. Caney 2010), for example through desertification, extreme weather conditions and rising sea levels. This is irreversible, but restricting emissions limits the extent to which the climate will change and whether (new) tipping points will be crossed. Continuing business as usual means that future generations may inherit a world that is unable to provide enough for all to lead good (enough) lives.

As a minimal theory of intergenerational justice, I will assume that this is impermissible: future generations are (at least[3]) owed a world in which good enough lives can be lived. This requires limiting CO_2 emissions so that they remain within a safe margin in order to prevent large parts of the planet becoming uninhabitable, unsafe[4] or incapable of producing food and other goods (e.g. Caney 2010). Three variables determine total emissions: population size, per capita consumption and the emissions per unit of consumption. There are three distinct strategies to limit the total amount of emissions: changing the number of people, limiting consumption or decreasing (e.g. using green technology) emissions per unit of consumption.[5]

Total global emissions are (partially) a function of the size of the population, and population growth is acknowledged as one of the most important drivers of rising emissions (Intergovernmental Panel on Climate Change 2014, 46). Are per capita emissions much more important than the size of the population, given that most emissions come from a minority of the global population? The average Ethiopian emits very little (0.1 metric tons of CO_2), but the average American emits 176 times as much (17.6 metric tons) (World Bank 2015). Given that population growth mostly takes place in countries where per capita emissions are very low, shouldn't we focus on reducing emissions in the world's richest countries instead? High fertility rates in Ethiopia, one may conclude, should not worry us for reasons relating to climate change because the country's contribution to growing global emissions is small.

Although the reduction of emissions in affluent countries is part of any plausible sustainability strategy, if one believes that poverty should be eradicated, then population growth in developing countries matters. Realizing a world in which all can lead good (enough) lives is harder with a larger population because the available CO_2 emissions rights will have to be shared with (many) more people, so per capita emissions will have to be lower. Although limiting CO_2-intensive consumption in high-emission countries is key to limiting emissions, population matters too.

Population size is a function of migration, fertility and mortality. Tweaking any of these three variables has an effect on population size, be it by changing patterns of migration, investments in health or the number of children people have (and the moment in their lives when they have them). Our concern is with the sustainability of the world as a whole, to and from which migration is impossible. Increasing mortality rates in order to limit population size is an unacceptable option, although some have defended it.[6] This leaves fertility as the only demographic variable available to influence population size.

Any plausible strategy to limit total emissions will probably involve *both* decreases in fertility and decreases in per capita emissions (through reducing consumption or through the use of low-emission technology). As noted earlier, the world population consists of over seven billion today, and this number is projected to grow to 10 or 11 billion in 2100. Reaching nine billion is inevitable, because the largest generation ever born is still to reach a reproductively active age. Even if this generation has fewer children on average, on aggregate, population growth will take place. But where population peaks exactly and what happens afterwards is a consequence of decisions and action taken now.

To what extent should fertility decrease in order to cap total emissions? How much procreation and how much per capita emissions are compatible with the minimal requirements of justice are highly intertwined questions. If limiting per capita emissions so that they are below a certain level is unacceptable, reductions in total emissions have to be accomplished by limiting fertility. If we think that a reduction in fertility is too much to ask for, a further decrease in per capita emissions or investments in an increased capacity of the planet to absorb CO_2 (e.g. reforestation) will be needed. In other words, the question is one of emphasis: the ways in which acceptable levels of CO_2 emissions can be achieved should be emphasized? To what extent is it fair to require people to refrain from procreating as part of a strategy to make the world more sustainable?

3 Against an unlimited right

One may think that people have a right to decide how many children[7] they have, be it none, one or many. This intuition is codified in several international treaties and declarations, often in reference to article 16.1 of the *Universal Declaration of Human Rights*, which states that 'men and women of full age, without limitation due to race, nationality or religion, have the right to marry and found a family' (United Nations 1948). The third Secretary-General of the UN explicitly links this to procreation:

> The Universal Declaration of Human Rights describes the family as the natural and fundamental unit of society. It follows that any choice and decision with regard to the size of the family must irrevocably rest with the family itself, and cannot be made by anyone else.
>
> (Thant 1967)

Later documents of the United Nations suggest that (prospective) parents have to be able to decide 'freely and responsibly ... taking into account the needs of their living and future children and their responsibility to the community' (United Nations 1994, 56–7). Although certain procreative decisions can apparently be judged to be *irresponsible*, the unlimited right is not put into doubt. Is this defensible? I will argue that it cannot be, by appealing to internal and external limitations on the right.

Let us start with external limitations. A limit is external if it is imposed in order to protect other rights or concerns. For something to be a human right, it has to be compossible with other human rights.[8] If one believes that rights come with claims, one cannot have a general human right to x and a right to y if it is impossible to protect both. How can an unlimited right to procreate clash with other putative rights? Having children affects both parents and the resulting children, but also present and future members of society, sometimes negatively.

The impact on others may be more than a mere setback in terms of (financial) interests.[9] In a world in which everybody had many children, extreme scarcity would arise and stable institutions could prove unsustainable. This would lead to violation of (rather uncontroversial) rights such as the right to life and to health and subsistence.[10] For example, for a great many people, competition may arise over resources needed for survival, such as fresh water sources or fertile ground. A right to procreate understood in its unlimited form would imply that it would be morally permissible for all to act on their procreative potential (the average maximum number of children per women stands at over 15 (Bongaarts 1978, 118). Even a minimal theory of justice which requires that future generations inherit a world in which their basic needs can be met leads to a limited understanding of procreative rights.

One could object that because very few people have that many children, this threat would not materialize. Even if this is true, the objection fails. In order for something to be a right it has to pass the universalizability test (e.g. O'Neill 1996): can an unlimited right to procreate be granted to all? The answer is no. At most, this objection establishes that if sustainability were not a problem, determining the limits of procreative freedom would not be a particularly pressing worry. It does not show that the right is unlimited.

The right to procreate has internal limits – limitations for the sake of protecting *the same* rights – too. Again, we can apply the universalizability test: a human right for some has to be compatible with the same right for all. If, as a result of overpopulation, future generations live in a depleted world, this may have two consequences. First, infertility is much higher among people with insufficient resources (Baudin, de la Croix and Gobbi 2015); in a poor world, many will lack the capacity to procreate. Second, if the life of children that are created would be very bad due to overpopulation, parents may have an obligation to refrain from procreation; arguably, it is impermissible to create a child that will have a very bad life. Hence, an unlimited right to procreate is incompatible with all having the same right.

One may attempt to use another strategy to defend a right to procreate without limits: preventing people from having children violates *other* rights, such as bodily integrity and privacy, or undermines gender equality; enforcing restrictions on procreative behaviour is impermissibly coercive or will disproportionately affect women. This is as true for the first child as it is for the tenth, and hence the right to procreate is unlimited. This argument fails to take into account the distinction between enforceable and unenforceable duties. It is possible to argue that people would be acting wrongly if they have many children while maintaining that others should not intervene. The argument establishes at most that enforcing limits on procreation is sometimes impermissible, but not that those having many children have acted permissibly (see also, for example, O'Neill 1979, 38).

This section attempted to establish that an unrestricted liberty right to procreate cannot be defended, because such a right may: (1) clash with other rights; and (2) is incompatible with the same right for all. The next question will present arguments for a restricted right to procreate.

4 Arguments for a limited right

The argument in the previous section does not mean that there is no right to procreate at all. Several philosophers argue that a preference for having children is like other preferences: some people love mountaineering, others like to travel by plane and yet others decide to have children. In the debates about parental justice, which focus on the question of *who* should pay for children (e.g. Casal and Williams 1995), it is often implicitly assumed that having children should be evaluated in a similar way to the other things people do in life. One important difference is that procreation involves the creation of a new human being with rights. This matters once the child exists, but here I focus on why it is important that people are allowed to *create* children.

Is what is at stake similar to what is at stake in other plans? This question matters, because if the interest is sufficiently important, it may be permissible to procreate *even if* this comes at some cost to others, for example in terms of less consumption. Take freedom of speech: even if what I say may harm the interest of others, I often (but not always) still have the right to say it. The interest that people have in freedom of speech trumps many other considerations. Young argues that procreation is not like this:

> I argue it is inconsistent to believe that overconsumption is wrong or bad yet believe that having children is morally permissible, insofar as they produce comparable environmental impacts, are voluntary choices and arise from similar desires.
>
> (Young 2001, 183)

Do the conditions after 'insofar' really hold? Having children does lead to emissions. Let's suppose that people have children voluntarily. This leaves the 'desires' that parenthood arises from: is the reason why having children and parenting matters equivalent to why other activities which contribute to emissions matter? Not every consumptive act is equal: the consumption of sufficient food is necessary for survival; some consumptive acts are key to formulating and realizing plans in life (e.g. education); and sometimes consumption allows preference satisfaction. I cannot do full justice to these issues here, but let me briefly review the reasons for thinking that procreation is something particularly important.

4.1 Continuation

There are two main reasons why procreation matters for society as a whole. First, without future generations, society or humankind will come to an end. This would mean that the projects we are a part of and the things we value would end with the deaths of the last individuals. Most people conceive of themselves as part of a larger whole: of a city, a country, a tradition, an ethnicity, a linguistic group or a profession, etc. These groups, which extend to both the past and the future, are constitutive of people's identity and the background against which they value and develop plans in life. Removing future people from the picture radically affects how we conceive of ourselves and what we consider worthwhile activities. Most people's plans and projects would have to be, if not abandoned, radically reformulated in light of the end of transgenerational projects. Scheffler, somewhat speculatively, says that a world without future people would be characterized by "widespread apathy, anomie, and despair; the erosion of social institutions and social solidarity; the deterioration of the physical environment; and by a pervasive loss of conviction about the value or point of many activities". (Scheffler 2013, 41–2)

Perhaps *some* plans would make sense in the face of human extinction. But the huge cost of giving up the key projects one values and identifies with and formulating new, different plans for those whose plans do not withstand the end of humanity is undeniable. For those who do not manage to confine the sources of value to within their own lives – which, I suppose, would be most of us – the prospect of the end of one's community would imply considerable costs. It is reasonable for people to claim that leading a meaningful life requires future people, even though it may not be impossible to lead a meaningful life without them. This is the *meaning argument* for the importance of creating future people.

Second, without sufficient new arrivals, the economy and society would decline and eventually collapse. New generations are necessary for pension and healthcare funding and for the general viability of the economic system. Perhaps, more importantly, new people are necessary for meeting the basic needs of the current population as it ages:

> A new generation is needed in order to avoid that people die from unnecessarily painful and probably premature deaths. Without a new generation,

the economy would collapse. It is unavoidable that many people end their lives in a state of dependency (the old, the ill, the disabled) and if there was no one to care for them they would die hungry, thirsty, without pain relief and other palliative care.

(Gheaus 2015, 94)

These two arguments together (economic and care) we could call the *dependency argument* for the importance of there being future people.

There are two reasons to worry about non-continuity. The dependency argument and the meaning argument establish that people have a weighty interest in sufficient new people coming into existence. This means that the right to procreate needs to be granted, at least to some, in order to create enough individuals to prevent the end or collapse of society. Any proposal aimed at making human behaviour compatible with the carrying capacity of the planet should take into account which demographic developments society can survive. A proposal to limit the population to the extent that it would lead to extinction or collapse would not be permissible. If that is the case, we should aim to further limit emissions (or invest in CO_2 mitigation). This does not tell us how the right to procreate should be distributed among prospective parents. For this we need to ask why procreation may matter for *individuals*.

4.2 (Biological) parenthood

What makes it important for individuals to be able to procreate? In the discussion that follows, I will assume, for simplicity's sake, that we are dealing with cases in which (1) people who have children are part of a couple and (2) they can procreate without assistance. There are at least two distinct arguments for the importance of the right.

First, parenthood is a position that grants access to the development of skills and certain goods. Brighouse and Swift argue that being able to engage in parental relationships matters greatly: 'The role enables them to exercise and develop capacities the development and exercise of which are, for many (though not, certainly, for all), crucial to their living fully flourishing lives.'(Brighouse and Swift 2006, 95). In addition, parenthood gives access to goods that are important for pursuing most plans in life. It is a way to create long-lasting intimate relationships, get access to love (and the special kind of love and intimacy that parent–child relationships provide), create an intimate personal sphere and make a contribution to a life that will (hopefully) outlast one's own.

Suppose that the following is correct: the goods and skills parenthood gives access to are important for leading a good (enough) life, although parenting may not be the only way to get access to these goods. Does a right to procreate follow? The goods mentioned stem from *parental* relationships, not from *procreation* as such: adoption may suffice. But the number of children available for adoption is limited, so procreation *may* be the only way to get access to a parental relationship. If that is the case, people have an important interest in being allowed to procreate.

One may object that parenting is not necessary for leading a good life. This chapter does not defend the claim that parenthood is a *need* or something people *ought* to do, but that having the possibility matters, compared with romantic relationships, without which some can lead fulfilling lives. This does not disprove that relationships are extremely important to those who do wish to engage in them. Only very weighty reasons suffice to require someone not to pursue these.

So far, the importance of the goods and skills that parenthood allows people to access has been emphasized. There may be additional reasons why having the right to procreate is important. Many value (biological) parenthood for non-instrumental reasons. Having children is part of how people think of their (future) selves and what they see as a normal human life. Requiring people not to procreate amounts to asking them to give up on something key to their plans and identity.

Nothing I have said so far suggests that having biological children is in any objective sense better than parenting children that are genetically unrelated. Insofar as this attachment to biological ties is culturally and not biologically determined, it is subject to change. Sustainability strategies may aim for ideational change of this commitment to biological parenthood so that procreation becomes a less crucial aspect of life for future generations.

These arguments support a right to procreate that is both limited and conditional. It is conditional because procreation is seen as instrumental to parenthood. If procreators are either unable or unwilling to parent the resulting child, they lack the right – unless others will parent said child (e.g. surrogate motherhood). It is limited because it establishes the right to parent *one child*. The right to have a first child and the right to have an additional child are fundamentally different. The first child gives access to parenthood, whereas the second child does not: the procreators are already parents.

We can now present an alternative reading of the right to found a family as formulated in the *Universal Declaration of Human Rights*. There are good reasons to grant people the right to found a family, but respecting this right requires the opportunity to have one child, not to have many. Having one child is sufficient to found a family: additional children enlarge but do not establish a family with parent–child relationships. This does not imply that having more than one child is *always* impermissible. It may be that having more children is permissible. The right kind of balance between limiting fertility and per capita emissions will probably depend on how much value people attach to having large families as opposed to being able to have high per capita emissions on which reduction can be enforced in a morally permissible way. What is at stake in these additional procreative entitlements is of lesser importance and hence is more easily overridden by reasons other than the right to have the first child.

This argument has clear implications for how procreative entitlements should be distributed, whereas *continuation* arguments have implications for the aggregate number of entitlements. A sustainability strategy that would aim at lowering fertility to acceptable levels but would distribute it unevenly among those who want to parent would not be acceptable.

Are parents entitled to less emissions rights because they already have children and this has an environmental impact? One could argue that the amount of CO_2 emissions available should be divided equally and those costs calculated in terms of CO_2 caused by having children taken out of people's share. Whether parents are subsequently entitled to fewer emissions is too difficult a question to discuss here. But the arguments presented here do establish that people's fair share *should* ideally include enough resources to procreate and parent (e.g. if procreation counts as CO_2 consumption, one should have at least enough emissions entitlements to parent and lead a good enough life).

What this section aimed to establish is that people have a weighty interest in engaging in parental relationships. This justifies a conditional right to procreate: *if* procreation is necessary for parenthood, people cannot (unless for very weighty reasons) reasonably be required not to have children, although it may not be unreasonable to require them to stop at one. Refusing people the right to one child needs very weighty considerations.

5 Poverty and procreation

What I have argued so far is that sustainability concerns can justify limits on the right to procreate, but that it should be non-nil. The following claim is compatible with what I have argued so far:

> P1: It is reasonable to morally require people to have no more than one child if this is needed to limit emissions, while protecting their right to have one child (i.e. it is unreasonable – in most circumstances – to ask people to have *zero* children).

This section considers whether P1 is reasonable in a world like ours (continuing to assume that all people live together as couples[11]). This one child requirement is nothing like *one child policies* that we are familiar with, such as the Chinese one. One can reject a one child policy because it asks too much of people or because the means used to enforce it are impermissible. I have only shown that the first kind of argument may fail (although it may not in the case of China): a sustainability strategy leaving room for a right to one child per couple does not necessarily place unreasonable demands on people. The second line of argument against one child policies is unaffected by what I say here.

There are several possible reasons to justify exemptions to P1. In some circumstances it may be reasonable to ask people not to have a child at all, say in a wrongful life case. In other circumstances it may not be reasonable to require people to have only one child. I will consider here whether it is reasonable to require all to have only one child, in light of global poverty and inequality.

Fertility rates are highest in the world's least developed regions, especially sub-Saharan Africa (May 2012, 27). There are two main reasons why P1 arguably places disproportionate demands on those who are already badly off. First, one may argue that it would be unfair to ask those who contribute very little to total emissions to make sacrifices in order to limit them. Second, the causes of high fertility are tied up with injustices. Asking the poor to have fewer children amounts to asking the victims of injustice to solve it. Although this may sometimes be unavoidable, it should be avoided if possible.

Although the determinants of fertility are greatly debated,[12] let me discuss three (sets of) mechanisms that are relatively uncontroversial. First, poverty and high child mortality correlate with high fertility. There are several explanations for this: children are (necessary) sources of cheap labour and – in the absence of pensions, social security or medical insurance – they are a protection against old age poverty. If child mortality is high, having many children is a good strategy to make sure a sufficient number of children survive. The *dependency argument* used on the collective level applies on a family scale here. If having many children is the only viable way to meet basic needs (now or in old age), P1 is too burdensome. Changing the circumstances that make this so – lowering child mortality and addressing (old age) poverty – is a requirement of justice on any plausible account. If this is right, it seems that instead of demanding lower fertility, priority should lie with meeting these demands of justice. As a side effect of meeting the requirements of justice, fertility rates will drop, and once people have a real choice their decisions may be subject to P1.

Second, access to and knowledge about birth control influences fertility rates. In the absence of these, refraining from sexual intercourse altogether is the only trustworthy alternative. Nussbaum lists 'opportunities for sexual satisfaction and for choice in matters of reproduction' as among the basic capabilities (under the heading of bodily integrity) (Nussbaum 2001,76). If she is right, the lack of contraception and knowledge about it would be sufficient to excuse those who do not act on P1. Making contraception available would have two important effects. To begin with, it would allow people to stop procreating once they didn't want additional children. This would only work if people already wanted fewer children. In addition, it would alter pre-existing preferences. The widespread availability of efficient birth control probably contributed to changes in family formation. By making childless unions and delayed childbearing and delayed marriage possibilities, it contributed to decoupling marriage and parenthood (van de Kaa 1996, 422). Delayed childbearing alone has a significant effect on the size of a population.[13] People may freely decide to have fewer children once contraception is available, limiting the need for P1. But requiring people with very little knowledge about, or insufficient access to, efficient birth control to stop procreating may be too much to ask.

Third, as has been emphasized since the 1994 Cairo Conference, the development and education of women correlates strongly with lower fertility rates (May 2012, 149–52). Sen has shown that fertility rates have dropped fastest in regions of India where the position of women has improved, faster than under repressive fertility regimes (Sen 2001a, 219–23). This should be expected because the *costs* of high fertility rates are carried almost exclusively by women. In Sen's words, many young women are 'shackled to a life of persistent bearing and raising of children' (Sen 2001b, 169). Emancipation makes having fewer children an option: '[S]ince women's interests are very badly served by high fertility rates imposed on them, they can be expected to correct this adversity given more decisional power' (Sen 2001b, 169). Whether lower fertility is an effect of increased earning potential and financial independence, increased opportunity costs and levels of education or a combination of several factors is hard to establish. However, it is safe to say that overall an increase in gender equality lowers fertility rates and child mortality (Sen 2001b, 173).[14] Blaming women in disadvantaged positions for not acting on P1 seems unreasonable in the light of these considerations.

A decline in fertility rates is in the interests of the global poor.[15] High fertility constitutes a kind of poverty trap: it is both (partially) a consequence and (partially) a cause of poverty and lack of development. However, it is often rational for *individual families* to have many children. Improving their position (in the ways suggested above) takes away this discrepancy between what is rational for the individual and what is best for both the poorer communities themselves and the world as a whole to a very large extent. Although people may still choose to have more than one child, they will now have a choice.

This section has aimed to argue two things. First, it suggests that addressing grave (global) injustices may be necessary before acting on P1 can be required. Second, it emphasizes that addressing inequality and poverty may very well limit the need for P1, because fertility levels will drop once injustices are addressed. Barry said that 'it is clear that everything that needs to be done to hold down population growth will at the same time contribute to the cause of justice' (Barry 2005, 263). 'Everything' may be too optimistic, but both objections raised at the beginning of this section can be resolved. Tackling grave injustices leads to lower fertility without unfairly asking the global poor to make sacrifices to reduce emissions.

6 Conclusion

In this chapter I have argued for four different claims. First, that there cannot be an unlimited right to procreate. Second, that there are good reasons to assign moral weight to the interest in procreation, sufficient to protect it by introducing a right to have one child per couple, and – on the collective level – enough procreative entitlements to sustain the community. The key idea is that in designing a sustainability strategy, emphasis should be placed on variables other than population (if possible) to the extent that this emphasis is necessary to protect the important interest that individuals and communities have in procreation. This may mean that investment in green technology or reducing per capita consumption are required. Similarly, it may mean that investment in mitigation strategies (to increase the total amount of CO_2 that can be permissibly emitted, through reforestation or other ways of absorbing CO_2) is required in order to accommodate additional people. Third, I have argued that there is a set of circumstances in which it would be unfair to require people to act on P1. A fourth, related, argument is that reducing global inequalities (including

Table 14.1 Which argument leads to what kind of right?

	Dependency (4.1)	Meaning (4.1)	Parenting (4.2)	Poverty (5)
Limited right for some.	Yes, sufficient procreation for sustainable economy and care.	Yes, sufficient procreation to make community continue	Yes, sufficient children to parent.	Yes, in order to protect the basic interest of the parents.
Limited right to one child for all.	No.	No.	Yes, if needed to become parent.	No.
Right to more than one child for some.	Yes, if needed for sustainable economy and care.	Yes, if needed for sustainable community.	No.	Yes, if no reasonable alternative.
Right to more than one child for all.	No.	No.	No.	No.
Unlimited right.	No.	No.	No.	No.

gender equality) can produce fairer intergenerational outcomes. For a summary of the kind of right each section aimed to justify, see Table 14.1.

What are the consequences of choosing a strategy to limit emissions to sustainable levels? When striking a balance between lowering per capita emissions and limiting procreation, a priority should be placed on limiting superfluous emissions that do not contribute to goals as important as parenting. This is in order to protect the interest people have in there being sufficient births for continuity and to allow people to become parents. Importantly, in an unequal world like ours, limiting fertility levels will have to go hand in hand with addressing global poverty; this will decrease fertility as well as open up the possibility for further fertility reduction because procreation becomes a choice rather than a necessity.

Notes

1 I am especially grateful to Axel Gosseries, who has commented on several drafts of this chapter. For comments and discussions I would like to thank Anca Gheaus, Andrea Felicetti, Cristián Fatauros, Danielle Zwarthoed, David Axelsen, Emanuele Murra, Gerhard Bos, Henry Shue, Ingrid Robeyns, Iñigo González, Juliana Bidadanure, Joachim Nieuwland, Jos Philips, Marcus Düwell, Maxime Lambrecht, Paula Gobbi, Sandrine Blanc, Siba Harb, Stephany Donze, Thierry Ngosso and Thomas Ferretti. Thanks are due also to the participants at workshops held at Utrecht University, the University of Louvain and the University of Glasgow and the participants at the ESF 'Rights to a Green Future' network meetings where earlier versions of this chapter were presented. I acknowledge the support of the F.R.S.-FNRS (FRESH), the ARC project on sustainability (French community of Belgium) and the ESF-funded networking programme 'Rights to a Green Future'.

2 A recent paper aims to show that 'there is an 80% probability that world population will increase to between 9.6 billion and 12.3 billion in 2100' (Gerland *et al.* 2014, 234).

3 One may think that we owe future generations more (e.g. equality) than sufficiency. For an overview of different views, see Gosseries 2008.

4 An additional advantage of a smaller population is that climate change is easier to deal with. Population pressure leads people to move into areas dangerous due to climate change (e.g. Bangladesh delta).

5 This draws on the IPAT formula: I for impact (in this case total emissions), which is a function of Population (P), Affluence (A) and Technology (T). More people, more affluence and the less advanced green technology all increase I (Ehrlich and Holdren 1971).

6 Some Malthusians have argued for letting 'Tertullian blessings' such as war, pests and famines take their course (Hardin 1974). These arguments are both empirically and morally indefensibly flawed (for an excellent rejection see Shue 1996, 97–104).

7 Procreating and parenting are two distinct activities, but I run them together here for simplicity's sake.

8 This is not an uncontroversial claim (e.g. Griffin 2008, ch. 3).

9 Some argue that these can already be good enough reasons to require people to either a) pay for children themselves or b) refrain from procreating (e.g. Casal and Williams 1995).

10 I borrow these rights from Caney (2010).

11 This is for simplicity's sake. We could work out what the arguments imply for other family arrangements.

12 For an overview of the literature on the determinants of fertility, see van de Kaa (1996) and Dasgupta (2000).

13 This is true even if fertility rates remain constant, because there is less overlap between generations.

14 Some point out that education also decreases childlessness (Baudin, de la Croix and Gobbi 2015, introduction). This will probably not offset the downward effect on total fertility because estimated 'unmet needs' for fertility control are huge: 137 million women who do not want additional children do not practice contraception (Bongaarts and Sinding 2009).

15 One of the advantages of a demographic transition towards lower fertility is a possible demographic dividend: higher per capita investment in the next generation (May 2012, 48–52).

References

Barry B. (2005) *Why social justice matters* Cambridge, Polity.

Baudin T., de la Croix D. and Gobbi P. (2015) *Development policies when accounting for the extensive margin of fertility* IRES Discussion Paper, Available at http://sites.uclouvain.be/econ/DP/IRES/2015003.pdf, accessed 30 August 2015.

Bongaarts J. (1978) 'A framework for analyzing the proximate determinants of fertility' *Population and Development Review*, 4(1) 105–32.

Bongaarts J. and Sinding S. (2009) 'A response to critics of family planning programs' *International Perspectives on Sexual and Reproductive Health*, 35(1) 39–44.

Brighouse H. and Swift A. 'Parents' rights and the value of the family' *Ethics*, 117(1) 80–108.

Caney S. (2010) 'Climate change, human rights, and moral thresholds' in Gardiner S. *et al.* eds *Climate ethics: essential readings* Oxford, Oxford University Press, 163–77.

Casal P. and Williams A. (1995) 'Rights, equality and procreation' *Analyse & Kritik*, 17(1) 93–116.

Dasgupta P. (2000) 'Population and resources: an exploration of reproductive and environmental externalities' *Population and Development Review*, 26(4) 643–89.

Ehrlich P. and Holdren J. (1971) 'Impact of population growth' *Science*, 171(3977) 1212–17.

Gerland P., Raftery A.E, Ševčíková H., Li N., Gu D., Spoorenberg T., Alkema L., Fosdick B.K., Chunn J., Lalic N., Bay G., Buettner T., Heilig G.K. and Wilmoth J. (2014) 'World population stabilization unlikely this century' *Science*, 346 234–7.

Gheaus A. (2015) 'Could there ever be a duty to have children?' in Hannan S., Brennan S. and Vernon R. eds, *Permissible progeny?* Oxford, Oxford University Press, 87–106.

Gosseries A. (2008) 'Theories of intergenerational justice: a synopsis' *S.A.P.I.EN.S. Surveys and Perspectives Integrating Environment and Society*, 1(1) 61–71.

Griffin J. (2008) *On human rights* Oxford, Oxford University Press.

Hardin G. (1974) 'Living on a lifeboat' *Bioscience*, 24(10) 561–8.

Intergovernmental Panel on Climate Change (2014) *Climate change 2014: synthesis report* Contribution of working groups I, II and III to the fifth assessment report of the Intergovernmental Panel on Climate Change, Geneva, IPCC.

May J. (2012) *World population policies* Dordrecht, Springer.

Nussbaum M.C. (2001) *Women and human development* Cambridge, Cambridge University Press.

O'Neill O. (1979) 'Begetting bearing and rearing' in O'Neill O. and Ruddick W. eds, *Having children* Oxford, Oxford University Press, 25–38.

O'Neill O. (1996) *Towards justice and virtue* Cambridge, Cambridge University Press.

Scheffler S. (2013) *Death and the afterlife* Oxford, Oxford University Press.

Sen A. (2001a) *Development as freedom* Oxford, Oxford University Press.

Sen A. (2001b) 'Population and gender equity' *Journal of Public Health Policy*, 22(2) 169–74.

Shue H. (1996) *Basic rights*, 2nd edn Princeton, Princeton University Press.

Thant U. (1967) Statement at Presentation of Declaration on Population Growth, 10 December, New York, Available at www.un.org/en/development/desa/population/theme/rights/, accessed 30 August 2012.

United Nations (1948) *Universal Declaration of Human Rights* New York, UN.

United Nations (1994) *Report of the International Conference on Population and Development*, Cairo 5–13 September, New York, UN.

van de Kaa D. J. (1996) 'Anchored narratives: the story and findings of half a century of research into the determinants of fertility' *Population Studies*, 50(3) 389–432.

World Bank (2015) 'CO_2 emissions (metric tons per capita)' see CO_2 emissions 2010–2014, Available at http://data.worldbank.org/indicator/EN.ATM.CO2E.PC, accessed 24 June 2015.

Young T. (2001) 'Overconsumption and procreation: are they morally equivalent?' *Journal of Applied Philosophy*, 18(2) 183–92.

15 The institutional representation of future generations

Sandor Fulop

1 Introduction

Intergenerational justice was the main element of the term "sustainable development" – at least in the definition developed by the Brundtland Commission in 1987 when it formulated its famous sentence: "We act as we do because we can get away with it: future generations do not vote, they have no political or financial power; they cannot challenge our decisions." Can they? The obvious answer is that they can if they have proper representation, which has appeared relatively slowly and decades later than the Brundtland Commission established the logical premises for it. In the years following 2000, certain state bodies started to appear here and there that were wholly or partly responsible for future generations, for example the parliamentary commissions in Finland and Israel and the Hungarian Ombudsman for Future Generations.

Since the planetary boundaries we trespass are of a global nature, sooner or later the institutional representation of future generations will emerge as a global governance issue, too. In this article we are going to analyse three major international legal documents: a report of the Secretary-General of the UN; a final report of the UN Special Rapporteur, John Knox; and the draft Sustainable Development Goals. These documents either raise directly the necessity of institutional representation of future generations or discuss the global ecological problems that could only be solved by having such an extraordinary institutional arrangement.

The national-level organisations for future generations (hereafter FGOs) have developed some typical functions: legal advocacy, a think tank and a complaint office role. My hypothesis is that the functions ensuing from the three environmental and human rights documents under consideration fall into these categories. Furthermore, these documents provide abundant information not only on the types of functions of the FGOs, but also on the conditions of their effective operation.

2 Is there a legal–institutional solution for the ecological crises?

Before we enter into the analysis of these important legal texts, let us consider the merits of the legal–institutional solutions as compared to the more organic social developments for protecting our civilisation from the consequences of ecological crises.

The problem of intergenerational justice overlaps with the present environmental problems because of the foreseeable and, according to many, unavoidable scenario of ecological crises. The warnings about these come from the outputs of reliable global scientific programmes such as the Millennium Assessment (MA) reports, reports from the Intergovernmental Panel on Climate Change (IPCC) and the Global Environmental Outlook (GEO) series of publications. These are joint efforts of thousands of international and national institutions affiliated with the UN and with many governments and universities. Private networks, such as the Club of Rome, the Balaton Group, the World Future Council (WFC) and the Oxford Martin Commission for Future Generations are also effective in developing holistic pictures of the environmental and related sociopolitical problems, and they sketch out scenarios that would require urgent but effective responses from all levels of decision-makers in the world.

The ideal way of solving/surviving the ecological crises and avoiding/mitigating the fact that we bring our offspring into a much worse situation than our ancestors did would be to have an organic trajectory, an arch starting from the widespread awareness of the results of the work of natural scientists, through to the interpretation work of social scientists, and then finishing with several levels of deliberative procedures. In this process, people, nations and the global community would ponder the moral weight of the situation and discuss the best ways of solving it. This would be followed by dramatic changes in the mindsets and wills of the overwhelming majority of individuals, communities, political parties, governments and international fora and this would all result in the necessary, concerted actions to amend the whole situation.[1] However, there is definitely not enough time for this, and time is just part of the problem. The value system of the consumer society and the vested interests of the economic groups that dictate political programmes to their parties prevail. Furthermore, national and international institutions show a high level of inertia and several actors defend their old convictions and moral bases quite fiercely. Logging companies in Oregon, in the US, can successfully campaign with such slogans as "Spotted owl? I like them – fried!",[2] or the Canadian oil industry can support exponents who say "Why should I do anything for posterity? What has posterity ever done for me?" (Elshof 2011, 34). While, hopefully, these sentences sound odd to the readers of this article, they might sound pleasant to the ears of those whose economic interests, moral weakness and/or psychological defence mechanisms prevent them from realising that there are obvious threats the ecological crises have for us and for our children. The slow-moving "chemistry" of this situation cries out for a "catalyst", a hub that makes the wheels of the cranking machinery spin much faster.

Organisations[3] that serve the interests of future generations can help to translate the scientific reports on ecological catastrophes into an understandable language to motivate their respective societies. They can keep on the agenda our urgent responsibilities to mitigate the effects of and adapt to the consequences of these catastrophes and, most importantly, they can fight the inertia and selfish short-sightedness of our political and economic decision-makers. However, there are plenty more institutional tasks that FGOs will have to perform regularly, and many of them are acknowledged by the three important international legal documents we will analyse. Some of these tasks can be undertaken without any difficulty, while in relation to others, the FGOs have to gauge the social and political risks. After a year or two of successful balancing between cooperative and confrontational strategies, FGOs tend to be accepted by their respective societies.[4] They can perform certain watchdog activities and even initiate legal steps when *environmental constitutional rights* of present or future generations are infringed or endangered. The usefulness and effectiveness of such institutions are, however, recurrently questioned by legal sceptics, who say that without a dramatic change in attitude on economic, political, social and personal levels there is no hope that ecological disasters will be dealt with successfully. Yet "unorganic", discontinuous changes in the legal–institutional arrangements are the quickest possible national and global reactions to the challenges of the scenario of imminent ecological crises (World Future Council 2014, 31).

3 Three major international documents that presuppose the existence of FGOs

Even though the first FGOs appeared on the national level, the most logical setting for the institutional breakthrough described in the previous section is the global level. Because of the almost two hundred possible participant nations, the discussions at UN fora have a better chance of overcoming the national-level power biases and short-term economic pressures. Global, long-term interests might be better revealed and served by the international-level decision-making procedures, especially by the UN system and by the fast-evolving global NGO networks; furthermore, the interplay of these two might be advantageous. The three legal documents that are being analysed reinforce my speculations and, together with other important legal and institutional global initiatives,[5] they might turn out to include the strongest arguments for the institutional support of the case of intergenerational justice globally.

3.1 The Ban Ki-moon (UNDESA) report

The draft of the 2012 Rio + 20 world summit's closing document, entitled "The future we want", contained a paragraph that ensured the institutional representation of future generations – until the very last day of this high-level conference. Thereafter, this paragraph, Paragraph 86, fell prey to the diplomatic manoeuvres of some of the G77 countries who were afraid of having yet another international body that might criticise their national practices from a new angle. In place of the deleted section, the parties accepted a more vague text that requested the Secretary-General of the UN to present a report on the institutional representation of future generations after the summit. The enthusiasm of the supporters of this case diminished further when it turned out that the task of preparing the report was being allocated to UNDESA, the economic development body of the United Nations. However, with the active participation of several Major Groups, large international NGOs and private experts,[6] the text of the report, *Intergenerational Solidarity and the Needs of Future Generations*[7] (hereafter Rep.) is quite progressive. It provides a widespread analysis of the existing national-level institutions and offers several institutional solutions for representing future generations globally. The climax of this effort is most certainly Point 13, where the text quotes Article 1 of the *Universal Declaration of Human Rights*[8] and establishes the following as a consequence: "Yet it is not immediately obvious on what ethical grounds human beings should be treated differently based on their date of birth, as this has no bearing on their humanity." The report also highlights the fact that in the last three decades more than 30 international legal documents have referred to the rights or interests of future generations[9] and in addition it devotes a whole paragraph to each of the national-level examples of the institutional representation of future generations in Canada, Finland, Hungary, Israel, New Zealand, Germany and Wales.[10]

3.2 The John Knox report on human rights and the environment

On his appointment to the UN Human Rights Council, Professor John Knox thoroughly examined human rights threatened by environmental harm on the one hand, and human rights obligations that might be raised as an argument for a higher level of environmental protection, on the other. He established a very wide network of scientists and NGOs to consult with, and he also took part personally in numerous international conferences partly or wholly dealing with the interrelationship between human rights and environmental protection.

A major statement from John Knox's "Mapping Report" (United Nations 2014b) (hereafter Map.) says that human rights thinking should incorporate the precautionary principle from environmental law in order to be able to recognise in good time and acknowledge the environmental hazards that threaten basic human rights, such as the right to life, health, water, and sanitation and housing. The report did not hide the limitations of the human rights approach either: human rights might have difficulties, it said, first, with territorial extensions, and second, with time extensions of their concepts. In addition, the report stated that human rights are inherently anthropocentric, meaning that this branch of law is less inclined to acknowledge the unconditional primacy of life conditions even if basic rights, such as the right to life and health, are at stake, when other human rights, such as the right to dignity or any social and economic rights, are being overshadowed.

3.3 The draft proposal of the UN sustainable development goals[11]

In view of the fact that the Millennium Development Goals expire in 2015, the UN system has started widespread consultations between the member states about a new, comprehensive set of goals, this time with more attention given to sustainability. The draft that is available at the time of writing is the *Open Working Group Proposal for Sustainable Development Goals*[12] (hereafter SDG) and seems to be a summary of almost all of the problems of humankind, from environmental degradation to organised crime, and from the abuse of women and children to minority rights and even traffic accidents. We need to ask: is it a really holistic picture? It certainly isn't if we compare it to such global analyses as the report of the Oxford Martin Commission for Future Generations *Now for the long-term* (Oxford Martin Commission for Future Generations 2013)[13] or the Global Policy Action Plan (GPACT) of the WFC.[14] However, taking into consideration that the 17 groups of SDG goals were and still are subject to the discussion and consensus of all UN nations, the coherence of the material is the best possible. This was also ensured by including recurrent elements of sustainable development content and several other integrative efforts.

4 Legislative advocacy tasks in the three documents

It is a big step forward that the international community has reached a level at which intergenerational justice is reflected in several international documents and that major UN policy papers – directly or indirectly – have started to raise the question of institutional representation of future generations. In the following pages we are going to argue that global and thereafter (with the encouragement of the success of the global institution) regional and national institutional representation too is indeed a logical next step; without this, the goodwill encompassed in the previously mentioned documents remains only a collection of wishful thoughts. Our thesis is that in the three recent major international documents we examine there is an inherent necessity for the institutional representation of future generations; in other words, many specific tasks that are discussed could not be performed unless such representation is established. Moreover, these tasks form a system in which the advocacy functions, the think tank functions and the functions that are connected with individual environmental conflicts support each other with information, professional connections and publicity, and in many other ways.

4.1 Bridging science, education and public awareness

The legal advocacy function of an FGO starts with clear recognition of the problems involving the long-term environmental and resource-depletion effects of present activities, and then continues when it conveys the findings to the political decision-makers and to the general public as well, in a proper form, which includes frequent, forceful messages. In other words, FGOs will build a solid bridge between science, education and public awareness in the field of sustainable development. The Rep. approaches this mediating, capacity-building function from several angles. It provides: a natural sciences perspective, "to understand and manage long-term threats to environmental quality"; a philosophy perspective to allow "open and critical engagement with moral and ethical choices"; an education and training perspective for "strengthening education for sustainable development and global citizenship"; "leadership training to foster attitude changes advancing intergenerational solidarity and justice"; and the adoption of an approach that relies on the basic tenets of economics. The report calls attention to the fact that the discount rate that economists use to evaluate the future effects of present activities, which the report says is too high, devalues the life and interests of our offspring unjustly, and, "furthermore, the conventional cost-benefit rationale is unsuitable for the valuation of irreversibilities" (United Nations 2013, 27–8, 30–1, 63).

While the few existing national-level FGOs do a lot to convey these messages to their policymakers and to the widest possible circles of their respective societies, it seems obvious that this vital task should be institutionalised in many more countries and globally, too. We have to point out that although the scientific findings on the fast approaching and solidly growing ecological crises, their moral consequences and the necessity of capacity-building, and environmental education on these issues do appear in the major policy documents (such as international declarations, regional and national environmental plans and sustainable development plans), to "cascade them down" into proper constitutional principles, and laws and regulations is much more difficult. The FGOs should be led by the so-called *finality principle* in their legal advocacy work, i.e. they should not lean back contentedly when the first results in state planning documents are achieved, because these are only the initial steps in a long procedure that is more frequently abandoned than carried out.

4.2 Balancing intergenerational and intra-generational justice

No legislative advocacy for intergenerational justice can be successful without including the issue of intra-generational justice.[15] The issue of balancing intergenerational and intra-generational justice is well represented in the three documents under consideration. The Rep. poses this very question at the start of one of its chapters – "Sacrificing the interests of current generations?" – and quickly establishes that "addressing the needs of future generations is not meaningful if delinked from addressing the needs of those living [now]". This does not mean that we should establish an artificial contradiction between the interests of present and future generations as a zero-sum game. On the contrary, together we form a "transgenerational community" that leads us to feel, as a human race, a responsibility to sustain our culture and history. Also, there are several win-win solutions that can be found with the help of FGOs and with the mindset of striving for mutual gains for present and future generations. While we are aware of the interests of present generations (are we, really?), the "less harm" alternatives for future generations can usually be found by acting in the spirit of the precautionary principle. On that basis, concludes the Rep., a global FG High Commissioner "could act as an advocate for intergenerational solidarity" (United Nations 2013 17, 23, 26, 63).

The Map. highlights two important instances when the infringements of the basic human rights of present and future generations are almost identical or overlap. As previously mentioned here in connection with discounting, irreversible changes in the basic resources of life, such as the lands of small island states sinking into the ocean, represent a harm for all generations of humankind. Furthermore, children's rights imply both the rights of present children and, to some extent, of future generations. It is our responsibility to combat children's diseases and malnutrition now and in the future, too. The Map. warns that environmental degradation endangers these rights seriously in many instances and therefore that states should "regulate and monitor the environmental impact of business activities that may compromise children's right to health, food security and access to safe drinking water and to sanitation"; furthermore, it advocates that they should also "put children's health concerns at the centre of their climate change adaptation and mitigation strategies". These latter notes from the Map. shed light on the real background of the often artificial confrontation between the rights of present and future generations: usually, it is not environmental protection activities but rather reckless business operations that are in antagonistic contradiction with the interests of our offspring (United Nations 2014b 22, 74).

In view of the contents of the above-mentioned documents, it seems to be quite appropriate that to "[e]nd poverty in all its forms everywhere" is proposed as the very first of the Sustainable Development Goals. Indeed, this is the only solution to the dilemma: objectively poor and extremely poor countries and poor people cannot be asked to sacrifice themselves for the living conditions of future generations, also taking into consideration the fact that environmental degradation burdens the vulnerable the most. While environmentally sustainable, small-scale food production offers sustainable living to poor local communities, large-scale industrial agriculture usually generates only business profits and poor quality food, and also causes irreversible damage to the soil which threatens the resources of future generations. Similarly, in ensuring healthy drinking water and sanitation, the interests of the enterprises supplying these must be secondary, and genuinely healthy solutions and intra- and intergenerational justice should prevail. The third major area of the economy in which business interests will be controlled by longer-term sustainability interests is energy production (United Nations 2014a, see SDG 1, 2.3, 6.6, 7).

The statements in the three major international documents under consideration that relate to onerous actions which need to be carried out to achieve intra- and intergenerational justice put FGOs in an extremely difficult position. Environmental protection in itself is a highly contradictory portfolio, therefore NGOs and state bodies that deal with it are quite frequently subject to unjust attacks from business and political circles. What will happen to them once they enter into discussions about social justice and justice in the economic world order? One can again suggest that the most straightforward, immediate action for FGOs is to protect the environment and save resources wherever possible; long-term social changes will have to be left to history. We revisit this issue in the last part of this chapter when we try to elicit information from our three sources about the effectiveness of FGOs.

4.3 Critical analysis of existing legal sources

The third logical stage in the advocacy work of FGOs would be to conduct a survey of the effects of existing legal sources on the fate of future generations. This would involve a global or regional FGO considering relevant international law, which would include environmental treaties. In this work, some general principles might form the starting point, such as Principle 1 of the 1972 Stockholm Declaration on the human environment or Principle 3 of the Rio Declaration. This latter is a rephrasing of the definition of sustainable development as "the right to development must be fulfilled so as to equitably meet developmental and environmental needs of present and future generations". Based on these general principles, the Rep. can quote a list of binding international treaties, such as the treaties on climate change (1992), biodiversity (1992), desertification (1994), radioactive waste (1997) and persistent organic pollutants (2001). It adds that these otherwise binding legal texts contain the language of future generations only in their preambles (United Nations 2013, 33–6). Contrary to the conclusion drawn by the Rep., we do not evaluate this legal solution as not binding; we interpret it as one step further in the direction of accepting concrete legal responsibilities for the protection of the interests of future generations. We note, however, that the willingness of states to undertake international commitments for the sake of future generations even on this almost declarative level seems to have tapered off during the last decade and a half. A global or regional organisation that represents future generations should focus a great deal of attention on international legislative efforts and should lobby for more significant inclusion of the interests of future generations – or otherwise the promising start of the development of relevant international law will not continue in the foreseeable future.

The language of future generations features strongly in the newer constitutional texts of many countries, for example Bolivia, Ecuador, Germany, Kenya, Norway, South Africa, Hungary and others. Encouraging mutual reinforcement, that is a kind of cross-fertilisation between the global and national developments in the field of intergenerational justice, would be an important task for a global FGO to carry out. Such a mediator role is missing nowadays. Even a simple but systematic collection of relevant legal and scientific data – a clearing house for future generations if you like – is still to be realised. Naturally, it is not only the global FGO that could benefit from the accumulated experiences of the states; the global example could encourage national-level efforts, too, especially in difficult situations when a national FGO might become a little bit too confrontational. Those who would find this inconvenient would call it a "system alien" or would use it as a scapegoat with regard to negative social or economic developments (United Nations 2013 37–8, 54). We can conclude, therefore, that a key task when the international community designs a global FGO is preventing the representatives of nations from accepting "the lowest common denominator" solutions and encouraging them to use the most progressive elements of the national-level solutions as building blocks in the creation of an effective global institution.

5 Think tank function in the three documents

While the major data relating to the scenario of future ecological crises are available and grow continuously, there is still plenty of room for certain targeted research activities, especially in the field of social sciences. In addition, the existing scientific findings should not, of course, only be disseminated in society by way of the formal planning–legislative–implementation tools of the state administration. Widespread networking, via research and discussion of the results, is to be engaged in by the FGO-type organisations. We can label this task as the "think tank" function of FGOs. Let us consider some examples with the help of the three documents under consideration.

Ideas about alternative ways of survival and resilience, so-called social experiments, were suggested a long time ago by Dennis Meadows and his circle (the Balaton Group). Similar suggestions are encompassed in the draft Sustainable Development Goals, too, under the heading SDG 9: "Build resilient infrastructure, promote inclusive and sustainable industrialisation and foster innovation". Such an infrastructure should be internationally harmonised for the sake of better safety when facing ecological problems on a global scale – this could be an important mediation task for a global FGO.

There is a striking contradiction between the age of networking, in which scientific and technical information flows more and more freely, and the fact that only a narrow minority can harness it; at the same time, the difference in wealth is growing – together with survival chances with regard to the most frequently occurring catastrophes – on both a national and a global scale. Solutions for achieving a higher level of social justice will not evolve automatically on their own, either in intra-generational or intergenerational terms (United Nations 2014a, SDG 9). Dissemination of best practices, information servicing and other capacity-building activities form an important part of the portfolio of an FGO.

Alternative indicator projects appear in many places, and some of them, such as the Ecological Footprint and the Happy Planet Index, have achieved global acknowledgement. However, their efforts are still sporadic and their effects with regard to decision-making on all scales are not traceable for the time being. There is no hope of progressing to a more sustainable social and economic order until ecological catastrophes raise the GDP and as such herald success for political leaders. In addition, many factors regarding human well-being are simply overlooked in the official indicator systems (United Nations 2014a, SDG 17.18, 17.19). Again, strong networking between the great minds who invent and put into practice alternative social and economic indicators and the widest possible audience is a must, and currently no one is carrying out this task – but it could be done by a global FGO.

While our discussion focuses primarily on the global theatre, the fight for the survival of our civilisation, according to many experts, is located decisively at the local level. Some communities do not wait for central directives but start local sustainable programmes, although usually in a complex way, beginning with sustainable food production and services, sustainable energy production and water and waste management; however, these are rarely connected to alternative cultural and economic practices such as, for example, introducing local currency. These initiatives and their networks, being the representatives of such local communities, might form the most important allies for a global FGO, and it is in the vested interest of any global-level FGO to support such sustainable local communities by carrying out systematic research, networking (supporting their conferences, newsletters and Internet communication, etc.), offering legal support (e.g. in relation to matters of access to local markets for healthy food, sustainable consumption and production patterns) and helping morally, too. Those who have drafted the Sustainable Development Goals are at the forefront of our historical development process and have included important goals in connection with sustainable consumption and production patterns, efficient use of natural resources, avoiding food waste and preventing excessive chemical treatment that poisons the living systems of arable soils, "ensuring that people everywhere have the relevant information and awareness for sustainable development and lifestyles in harmony with nature" (United Nations 2014a, SDG 12).

6 Dealing with individual cases – the complaint office function in the three documents

A global FGO should be attentive to local- and national-level environmental conflicts. However, in international diplomacy the reference to state sovereignty would prevent it from interfering in such issues in a decisive way. There are several examples of international economic bodies and the UN human rights organisations too, having a strong presence in national matters, sometimes seriously limiting national sovereignty. Even if this is true, a new type of organisation, such as a global FGO, could not claim similar status at first; it would have to wait for the historical moment when every stakeholder acknowledges the right to a healthy environment as a key factor in sustaining other basic human rights. The lack of a right to directly interfere with national-level processes is not a major problem with regard to a global or regional FGO performing its tasks because there are many levels of international legal measures that are much less strict and represent welcome, non-binding support for states that are trying to overcome their environmental conflicts. The mere fact that a global institution becomes aware of negative processes and can follow the patterns and negative trends can help a great deal in achieving a more just and time-proof ecological world regime. Furthermore, having limited functions on a national level would not prevent a global FGO from keeping intergenerational justice on the agenda on all levels: The existence of such an office at the United Nations would help address, in a focused manner, the long-term consequences of present-day actions, by spotlighting impact on the future in tangible, non-abstract terms and by rallying support for integrating sustainability into planning decisions by governments, business and individuals. The office would also play an advocacy role by highlighting the moral imperative of leaving behind a healthy world in which future generations will live out their lives (United Nations 2013, 56–7).

6.1 Public participation as an inalienable part of the work of FGOs

Without strong local environmental movements there is no meaningful environmental protection, even in countries with the most committed and equipped environmental administration. Without the thousands of eyes and ears of public participation our global environment would eventually be consumed and polluted piece by piece.[16] The Rep. carefully examines examples of the existing national-level FGOs and finds that almost all of them maintain strong connections with the stakeholders of local-level environmental conflicts, which are usually triggered by complaints or by other forms of information from the local communities and NGOs. Often this information is complemented by the information-gathering activities of the FGOs (United Nations 2013, 39–48).

The Map. summarises the duty to facilitate public participation in environmental decision-making on a human rights (including due process) basis, including the rights of freedom of expression and association: "human rights bodies have built on this baseline in the environmental context, elaborating a duty to facilitate public participation in environmental decision-making in order to safeguard a wide spectrum of rights from environmental harm". Support for public participation and capacity-building (including fighting against activities that destroy the ability of the public to participate in the decision-making procedures concerning their rights and interests) is much needed in our time, where gaps in environmental democracy still exist and counter-movements are only just gaining momentum. Some of these movements refer to the economic crises, while others just rely on the old professional biases of the administrators against any interference by laymen in their cases and procedures. In other words, FGOs at all levels should not only use the information and help gained from public participation, but also deal with the topic of public participation itself; they should take note of its solid legislative basis and strive for its effective implementation. Capacity-building is a must in order to sustain one of the best sources of information on and solutions to widespread local environmental conflicts (United Nations 2014b, 36, 39–40).

6.2 New kinds of environmental conflicts that require alternative, creative solutions

The Map. refers to authoritative sources from several continents[17] that unanimously agree that international human rights responsibilities bind states together in each individual case where environmental pollution could endanger not only several human rights concerning life and health but also certain social and economic rights. The human rights approach to be used in environmental crises creates a clear international legal responsibility of countries with regard to their own individual cases and makes futile their references to state sovereignty when they are speaking of issues involving serious environmental harm. Furthermore, a logical extension of this concept is when the individual infringement of human rights takes place in another country, not even necessarily a neighbouring one.

We repeat, however, that a newly established global or regional FGO will neither be prestigious enough, as far as the international human rights (and market protection bodies) are concerned, nor have enough resources at its disposal in order to directly intervene in countries' individual cases. Collecting knowledge about the individual problems, drawing general conclusions from them and initiating international actions to change the conditions and patterns of such cases is certainly possible; however, the moral and logistical support of the respective networks of experts and NGOs that support local communities in such vital conflicts is needed too (United Nations 2014b 58–63, 66).

6.3 Comparative advantages of FGOs

The support of local communities for several levels of FGOs is not only a possibility, but a key issue in the effectiveness of their fight for a liveable environment and long-term sustainability. Contrary to the tunnel vision we frequently experience in the actions of the modern, compartmentalised governmental system, this new office offers trans-disciplinary, holistic, problem-oriented solutions. These features bring FGOs very close to public participation, and in this way such an organisation is an ideal partner for local communities and NGOs.

Once it had access to a database of best practices from all over the world, a global FGO could serve – upon request – by providing support and advice on the most effective policy measures for solving local environmental conflicts in such a way that the solutions themselves would be sustainable, too. For this to happen, all the social and economic interests at stake should be duly considered – as we mentioned earlier, good compromises can usually be found in places where environmental protection and intergenerational justice do not entail an excessive financial burden or painful social changes. The only problem is that not everyone is aware of these solutions, and some powerful actors would wish not only to fulfil their own interests but to conquer their "enemies" in the dispute. Social–psychological motivations represent the key factor in local environmental conflicts more often than we might think, even in cases of major investment projects – careful clarification of facts and separating them from the emotions of the participants requires a broader network of all interested parties and experts, including FGOs. Social conflict engineering, mediation and forging win-win situations are functions that fit very well with FGOs. (United Nations 2013, 63).

7 Conditions of effective operation of FGOs in the three documents

The stakes are too high to create any weak, ineffective bodies either on a national or an international level to represent future generations. The literature about this is abundant, and the three major international documents under consideration make it clear that there is full awareness of this requirement.

All the national-level FGOs examined in the Rep. have gained considerable prestige, and even though they are state bodies they have a relatively high level of *independence*. None of the examples mentioned in the three documents is part of the government; instead they are affiliated to the national parliament or, as in one exceptions, to a parliamentary body (the general auditor) (United Nations 2013, 39–48). Independence should mean *methodological independence*, too: FGOs usually run iterative, deliberative procedures; they perform transdisciplinary clarification of facts. These requirements are very much in harmony with the last goal of the SDG that gives some hints about the "means of implementation and revitalisation of the global partnership for sustainable development" (United Nations 2014a, SDG 17, especially 17.16 on multi-stakeholder partnerships). This methodological independence is the precondition of an ability to solve irregular conflicts that either fall outside the scope of operation of the governmental bodies or for which solutions can only be formal, for example because the social or political pressure on them is too great. FGOs should operate in significantly different ways, because it is pointless to duplicate the functions and operation of existing state institutions that deal with monitoring and legal redress.

Legitimacy and *access to information* are highlighted by the Map. as the conditions required for strong control over the national governmental and municipal administrations and also for being able to draw a realistic picture of the nature and extent of environmental conflicts (United Nations 2014b, 31–5). Legitimacy is reinforced by *strong support from basic social networks*: science, professional bodies, churches and NGOs, for example. Furthermore, it goes without saying that in order to sustain their full legitimacy, internal governance of the FGOs should meet the highest expectations. *Transparency* and *accountability* are the basic requirements the FGOs demand from the national governmental and international bodies they work with – it would be quite strange to neglect these features in their own operations (United Nations 2014a, SDG 14).

Different histories and different levels of social acceptance and embeddedness lead to significant differences between FGOs and human rights bodies in the selection of strategies based on a scale ranging from conflict to cooperation.[18] As is clear from the Map., international human rights bodies do not hesitate to engage with the hottest issues, such as large-scale oil developments or nuclear power plants (United Nations 2014b, 18–19). Naturally, the strategy of an FGO should be more subtle and pay more attention to the *compromise elements* that the definition of sustainable development has gained during its history.[19]

8 Conclusion

In the last few decades, international NGO networks and scientific discussions have prepared the way for the institutional representation of future generations. In some countries we have witnessed early experiences of establishing FGOs; furthermore, in some countries such institutions could continue to exist in the long term. At the time of writing, 2015, we have arrived at a new stage in this development, with major international legal documents indicating the necessity of creating FGOs. We can have no doubts about the urgent tasks of ensuring intergenerational justice and human rights for all and sustainable development in general, as clearly described in the Rep., the Map. and in the SDG, and these aims cannot be achieved unless there is a specific, carefully constructed institutional background.

The unequivocal findings on imminent ecological catastrophes issued by the highest-level international scientific programmes don't alarm the decision-makers at all. No one makes effective, concerted global efforts to mitigate the already irreversible changes in the fields of climate change, biodiversity loss, soil eradication and many others. No one spends significant resources on vital areas of social and scientific experiments, such as a network of sustainable local communities and alternative indicators of the achievements of a state or a nation in promoting the well-being and happiness of its people. No one will prevent shrewd manipulators of public opinion from making the social injustices of the present into intergenerational injustices. No one will prevent diplomats who are members of global legislative fora from taking the most convenient, lowest common denominator standpoints from which they create new and separate paper tigers against global warming, dramatic loss of biodiversity and arable lands, and many other issues that threaten our civilisation with extinction. These issues will not be managed, especially not in their entirety and with their synergies and reverberations, in a systematic way unless there is a new type of institution that gives a voice and legal representation to future generations and, under the same remit, provides these things in relation to our own future.

Due to considerable scientific efforts, the efforts of NGOs, and also to the three excellent international legal documents we have examined in this chapter, the formats of such FGOs are now much clearer.

Notes

1 We do not say that this organic procedure is not possible, especially in relation to issues that are not too burdensome technically or economically, such as the successful reversing of the depletion of the ozone layer as discussed in Rockström et al. 2009, 472. Some scientists tend to take this possibility quite seriously, e.g. that owing to the IPCC's efforts, "Socio political and psycho sociological climate began to change dramatically and rapidly" (Weston and Bach 2009, ix).

2 A personal communication from the attorneys of the Sierra Club.

3 For an overall sociological and philosophical definition of organisations and meta-organisations (the closest one to the term "institution" we are going to use in this article) within institutions, we refer to Seumas Miller (Miller 2010, 4–5).

4 The best example is the New Zealand Parliamentary Commissioner for the Environment (PCE), whose office has been operating since 1987.

5 GPACT and the work of the Oxford Martin Commission for Future Generations initially.

6 The two major achievements of these experts and the NGOs' networking process played an active role in the Expert Panel on Intergenerational Solidarity, May 2013, New York, UN headquarters and the co-organisation of the UNDESA World Future Council Conference, July 2013, Palais de Nations, Geneva.

7 United Nations, General Assembly, sixty-eighth session, agenda item 19, No. A/68/100.

8 "All human beings are born free and equal in dignity and rights. They are endowed with reason and conscience and should act towards one another in a spirit of brotherhood."

9 Other sources, such as Halina Ward (Ward 2012, 6–7), claim that this occurs in more than 60 such documents. We note that, except in a few instances, such as the Aarhus Convention, the language of future generations is used in soft laws. Time will tell when the critical mass and the critical time are reached and when the protection of the interests of future generations will at least become part of international customary law.

10 This list is not exhaustive, especially if we consider the countries where establishing similar organisations has been suggested and taken into consideration recently, such as Malta, the Netherlands, Norway and Sweden. An interesting analysis of these institutions can be read in Mahito Shindo's work (Shindo 2013) This study, which is nearly 500 pages long, is based on a careful analysis of the similar institutions in New Zealand, Hungary and the Australian Capital Territory, and it is noted that the proposal for Japan rests upon the failure of the administration to handle recent major environmental catastrophe situations.

11 After the collection of documents that was referred to during the writing of this proposal was closed, the document was renamed "Road to Dignity by 2030" https://sustainabledevelopment.un.org/index.php?page=view&type=111&nr=5809&menu=35.

12 UN General Assembly, sixty-eighth session, agenda items 14, 19(a) and 118, No. A/68/970.

13 This report focuses on the so-called megatrends in technology, demographics, mobility, society and health, etc. the challenges arising from them and the shaping factors (and hindrances) of change and proposals, such as creative coalitions, innovative institutions, re-evaluation of the future in the hierarchy of social values and investing in younger generations.

14 The starting point for GPACT is a more responsible governance, and thereafter it is concerned with equity and dignity, peace and security, the climate and ecosystems, and more than just sharing wealth and a reformed world of enterprises. A special value of GPACT is that all of the elements of its system are bolstered with the experiences of actual, long-term programmes that the WFC has been running in the last couple of years as at the time of writing.

15 One of the most promising theories concerning intra-generational justice is the convergence theory as "fair access to the bio-capacity of the planet within planetary biophysical boundaries"; see its discussion in the context of intergenerational justice by Barbara Adam (Adam 2012, 1, 5–6).

16 Similarly, consider the underlying importance of citizen suits in intergenerational justice in Weston and Bach (2009, 48).

17 Special Representative of the Secretary-General on Human Rights and Transnational Corporations and other Business Enterprises, the *Guiding Principles on Business and Human Rights* endorsed by the Human Rights Council, the Committee on Economic, Social and Cultural Rights, the African Commission, the Inter-American Commission on Human Rights and the European Court.

18 An interesting aspect of the same dilemma is the collective acceptance theory and the teleological theory of institutions (Miller 2010, Chapters 2 and 3).
19 Not everyone is so tolerant. In 2013, 170,000 signatures were collected by European youth groups in order to issue a European Citizens' Initiative for criminalisation of the most grievous wrongdoings in environmental protection. See the conference organised by End Ecocide: A Global Citizens' Initiative to Protect Ecosystems, held 13–14 October 2014, Brussels. Environmental criminal law was the major tool of the New Jersey chief environmental prosecutor between 1990 and 1994 which was very successful until it was totally eradicated by a new governor (Madonna and Breslin 1992).

References

Adam B. (2012) *Responsibility for future generations* A Schumacher Institute Challenge Paper, Available at www.schumacherinstitute.org.uk/sites/schumacherinstitute.org.uk/files/downloadable/Challenge%20Papers/BAdam%20Challenge%20-%20Responsibility%20to%20Future.pdf, accessed 25 July 2015.

Elshof L. (2011) "Can education overcome climate change inactivism?" *Journal for Activism in Science & Technology Education*, 3(1) 15–51, 34.

Madonna S.J. and Breslin K.M. (1992) "The environmental prosecutor: New Jersey's innovative approach to environmental enforcement" *Vill. Envtl L.J.*, 3 47–69.

Miller S. (2010) "Social institutions" in Zalta E.N. ed., *The Stanford encyclopedia of philosophy* winter 2014 edition, Available at http://plato.stanford.edu/archives/win2014/entries/social-institutions, accessed 25 July 2015.

Oxford Martin Commission for Future Generations (2013) *Now for the long term* The report from the Oxford Martin Commission for Future Generations, Oxford, Oxford Martin School, University of Oxford, 1–86.

Rockström J., Steffen W., Noone K., Persson Å., Chapin III F.S., Lambin E.F., Lenton T.M., Scheffer M., Folke C., Schellnhuber H.J., Nykvist B., de Wit C.A., Hughes T., van der Leeuw S., Rodhe H., Sörlin S., Snyder P.K., Costanza R., Svedin U., Falkenmark M., Karlberg L., Corell R.W., Fabry V.J., Hansen J., Walker B., Liverman D., Richardson K., Crutzen P. and Foley J.A. (2009) "A safe operating place for humanity" *Nature*, 461 472–5.

Shindo, M. (2013) "The environmental ombudsman and administrative decision-making: an assessment of its suitability for Japan" Unpublished PhD thesis, Macquarie Law School, Sydney, Australia, 1–479.

United Nations (2013) *Intergenerational solidarity and the needs of future generations* Report of the Secretary-General to the General Assembly of the United Nations, New York, UN.

United Nations (2014a) *Report of the Open Working Group of the General Assembly on Sustainable Development Goals*, New York, UN.

United Nations (2014b) *Report of the Independent Expert on the issue of human rights obligations relating to the enjoyment of a safe, clean, healthy and sustainable environment, John H. Knox: mapping report* 25th session, agenda item 3, No. A/HRC/25/53, New York, UN, Human Rights Council.

United Nations (2015) "Road to dignity by 2030" (https://sustainabledevelopment.un.org/index.php?page=view&type=111&nr=5809&menu=35) accessed 25 July 2015.

Ward H. (2012) *Committing to the future we want: a High Commissioner for Future Generations at Rio+20* discussion paper for the 2012 UN Conference on Sustainable Development, [no place], Foundation for Democracy and Sustainable Development/World Future Council, 1–21.

Weston B.H. and Bach T. (2009) *Recalibrating the law of humans with the laws of nature: climate change, human rights and intergenerational justice* Vermont Law School research paper series no. 10-06, Vermont, IO, Vermont Law School, 1–102.

World Future Council (2014) *Global policy action plan: incentives for a sustainable future* Hamburg, WFC, 1–35.

16 Human rights, sustainability and future people – a future discussion

Marcus Düwell and Gerhard Bos

1 Introduction

This chapter aims to identify various central aspects that future debates about the role of human rights in responding to contemporary ecological challenges should take into consideration. The chapter first reminds us why it is necessary to discuss questions about long-term responsibilities in relation to human rights. Necessary measures for effective, sustainable politics will have an impact on the legitimate exercise of liberties, and therefore it is not possible to avoid discussing how the rights of currently living people relate to the obligations we have with regard to future people on the basis of human rights principles. Next we identify three points that merit particular discussion. *First of all*, we have to ask what the consequences would be if we were aware of the role of future people within the human rights regime. What would this mean for the content of the human rights principles? *Second*, if we see future people as rights-holders, they would have to be represented in our political and legal order. What would that look like and how would this affect democratic decision-making? *Third*, effective measures of sustainability will necessarily imply a stronger international coordination and the forming of supra-national institutions. Human rights are traditionally, however, strongly understood as related to the state – as rights against the state or as rights protected by the state. What would this switch mean for the role of human rights? This short overview shows that seeing human rights in a long-term perspective is not only a challenge for human rights scholars but urges us to debate human rights from a broader range of interdisciplinary perspectives; it also shows that questions of sustainability must be on the research agenda of the social sciences and humanities in the years to come.

2 The problem

The chapters in this book focused on various questions concerning the relationship between human rights, sustainability and future generations. This relationship has scarcely been investigated at all. It seems obvious that the relationship is not a neutral one. The human rights framework has played a crucial role in the international political order since World War II insofar as human rights principles have limited the legitimate exercise of governmental power and helped to formulate political aspirations as well as guide the formation of the internal legal order of states. The faster the ecological challenges influence our life, the more intensely we will have to think about measures of sustainability that will significantly interact with the legal and political order that is guided by human rights principles. Because of the enormous increase in the world population, the industrialization of developing parts of the world and similar developments, it is obvious that those measures will have to be concerned with limitations of liberties that people have seen as a central part of those rights that they thought each human being should be able to enjoy. It is hardly possible to develop a sustainable way of living if we don't change habits with regard to energy use and travelling. Just to develop technologies that use less energy will probably not be sufficient. The same holds for population growth: it is difficult to see how sustainable development is compatible with the world population growing as rapidly as it is expected at the moment, especially when we recognize that consumption is growing as well. All measures to change this will imply limitations of liberties. The more intense measures of sustainability will influence the legal order of individual states and the international order as such, so it is even more pressing to clarify the relationship of these measures to the human rights framework. We should not just use human rights as a rhetorical tool to enhance the dramatic effect when talking about future generations; we should try to understand the whole extent of the challenge if we see human rights from the perspective of long-term responsibilities. This is a challenge for legal scholars, philosophers and political theorists and also for scholars from the social sciences and humanities. Understanding long-term responsibility in terms of human rights is concerned not only with addressing it by reference to a specific and dominant regulatory framework that exists alongside others, but also with the significant history of thinking about politics, morality, law and human nature. An interpretation of the relationship between human rights and sustainability will therefore have to deal with an understanding of the perspectives that are relevant for an understanding of the development and justification of the human rights framework. Such a broader debate about a reinterpretation of human rights has just started. For the benefit of this debate in the future, we would like to highlight some relevant points in the following sections.

3 Why human rights?

There are various understandings of the concept of human rights that partly overlap but partly exclude each other (see, for example, the contributions of Beyleveld, Bos, Claassen, Düwell, Philips and Preda in this volume). There are discussions about whether human rights have to be seen as protecting basic human interests or as protecting humans' ability to freely decide about the life they want to lead. There are also discussions about the scope of human rights protection, in which different views see it as ranging from having a quite minimalistic task to involving far-reaching guarantees of socio-economic rights. And there are discussions about the extent to which contemporary international human rights law has to be seen as a result of various – or even one particular – tradition(s) of moral and political thought or as a modern regulatory system that is relatively emancipated from the various intellectual sources that played a role in the long history of its development.

But to what extent are the ecological challenges related to all these debates? The answer could be twofold.

On the one hand, there is an obvious relationship. The more ecological changes affect our life conditions, the more it is obvious that our ability to act and our basic interests are affected. To the extent that these ecological changes are the result of human action, it is obvious that the rights of human beings are at stake. The faster climate change develops – and over the last few years international reports have given rise to the belief that it is developing much faster than expected – the more it is obvious that extreme ecological problems will arise within the twenty-first century. This means that they do not just affect the possible rights of future people; it is quite likely that the current generation will be affected too, probably younger people rather than older ones. The old question about whether future (non-existent) people can have rights is therefore still important philosophically but, whatever position one holds in this debate, it is quite certain that the rights of existing people will be affected in the future by the way we emit CO_2 and by the way we use resources today. Thus, independent of contested aspects of the human rights regime, the ecological challenge will be relevant from the human rights perspective.

On the other hand, the different ways of interpreting human rights are not irrelevant for these debates. We may see, for example, human rights just as protecting negative liberty, or as more extensive rights of human beings to be supported in their ability to live a flourishing life or only as protecting the individual against state intervention – all these different views on the idea of human rights will play a role in the reinterpretation of human rights according to a long-term perspective. The various ecological challenges are so far-reaching that we have to wonder what appropriate responses of the human rights regime could look like. It is quite likely that a human rights regime that takes these challenges seriously would in some respects look different to the human rights regime we know so far – we will discuss some of these aspects shortly. Therefore, it is important to get an understanding of how changes in the human rights regime can be conceptually reconstructed and rationally justified. If we do not see human rights as arbitrary but as a fundamental political achievement, then we should expect that any changes in the human rights regime are in accordance with the logical and conceptual presuppositions that are required to substantiate the claim of universal acceptability that forms a central feature of the human rights tradition. In the light of such an understanding, we will be better able to comprehend what appropriate responses of the human rights regime to the ecological challenges could look like. This means that a broader discussion about the political, historical and moral role of human rights is necessary.

4 Challenges of a long-term perspective for the human rights regime

But why are the ecological challenges so far-reaching? Let us mention just three aspects:

First, there is no evidence to suggest that we will be able to meet the challenges of climate change without a drastic reduction in emissions, and this will not be possible without severely limiting the exercise of people's basic liberties. Of course, new technologies will help to reduce the emissions resulting from various activities. But it is not plausible to assume that those technologies that emit less will compensate for the fact that there are more people than there used to be and that those people live longer, travel more, buy more luxury goods, use more energy etc. If we take appropriate measures to deal with the long-term ecological challenges, we will have to regulate mobility and energy use in general, food production and consumption (see Meijboom in this volume) and reproductive behaviour (see Meijer in this volume), to mention just some of the central elements. This means that it is hard to see how we could reach a sustainable lifestyle without limiting the exercise of our liberties. Thus, a possible tension between sustainability and human rights appears. If we see human rights simply as people's entitlement to exercise their liberties without asking what kind of ecological consequences the exercise of those liberties will have and how these consequences affect the rights of (current or future) human beings, the human rights regime appears as one of the causes of the ecological crisis rather than its remedy'. And indeed, public and legal debates focus on human rights primarily when the exercise of people's liberties is at stake, and those debates are mainly concerned with current and manifest conflicts. If we see human rights from the perspective of long-term responsibilities, it is quite likely that we will have to ask how the relationship within the human rights regime between the protection of future ecological conditions and the possible current constraints on individual liberties can be regulated. This question also requires some theorizing about the relative weight different liberties may have within the human rights regime (see Beyleveld in this volume). Not every restriction of individual liberties will be important to the same degree. The more we extend the human rights regime to the future, the more urgent it will be to gain a better understanding of how we can weigh the different rights against each other in a justified manner and how we can prioritize different aspects. A particularly relevant question will be about the extent to which the concept of human dignity, which is the fundamental concept of the human rights regime, can provide a normative orientation with regard to these questions (see Düwell in this volume).

Second, if we had to see future people as being protected by the human rights regime, this would have consequences for their status within the legal realm. In the light of the legal contributions of this volume (Pirjatanniemi, Lawrence, Gaillard and Riley), we can assume that to some extent legal scholars are starting to deal with this topic. In general, we assume that having the dignity of a right-holder gives a person a position within the democratic order. This position would imply that we have to take their basic rights into consideration. But if we have reason to believe that we are obliged to directly or indirectly respect the basic interests of future people on the basis of the normative starting points of the human rights regime they would have a legal status of their own. This consideration has consequences for the way we understand the legal space in which we act and live and the kind of legal and political responsibilities we have with regard to future right-holders. If constitutional democracy is understood as the legal and political order in which all right-holders have to be represented in the decision-making process and have all their rights at least respected if not secured, there would have to be a representation of future people as well. This means that taking their perspective into account would not just be a matter of our pity for future people. Rather, it would have to be part of the constitutional order, according to the requirements of human rights, to organize the state in a way that would take those interests into account. This would probably have consequences for the political order and not just for the material decisions that are made. One would have to wonder what such a representation of future people would look like (see Sandor Fulop in this volume).

At the same time, we would be forced to reconsider our understanding of democracy. Under the human rights regime we already understand democracy as regulated by the political rights of citizens and constrained by the constitutional rights of presently existing citizens and the human rights of non-citizens. The number of constraints would probably increase and we might be afraid that the role of the courts would be too dominant. But this only means that there are important theoretical and practical problems to be discussed if we include future people within the scope of the human rights regime – some of these are tackled in the previous chapters. A legal system that would appropriately represent future people would probably have to develop new political and legal procedures. But in all these debates, we should be aware of what is at stake if we discuss the role of human rights with regard to ecological challenges.

Third, if ecological challenges had to be regulated within the scope of the human rights regime, this would have consequences for the role of the state and supra-national actors and also for the role of those institutions that have to fulfil the duties that correspond to the rights. The traditional provisions of the human rights regime focus primarily on the individual state as duty-bearer. Human rights are understood as rights against the state – in the sense that the rights protect a space of the individual that may not be infringed upon by the state – or in terms of the state having the task of establishing an order in which the protection of the rights of the individual can be guaranteed. This traditional picture has already expanded in several respects during the last few decades. On the one hand, the currently accepted scope of human rights provisions includes not only liberty rights but socio-economic and cultural rights, whose precise status within the human rights regime is contested but, which, nevertheless, are certainly part of the current human rights regulations. If that is the case, the rights cannot only be addressed negatively against the state, but the state has to be active in promoting and encouraging activities that support the realization of these rights. This would necessarily involve a positive role for non-state actors, since citizens' enjoyment of these rights does not solely depend on the state. On the other hand, there have been some shifts in the last few decades towards international agencies having a more direct role in the realization of human rights requirements. Moreover, the logic of human rights entails a normative orientation for the public domain, on top of the normative relations it denotes between individuals and the state (see Reder and Köhler in this volume). One can make all kinds of comments on these developments, but in any case we can see that a sole focus on the individual state as duty-bearer as it was traditionally discussed in human rights debates is not so self-evident now.

This point is particularly relevant in the context of this volume, since it is quite obvious that seeing human rights from a long-term perspective and giving appropriate normative responses to global ecological challenges will require a high level of international coordination and probably the creation of supra-national institutions; perhaps it will lead to a new global world order in which the national states as we know them in Europe will only play a minor role and great political blocks, like China, the USA and the European Union, will be the most important actors. This will change the possible role of human rights significantly, and we can only wonder what democratic decision-making in such political orders might look like.

More topics should be mentioned here, such as the extent to which it is compatible with the rights of future people to take decisions that very significantly determine their life conditions. One might think of the old debate about nuclear waste here, but also about possible decisions regarding geo-engineering. How should we think about these decisions against the background of the human rights regime? How should we evaluate 'nudging' strategies, where technologies are developed to influence people's behaviour so that it becomes more sustainable by bypassing their conscious decision-making? Should these strategies be permitted, prohibited or encouraged from a human rights perspective? But all these questions show that the debate should not just focus on some of the questions concerning the application of the human rights regime, but should ultimately be about the interpretation of human rights in general. What we need is a much broader perspective on the challenge that the ecological changes form for the human rights idea.

5 Towards a philosophy of human rights in times of global ecological changes

When we emphasized above that various fundamental philosophical questions concerning human rights have to be discussed, the aim was not to find a new excuse for not taking necessary actions against the dangers of climate change. The need for political measures is real and they should be enforced now. But it would be an underestimation of the dimensions of the current global ecological changes if we didn't understand that appropriate measures will probably affect all areas of our life and our political and legal institutions as well. They will affect our personal behaviour, technological developments and the actions of national and international institutions. This, however, has the implication that we have to reconsider a broad range of moral convictions, patterns of actions and the role of various institutions. Human rights have formed the central reference point for the normative–political order since World War II, and the idea that our political actions should be guided by respect for human rights is even older. If it had to be part of this framework to protect current and future people against the damage that climate change can do, this would have far-reaching consequences for the concrete regulations of the human rights regime as well as for the institutions that are appropriate for their enforcement. The consequences could range from constraints on individual liberties whose exercise would result in emissions through constraints on reproductive liberties and obligations on states to take far-reaching measures to enforce a reduction in carbon emissions to financial transfers from rich to poor states to enable them to implement sustainable technologies. There is an alternative option; this would force us to conclude that the human rights idea was just useful when it came to dealing with the problems people had after World War II. Perhaps the idea of human rights is appropriate to govern our actions when it is necessary to limit the exercise of our liberties in a way that does not infringe upon the liberties of others, but perhaps this idea has no normative power when it comes to responses to ecological challenges. But if the latter were the case, the consequences would go far beyond the realm of climate policy. It would mean that human rights would lose their role as the central reference point of our normative–political order. From the perspective of ethics, it is a task of primary importance to investigate the role human rights can play with regard to long-term responsibilities and global ecological challenges. One could even say that there is no way of understanding our current normative–political order appropriately without thinking about this question. The discussions in this volume have tried to take a step in the right direction, but obviously it is only one step – a lot of others have to follow.

Index

Page numbers in *italics* denote tables.

Taylor & Francis eBooks

Helping you to choose the right eBooks for your Library

Add Routledge titles to your library's digital collection today. Taylor and Francis ebooks contains over 50,000 titles in the Humanities, Social Sciences, Behavioural Sciences, Built Environment and Law.

Choose from a range of subject packages or create your own!

Benefits for you
- » Free MARC records
- » COUNTER-compliant usage statistics
- » Flexible purchase and pricing options
- » All titles DRM-free.

REQUEST YOUR **FREE** INSTITUTIONAL TRIAL TODAY

Free Trials Available
We offer free trials to qualifying academic, corporate and government customers.

Benefits for your user
- » Off-site, anytime access via Athens or referring URL
- » Print or copy pages or chapters
- » Full content search
- » Bookmark, highlight and annotate text
- » Access to thousands of pages of quality research at the click of a button.

eCollections – Choose from over 30 subject eCollections, including:

Archaeology	Language Learning
Architecture	Law
Asian Studies	Literature
Business & Management	Media & Communication
Classical Studies	Middle East Studies
Construction	Music
Creative & Media Arts	Philosophy
Criminology & Criminal Justice	Planning
Economics	Politics
Education	Psychology & Mental Health
Energy	Religion
Engineering	Security
English Language & Linguistics	Social Work
Environment & Sustainability	Sociology
Geography	Sport
Health Studies	Theatre & Performance
History	Tourism, Hospitality & Events

For more information, pricing enquiries or to order a free trial, please contact your local sales team: www.tandfebooks.com/page/sales

For Product Safety Concerns and Information please contact our EU
representative GPSR@taylorandfrancis.com
Taylor & Francis Verlag GmbH, Kaufingerstraße 24, 80331 München, Germany